ANNE OF WINDY POPLARS

by
L. M. MONTGOMERY

NEW YORK
FREDERICK A. STOKES COMPANY
PUBLISHERS

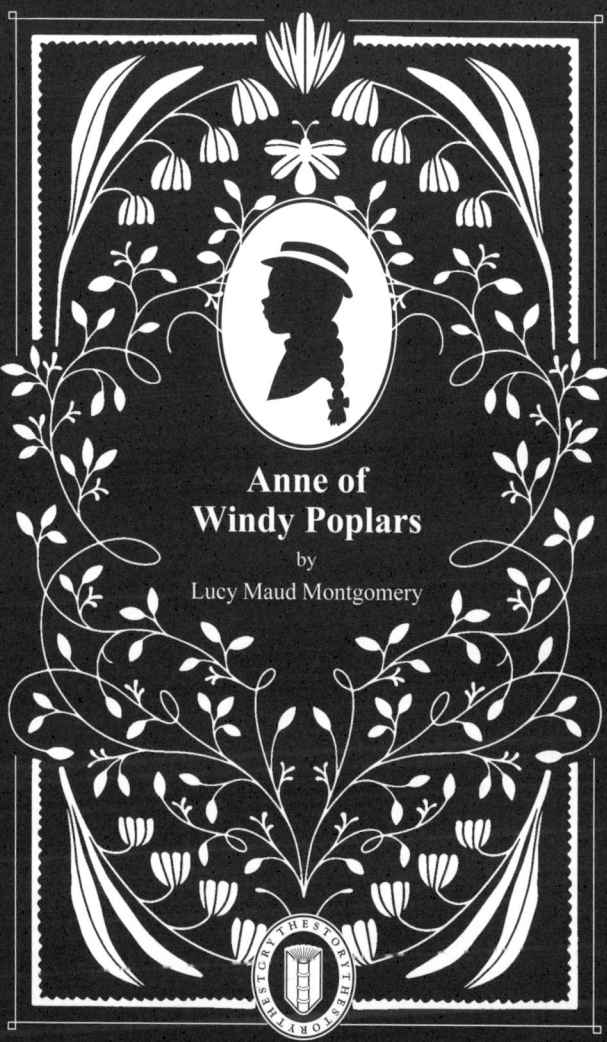

Anne of
Windy Poplars
by
Lucy Maud Montgomery

Copyright, 1936
by FREDERICK A. STOKES COMPANY

All rights reserved

The First Year

__ 6

The Second Year

__ 176

The Third Year

__ 281

THE FIRST YEAR

1

(Letter from Anne Shirley, B.A., Principal of Summerside High School, to Gilbert Blythe, medical student at Redmond College, Kingsport.)

"Windy Poplars,
"Spook's Lane,
"S'side, P. E. I.,
"Monday, September 12th.

"DEAREST:

"Isn't that an address! Did you ever hear anything so delicious? Windy Poplars is the name of my new home and I love it. I also love Spook's Lane, which has no legal existence. It should be Trent Street but it is never called Trent Street except on the rare occasions when it is mentioned in the Weekly Courier... and then people look at each other and say, 'Where on earth is that?' Spook's Lane it is...although for what reason I cannot tell you. I have already asked Rebecca Dew about it, but all she can say is that it has always been Spook's Lane and there was some old yarn years ago of its being haunted. But she has never seen anything worse-looking than herself in it.

"However, I mustn't get ahead of my story. You don't know Rebecca Dew yet. But you will, oh, yes, you will. I foresee that Rebecca Dew will figure largely in my future correspondence.

"It's dusk, dearest. (In passing, isn't 'dusk' a lovely word? I like it better than twilight. It sounds so velvety and shadowy and...and...dusky.) In daylight I belong to the world...in the night to sleep and eternity. But in the dusk I'm free from both and belong only to myself...and you. So I'm going to keep this hour sacred to writing to you. Though this won't be a love-letter. I have a scratchy pen and I can't write love-letters with a scratchy pen...or a sharp pen...or a stub pen. So you'll only get that kind of letter from me when I have exactly the right kind of pen. Meanwhile, I'll tell you about my new domicile and its inhabitants. Gilbert, they're such dears.

"I came up yesterday to look for a boarding-house. Mrs. Rachel Lynde came with me, ostensibly to do some shopping but really, I know, to choose a boarding-house for me. In spite of my Arts course and my B.A., Mrs. Lynde still thinks I am an inexperienced young thing who must be guided and directed and overseen.

"We came by train and oh, Gilbert, I had the funniest adventure. You know I've always been one to whom adventures came unsought. I just seem to attract them, as it were.

"It happened just as the train was coming to a stop at the station. I got up and, stooping to pick up Mrs. Lynde's suitcase (she was planning to spend Sunday with a friend in Summerside), I leaned my knuckles heavily on what I thought was the shiny arm of a seat. In a second I received a violent crack across them that nearly made me howl. Gilbert, what I had taken for the arm of a seat was a man's bald head. He was glaring fiercely at me and had evidently just waked up. I apologized abjectly and got off the train as quickly as possible. The last I saw of him he was still glaring. Mrs. Lynde was horrified and my knuckles are sore yet!

"I did not expect to have much trouble in finding a boarding-house, for a certain Mrs. Tom Pringle has been boarding the various principals of the High School for the last fifteen years. But, for some unknown reason, she has grown suddenly tired of 'being bothered' and wouldn't take me. Several other desirable places had some polite excuse. Several other places weren't desirable. We wandered about the town the whole afternoon and got hot and tired and blue and headachy...at least I did. I was ready to give up in despair...and then, Spook's Lane just happened!

"We had dropped in to see Mrs. Braddock, an old crony of Mrs. Lynde's. And Mrs. Braddock said she thought 'the widows' might take me in.

"'I've heard they want a boarder to pay Rebecca Dew's wages. They can't afford to keep Rebecca any longer unless a little extra money comes in. And if Rebecca goes, who is to milk that old red cow?'

"Mrs. Braddock fixed me with a stern eye as if she thought I ought to milk the red cow but wouldn't believe me on oath if I claimed I could.

"'What widows are you talking about?' demanded Mrs. Lynde.

"'Why, Aunt Kate and Aunt Chatty,' said Mrs. Braddock, as if everybody, even an ignorant B.A., ought to know that. 'Aunt Kate is Mrs. Amasa MacComber (she's the Captain's widow) and Aunt Chatty is Mrs. Lincoln MacLean, just a plain widow. But every one calls them "aunt." They live at the end of Spook's Lane.'

"Spook's Lane! That settled it. I knew I just had to board with the widows.

"'Let's go and see them at once,' I implored Mrs. Lynde. It seemed to me if we lost a moment Spook's Lane would vanish back into fairyland.

"'You can see them, but it'll be Rebecca who'll really decide whether they'll take you or not. Rebecca Dew rules the roost at Windy Poplars, I can tell you."

"Windy Poplars! It couldn't be true...no it couldn't. I must be dreaming. And Mrs. Rachel Lynde was actually saying it was a funny name for a place.

"'Oh, Captain MacComber called it that. It was his house, you know. He planted all the poplars round it and was mighty proud of it, though he was seldom home and never stayed long. Aunt Kate used to say that was inconvenient, but we never got it figured out whether she meant his staying such a little time or his coming back at all. Well, Miss Shirley, I hope you'll get there. Rebecca Dew's a good cook and a genius with cold potatoes. If she takes a notion to you you'll be in clover. If she doesn't...well, she won't, that's all. I hear there's a new banker in town looking for a boarding-house and she may prefer him. It's kind of funny Mrs. Tom Pringle wouldn't take you. Summerside is full of Pringles and half Pringles. They're called "The Royal Family" and you'll have to get on their good side, Miss Shirley, or you'll never get along in Summerside High. They've always ruled the roost hereabouts...there's a street called after old Captain Abraham Pringle. There's a regular clan of them, but the two old ladies at Maplehurst boss the tribe. I did hear they were down on you.'

"'Why should they be?' I exclaimed. 'I'm a total stranger to them.'

"'Well, a third cousin of theirs applied for the Principalship and they all think he should have got it. When your application was accepted the whole kit and boodle of them threw back their heads and howled. Well, people are like that. We have to take them as we find them, you know. They'll be as smooth as cream to you but they'll work against you every time. I'm not wanting to discourage you but forewarned is forearmed. I hope you'll make good just to spite them. If the widows take you, you won't mind eating with Rebecca Dew, will you? She isn't a servant, you know. She's a far-off cousin of the Captain's. She doesn't come to the table when there's company...she knows her place then... but if you were boarding there she wouldn't consider you company, of course.'

"I assured the anxious Mrs. Braddock that I'd love eating with Rebecca Dew and dragged Mrs. Lynde away. I must get ahead of the banker.

"Mrs. Braddock followed us to the door.

"'And don't hurt Aunt Chatty's feelings, will you? Her feelings are so easily hurt. She's so sensitive, poor thing. You see, she hasn't quite as much money as Aunt Kate...though Aunt Kate hasn't any too much either. And then Aunt Kate liked her husband real well...her own husband, I mean...but Aunt Chatty didn't...didn't like hers, I mean. Small wonder! Lincoln MacLean was an old crank...but she thinks people hold it against her. It's lucky this is Saturday. If it was Friday Aunt Chatty wouldn't even consider taking you. You'd think Aunt Kate would be the superstitious one, wouldn't you? Sailors are kind of like that. But it's Aunt Chatty...although her husband was a carpenter. She was very pretty in her day, poor thing.'

"I assured Mrs. Braddock that Aunt Chatty's feelings would be sacred to me, but she followed us down the walk.

"'Kate and Chatty won't explore your belongings when you're out. They're very conscientious. Rebecca Dew may, but she won't tell on you. And I wouldn't go to the front door if I was you. They only use it for something real important. I don't think it's been opened since Amasa's funeral. Try the side door. They keep the key under the flower-pot on the window-sill, so if nobody's home just unlock the door and go in and wait. And whatever you do, don't praise the cat, because Rebecca Dew doesn't like him.'

"I promised I wouldn't praise the cat and we actually got away. Erelong we found ourselves in Spook's Lane. It is a very short side street, leading out to open country, and far away a blue hill makes a beautiful back-drop for it. On one side there are no houses at all and the land slopes down to the harbor. On the other side there are only three. The first one is just a house...nothing more to be said of it. The next one is a big, imposing, gloomy mansion of stone-trimmed red brick, with a mansard roof warty with dormer-windows, an iron railing around the flat top and so many spruces and firs crowding about it that you can hardly see the house. It must be frightfully dark inside. And the third and last is Windy Poplars, right on the corner, with the grass-grown street on the front and a real country road, beautiful with tree shadows, on the other side.

"I fell in love with it at once. You know there are houses which impress themselves upon you at first sight for some reason you can hardly define. Windy Poplars is like that. I may describe it to you as a white frame house...very white...with green shutters...very green...with a 'tower' in the corner and a dormer-window on either side, a low stone wall dividing it from the street, with aspen poplars growing at intervals along it, and a big garden at the back where flowers and vegetables are delightfully jumbled up together...but all this can't convey its charm to you. In short, it is a house with a delightful personality and has something of the flavor of Green Gables about it.

"'This is the spot for me...it's been foreordained,' I said rapturously.

"Mrs. Lynde looked as if she didn't quite trust foreordination.

"'It'll be a long walk to school,' she said dubiously.

"'I don't mind that. It will be good exercise. Oh, look at that lovely birch and maple grove across the road.'

"Mrs. Lynde looked but all she said was,

"'I hope you won't be pestered with mosquitoes.'

"I hoped so, too. I detest mosquitoes. One mosquito can keep me 'awaker' than a bad conscience.

"I was glad we didn't have to go in by the front door. It looked so forbidding...a big, double-leaved, grained-wood affair, flanked by panels of red, flowered glass. It doesn't seem to belong to the house at all. The little green side door, which we reached by a darling path of thin, flat sandstones sunk at intervals in the grass, was much more friendly and inviting. The path was edged by very prim, well-ordered beds of ribbon grass and bleeding-heart and tiger-lilies and sweet-William and southernwood and bride's bouquet and red-and-white daisies and what Mrs. Lynde calls 'pinies.' Of course they weren't all in bloom at this season, but you could see they had bloomed at the proper time and done it well. There was a rose plot in a far corner and between Windy Poplars and the gloomy house next a brick wall all overgrown with Virginia creeper, with an arched trellis above a faded green door in the middle of it. A vine ran right across it, so it was plain it hadn't been opened for some time. It was really only half a door, for its top half is merely an open oblong through which we could catch a glimpse of a jungly garden on the other side.

"Just as we entered the gate of the garden of Windy Poplars I noticed a little clump of clover right by the path. Some impulse led me to stoop down and look at it. Would you believe it, Gilbert? There, right before my eyes, were three four-leafed clovers! Talk about omens! Even the Pringles can't contend against that. And I felt sure the banker hadn't an earthly chance.

"The side door was open so it was evident somebody was at home and we didn't have to look under the flower-pot. We knocked and Rebecca Dew came to the door. We knew it was Rebecca Dew because it couldn't have been any one else in the whole wide world. And she couldn't have had any other name.

"Rebecca Dew is 'around forty' and if a tomato had black hair racing away from its forehead, little twinkling black eyes, a tiny nose with a knobby end and a slit of a mouth, it would look exactly like her. Everything about her is a little too short...arms and legs and neck and nose...everything but her smile. It is long enough to reach from ear to ear.

"But we didn't see her smile just then. She looked very grim when I asked if I could see Mrs. MacComber.

"'You mean Mrs. Captain MacComber?' she said rebukingly, as if there were at least a dozen Mrs. MacCombers in the house.

"'Yes,' I said meekly. And we were forthwith ushered into the parlor and left there. It was rather a nice little room, a bit cluttered up with antimacassars but with a quiet, friendly atmosphere about it that I liked. Every bit of furniture had its own particular place which it had occupied for years. How that furniture shone! No bought polish ever produced that mirror-like gloss. I knew it was Rebecca Dew's elbow grease. There was a full-rigged ship in a bottle on the mantelpiece which interested Mrs. Lynde greatly. She couldn't imagine how it ever got into the bottle...but she thought it gave the room 'a nautical air.'

"'The widows' came in. I liked them at once. Aunt Kate was tall and thin and gray, and a little austere...Marilla's type exactly: and Aunt Chatty was short and thin and gray, and a little wistful. She may have been very pretty once but nothing is now left of her beauty except her eyes. They are lovely...soft and big and brown.

"I explained my errand and the widows looked at each other.

"'We must consult Rebecca Dew,' said Aunt Chatty.

"'Undoubtedly,' said Aunt Kate.

"Rebecca Dew was accordingly summoned from the kitchen. The cat came in with her...a big fluffy Maltese, with a white breast and a white collar. I should have liked to stroke him, but, remembering Mrs. Braddock's warning, I ignored him.

"Rebecca gazed at me without the glimmer of a smile.

"'Rebecca,' said Aunt Kate, who, I have discovered, does not waste words, 'Miss Shirley wishes to board here. I don't think we can take her.'

"'Why not?' said Rebecca Dew.

"'It would be too much trouble for you, I am afraid,' said Aunt Chatty.

"'I'm well used to trouble,' said Rebecca Dew. You can't separate those names, Gilbert. It's impossible...though the widows do it. They call her Rebecca when they speak to her. I don't know how they manage it.

"'We are rather old to have young people coming and going,' persisted Aunt Chatty.

"'Speak for yourself,' retorted Rebecca Dew. 'I'm only forty-five and I still have the use of my faculties. And I think it would be nice to have a young person sleeping in the house. A girl would be better than a boy any time. He'd be smoking day and night...burn us in our beds. If you must take a boarder, my advice would be to take her. But of course it's your house.'

"She said and vanished...as Homer was so fond of remarking. I knew the whole thing was settled but Aunt Chatty said I must go up and see if I was suited with my room.

"'We will give you the tower room, dear. It's not quite as large as the spare room, but it has a stove-pipe hole for a stove in winter and a much nicer view. You can see the old graveyard from it.'

"I knew I would love the room...the very name, 'tower room,' thrilled me. I felt as if we were living in that old song we used to sing in Avonlea School about the maiden who 'dwelt in a high tower beside a gray sea.' It proved to be the dearest place. We ascended to it by a little flight of corner steps leading up from the stair-landing. It was rather small...but not nearly as small as that dreadful hall bedroom I had my first year at Redmond. It had two windows, a dormer one looking west and a gable one looking north, and in the corner formed by the tower another three-sided window with casements opening outward and shelves underneath for my books. The floor was covered with round, braided rugs, the big bed had a canopy top and a 'wild-goose' quilt and looked so perfectly smooth and level that it seemed a shame to spoil it by sleeping in it. And, Gilbert, it is so high that I have to climb into it by a funny little movable set of steps which in daytime are stowed away under it. It seems Captain MacComber bought the whole contraption in some 'foreign' place and brought it home.

"There was a dear little corner cupboard with shelves trimmed with white scalloped paper and bouquets painted on its door. There was a round blue cushion on the window-seat...a cushion with a button deep in the center, making it look like a fat blue doughnut. And there was a sweet washstand with two shelves...the top one just big enough for a basin and jug of robin's-egg blue and the under one for a soap dish and hot water pitcher. It had a little brass-handled drawer full of towels and on a shelf over it a white china lady sat, with pink shoes and gilt sash and a red china rose in her golden china hair.

"The whole place was engoldened by the light that came through the corn-colored curtains and there was the rarest tapestry on the whitewashed walls where the shadow patterns of the aspens outside fell...living tapestry, always changing and quivering. Somehow, it seemed such a happy room. I felt as if I were the richest girl in the world.

"'You'll be safe there, that's what,' said Mrs. Lynde, as we went away.

"'I expect I'll find some things a bit cramping after the freedom of Patty's Place,' I said, just to tease her.

"'Freedom!' Mrs. Lynde sniffed. 'Freedom! Don't talk like a Yankee, Anne.'

"I came up today, bag and baggage. Of course I hated to leave Green Gables. No matter how often and long I'm away from it, the minute a vacation comes I'm part of it again as if I had never been away, and my heart is torn over leaving it. But I know I'll like it here. And it likes me. I always know whether a house likes me or not.

"The views from my windows are lovely...even the old

graveyard, which is surrounded by a row of dark fir trees and reached by a winding, dyke-bordered lane. From my west window I can see all over the harbor to distant, misty shores, with the dear little sail-boats I love and the ships outward bound 'for ports unknown'...fascinating phrase! Such 'scope for imagination' in it! From the north window I can see into the grove of birch and maple across the road. You know I've always been a tree worshiper. When we studied Tennyson in our English course at Redmond I was always sorrowfully at one with poor Enone, mourning her ravished pines.

"Beyond the grove and the graveyard is a lovable valley with the glossy red ribbon of a road winding through it and white houses dotted along it. Some valleys are lovable...you can't tell why. Just to look at them gives you pleasure. And beyond it again is my blue hill. I'm naming it Storm King...the ruling passion, etc.

"I can be so alone up here when I want to be. You know it's lovely to be alone once in a while. The winds will be my friends. They'll wail and sigh and croon around my tower...the white winds of winter...the green winds of spring...the blue winds of summer...the crimson winds of autumn...and the wild winds of all seasons...'stormy wind fulfilling his word.' How I've always thrilled to that Bible verse...as if each and every wind had a message for me. I've always envied the boy who flew with the north wind in that lovely old story of George MacDonald's. Some night, Gilbert, I'll open my tower casement and just step into the arms of the wind...and Rebecca Dew will never know why my bed wasn't slept in that night.

"I hope when we find our 'house of dreams,' dearest, that there will be winds around it. I wonder where it is...that unknown house. Shall I love it best by moonlight or dawn? That home of the future where we will have love and friendship and work...and a few funny adventures to bring laughter in our old age. Old age! Can we ever be old, Gilbert? It seems impossible.

"From the left window in the tower I can see the roofs of the town...this place where I am to live for at least a year. People are living in those houses who will be my friends, though I don't know them yet. And perhaps my enemies. For the ilk of Pye are found everywhere, under all kinds of names, and I understand the Pringles are to be reckoned with. School begins tomorrow. I shall have to teach geometry! Surely that can't be any worse than learning it. I pray heaven there are no mathematical geniuses among the Pringles.

"I've been here only for half a day, but I feel as if I had known the widows and Rebecca Dew all my life. They've asked me to call them 'aunt' already and I've asked them to call me Anne. I called Rebecca Dew 'Miss Dew'...once.

"'Miss What?' quoth she.

"'Dew,' I said meekly. 'Isn't that your name?'

"'Well, yes, it is, but I ain't been called Miss Dew for so long it gave me quite a turn. You'd better not do it any more, Miss Shirley, me not being used to it.'

"'I'll remember, Rebecca...Dew,' I said, trying my hardest to leave off the Dew but not succeeding.

"Mrs. Braddock was quite right in saying Aunt Chatty was sensitive. I discovered that at supper-time. Aunt Kate had said something about 'Chatty's sixty-sixth birthday.' Happening to glance at Aunt Chatty I saw that she had...no, not burst into tears. That is entirely too explosive a term for her performance. She just overflowed. The tears welled up in her big brown eyes and brimmed over, effortlessly and silently.

"'What's the matter now, Chatty?' asked Aunt Kate rather dourly.

"'It...it was only my sixty-fifth birthday,' said Aunt Chatty.

"'I beg your pardon, Charlotte,' said Aunt Kate...and all was sunshine again.

"The cat is a lovely big Tommy-cat with golden eyes, an elegant coat of dusty Maltese and irreproachable linen. Aunts Kate and Chatty call him Dusty Miller, because that is his name, and Rebecca Dew calls him That Cat because she resents him and resents the fact that she has to give him a square inch of liver every morning and evening, clean his hairs off the parlor arm-chair seat with an old tooth-brush whenever he has sneaked in and hunt him up if he is out late at night.

"'Rebecca Dew has always hated cats,' Aunt Chatty tells me, 'and she hates Dusty especially. Old Mrs. Campbell's dog...she kept a dog then...brought him here two years ago in his mouth. I suppose he thought it was no use to take him to Mrs. Campbell. Such a poor miserable little kitten, all wet and cold, with its poor little bones almost sticking through its skin. A heart of stone couldn't have refused it shelter. So Kate and I adopted it, but Rebecca Dew has never really forgiven us. We were not diplomatic that time. We should have refused to take it in. I don't know if you've noticed...' Aunt Chatty looked cautiously around at the door between the dining-room and kitchen...'how we manage Rebecca Dew.'

"I had noticed it...and it was beautiful to behold. Summerside and Rebecca Dew may think she rules the roost but the widows know differently.

"'We didn't want to take the banker...a young man would have been so unsettling and we would have had to worry so much if he didn't go to church regularly. But we pretended we did and Rebecca Dew simply wouldn't hear of it. I'm so glad we have you, dear. I feel sure you'll be a very nice person to cook for. I hope you'll like us all. Rebecca Dew has some very fine qualities. She was not so tidy when she came fifteen years ago as she is now. Once Kate had to write her name..."Rebecca Dew"...right across the parlor mirror to show the dust. But she never had to do it again. Rebecca Dew can take a hint. I hope you'll find your room comfortable, dear. You may have the window open at night. Kate does not approve of night air but she knows boarders must have privileges. She and I sleep together and we have arranged it so that one night the window is shut for her and the next it is open for me. One can always work out little problems like that, don't you think? Where there is a will there is always a way. Don't be alarmed if you hear Rebecca prowling a good deal in the night. She is always hearing noises and getting up to investigate them. I think that is why she didn't want the banker. She was afraid she might run into him in her nightgown. I hope you won't mind Kate not talking much. It's just her way. And she must have so many things to talk of...she was all over the world with Amasa MacComber in her young days. I wish I had the subjects for conversation she has, but I've never been off P. E. Island. I've often wondered why things should be arranged so...me loving to talk and with nothing to talk about and Kate with everything and hating to talk. But I suppose Providence knows best.'

"Although Aunt Chatty is a talker all right, she didn't say all this without a break. I interjected remarks at suitable intervals, but they were of no importance.

"They keep a cow which is pastured at Mr. James Hamilton's up the road and Rebecca Dew goes there to milk her. There is any amount of cream and every morning and evening I understand Rebecca Dew passes a glass of new milk through the opening in the wall gate to Mrs. Campbell's 'Woman.' It is for 'little Elizabeth,' who must have it under doctor's orders. Who the Woman is, or who little Elizabeth is, I have yet to discover. Mrs. Campbell is the inhabitant and owner of the fortress next door...which is called The Evergreens.

"I don't expect to sleep tonight...I never do sleep my first night in a strange bed and this is the very strangest bed I've ever seen. But I won't mind. I've always loved the night and I'll like lying awake and thinking over everything in life, past, present and to come. Especially to come.

"This is a merciless letter, Gilbert. I won't inflict such a long one on you again. But I wanted to tell you everything, so that you could picture my new surroundings for yourself. It has come to an end now, for far up the harbor the moon is 'sinking into shadow-land.' I must write a letter to Marilla yet. It will reach Green Gables the day after tomorrow and Davy will bring it home from the post-office, and he and Dora will crowd around Marilla while she opens it and Mrs. Lynde will have both ears open...Ow...w...w! That has made me homesick.

Good-night, dearest, from one who is now and ever will be,

"Fondestly yours,

"ANNE SHIRLEY."

2

(Extracts from various letters from the same to the same.)

"September 26th.

"Do you know where I go to read your letters? Across the road into the grove. There is a little dell there where the sun dapples the ferns. A brook meanders through it; there is a twisted mossy tree-trunk on which I sit, and the most delightful row of young sister birches. After this, when I have a dream of a certain kind...a golden-green, crimson-veined dream...a very dream of dreams...I shall please my fancy with the belief that it came from my secret dell of birches and was born of some mystic union between the slenderest, airiest of the sisters and the crooning brook. I love to sit there and listen to the silence of the grove. Have you ever noticed how many different silences there are, Gilbert? The silence of the woods...of the shore...of the meadows...of the night...of the summer afternoon. All different because all the undertones that thread them are different. I'm sure if I were totally blind and insensitive to heat and cold I could easily tell just where I was by the quality of the silence about me.

"School has been 'keeping' for two weeks now and I've got things pretty well organized. But Mrs. Braddock was right...the Pringles are my problem. And as yet I don't see exactly how I'm going to solve it in spite of my lucky clovers. As Mrs. Braddock says, they are as smooth as cream...and as slippery.

"The Pringles are a kind of clan who keeps tabs on each other and fight a good bit among themselves but stand shoulder to shoulder in regard to any outsider. I have come to the conclusion that there are just two kinds of people in Summerside... those who are Pringles and those who aren't.

"My room is full of Pringles and a good many students who bear another name have Pringle blood in them. The ring-leader of them seems to be Jen Pringle, a green-eyed bantling who looks as Becky Sharp must have looked at fourteen. I believe she is deliberately organizing a subtle campaign of insubordination and disrespect, with which I am going to find it hard to cope. She has a knack of making irresistibly comic faces and when I hear a smothered ripple of laughter running over the room behind my back I know perfectly well what has caused it, but so far I haven't been able to catch her out in it. She has brains, too...the little wretch!...can write compositions that are fourth cousins to literature and is quite brilliant in mathematics...woe is me! There is a certain sparkle in everything she says or does and she has a sense of humorous situations which would be a bond of kinship between us if she hadn't started out by hating me. As it is, I fear it will be a long time before Jen and I can laugh together over anything.

"Myra Pringle, Jen's cousin, is the beauty of the school...and apparently stupid. She does perpetrate some amusing howlers...as, for instance, when she said today in history class that the Indians thought Champlain and his men were gods or 'something inhuman.'

"Socially the Pringles are what Rebecca Dew calls 'the e-light' of Summerside. Already I have been invited to two Pringle homes for supper...because it is the proper thing to invite a new teacher to supper and the Pringles are not going to omit the required gestures. Last night I was at James Pringle's...the father of the aforesaid Jen. He looks like a college professor but is in reality stupid and ignorant. He talked a great deal about 'discipline,' tapping the tablecloth with a finger the nail of which was not impeccable and occasionally doing dreadful things to grammar. The Summerside High had always required a firm hand...an experienced teacher, male preferred. He was afraid I was a leetle too young...'a fault which time will cure all too soon,' he said sorrowfully. I didn't say anything because if I had said anything I might have said too much. So

I was as smooth and creamy as any Pringle of them all could have been and contented myself with looking limpidly at him and saying inside of myself, 'You cantankerous, prejudiced old creature!'

"Jen must have got her brains from her mother...whom I found myself liking. Jen, in her parents' presence, was a model of decorum. But though her words were polite her tone was insolent. Every time she said 'Miss Shirley' she contrived to make it sound like an insult. And every time she looked at my hair I felt that it was just plain carroty red. No Pringle, I am certain, would ever admit it was auburn.

"I liked the Morton Pringles much better...though Morton Pringle never really listens to anything you say. He says something to you and then, while you're replying, he is busy thinking out his next remark.

"Mrs. Stephen Pringle...the Widow Pringle...Summerside abounds in widows...wrote me a letter yesterday...a nice, polite, poisonous letter. Millie has too much home work...Millie is a delicate child and must not be overworked. Mr. Bell never gave her home work. She is a sensitive child that must be understood. Mr. Bell understood her so well! Mrs. Stephen is sure I will, too, if I try!

"I do not doubt Mrs. Stephen thinks I made Adam Pringle's nose bleed in class today by reason of which he had to go home. And I woke up last night and couldn't go to sleep again because I remembered an i I hadn't dotted in a question I wrote on the board. I'm certain Jen Pringle would notice it and a whisper will go around the clan about it.

"Rebecca Dew says that all the Pringles will invite me to supper, except the old ladies at Maplehurst, and then ignore me forever afterwards. As they are the 'e-light,' this may mean that socially I may be banned in Summerside. Well, we'll see. The battle is on but is not yet either won or lost. Still, I feel rather unhappy over it all. You can't reason with prejudice. I'm still just as I used to be in my childhood...I can't bear to have people not liking me. It isn't pleasant to think that the families of half my pupils hate me. And for no fault of my own. It is the injustice that stings me. There go more italics! But a few italics really do relieve your feelings.

"Apart from the Pringles I like my pupils very much. There are some clever, ambitious, hard-working ones who are really interested in getting an education. Lewis Allen is paying for his board by doing housework at his boarding-house and isn't a bit ashamed of it. And Sophy Sinclair rides bareback on her father's old gray mare six miles in and six miles out every day. There's pluck for you! If I can help a girl like that, am I to mind the Pringles?

"The trouble is...if I can't win the Pringles I won't have

much chance of helping anybody.

"But I love Windy Poplars. It isn't a boardinghouse...it's a home! And they like me...even Dusty Miller likes me, though he sometimes disapproves of me and shows it by deliberately sitting with his back turned towards me, occasionally cocking a golden eye over his shoulder at me to see how I'm taking it. I don't pet him much when Rebecca Dew is around because it really does irritate her. By day he is a homely, comfortable, meditative animal...but he is decidedly a weird creature at night. Rebecca says it is because he is never allowed to stay out after dark. She hates to stand in the back yard and call him. She says the neighbors will all be laughing at her. She calls in such fierce, stentorian tones that she really can be heard all over the town on a still night shouting for 'Puss...puss...PUSS!' The widows would have a conniption if Dusty Miller wasn't in when they went to bed. 'Nobody knows what I've gone through on account of That Cat... nobody,' Rebecca has assured me.

"The widows are going to wear well. Every day I like them better. Aunt Kate doesn't believe in reading novels, but informs me that she does not propose to censor my reading-matter. Aunt Chatty loves novels. She has a 'hidy-hole' where she keeps them...she smuggles them in from the town library...together with a pack of cards for solitaire and anything else she doesn't want Aunt Kate to see. It is in a chair seat which nobody but Aunt Chatty knows is more than a chair seat. She has shared the secret with me, because, I strongly suspect, she wants me to aid and abet her in the aforesaid smuggling. There shouldn't really be any need for hidy-holes at Windy Poplars, for I never saw a house with so many mysterious cupboards. Though to be sure, Rebecca Dew won't let them be mysterious. She is always cleaning them out ferociously. 'A house can't keep itself clean,' she says sorrowfully when either of the widows protests. I am sure she would make short work of a novel or a pack of cards if she found them. They are both a horror to her orthodox soul. Rebecca Dew says cards are the devil's books and novels even worse. The only things Rebecca ever reads, apart from her Bible, are the society columns of the Montreal Guardian. She loves to pore over the houses and furniture and doings of millionaires.

"'Just fancy soaking in a golden bathtub, Miss Shirley,' she said wistfully.

"But she's really an old duck. She has produced from somewhere a comfortable old wing chair of faded brocade that just fits my kinks and says, 'This is your chair. We'll keep it for you.' And she won't let Dusty Miller sleep on it lest I get hairs on my school skirt and give the Pringles something to talk about.

"The whole three are very much interested in my circlet of pearls...and what it signifies. Aunt Kate showed me her engagement ring (she can't wear it because it has grown too small) set with turquoises. But poor Aunt Chatty owned to me with tears in her eyes that she had never had an engagement ring...her husband thought it 'an unnecessary expenditure.' She was in my room at the time, giving her face a bath in buttermilk. She does it every night to preserve her complexion, and has sworn me to secrecy because she doesn't want Aunt Kate to know it.

"'She would think it ridiculous vanity in a woman of my age. And I am sure Rebecca Dew thinks that no Christian woman should try to be beautiful. I used to slip down to the kitchen to do it after Kate had gone to sleep but I was always afraid of Rebecca Dew coming down. She has ears like a cat's even when she is asleep. If I could just slip in here every night and do it...oh, thank you, my dear.'

"I have found out a little about our neighbors at The Evergreens. Mrs. Campbell (who was a Pringle!) is eighty. I haven't seen her but from what I can gather she is a very grim old lady. She has a maid, Martha Monkman, almost as ancient and grim as herself, who is generally referred to as 'Mrs. Campbell's Woman.' And she has her great granddaughter, little Elizabeth Grayson, living with her. Elizabeth...on whom I have never laid eyes in spite of my two weeks' sojourn...is eight years old and goes to the public school by 'the back way'...a short cut through the back yards...so I never encounter her, going or coming. Her mother, who is dead, was a granddaughter of Mrs. Campbell, who brought her up also...Her parents being dead. She married a certain Pierce Grayson, a 'Yankee,' as Mrs. Rachel Lynde would say. She died when Elizabeth was born and as Pierce Grayson had to leave America at once to take charge of a branch of his firm's business in Paris, the baby was sent home to old Mrs. Campbell. The story goes that he 'couldn't bear the sight of her' because she had cost her mother's life, and has never taken any notice of her. This of course may be sheer gossip because neither Mrs. Campbell nor the Woman ever opens her lips about him.

"Rebecca Dew says they are far too strict with little Elizabeth and she hasn't much of a time of it with them.

"'She isn't like other children...far too old for eight years. The things that she says sometimes! "Rebecca," she sez to me one day, "suppose just as you were ready to get into bed you felt your ankle nipped?" No wonder she's afraid to go to bed in the dark. And they make her do it. Mrs. Campbell says there are to be no cowards in her house. They watch her like two cats watching a mouse, and boss her within an inch of her life. If she makes a speck of noise they nearly pass out. It's "hush, hush" all the time. I tell you that child is being hush-hushed to death. And what is to be done about it?'

"What, indeed?

"I feel that I'd like to see her. She seems to me a bit pathetic. Aunt Kate says she is well looked after from a physical point of view...what Aunt Kate really said was, 'They feed and dress her well'...but a child can't live by bread alone. I can never forget what my own life was before I came to Green Gables.

"I'm going home next Friday evening to spend two beautiful days in Avonlea. The only drawback will be that everybody I see will ask me how I like teaching in Summerside.

"But think of Green Gables now, Gilbert...the Lake of Shining Waters with a blue mist on it...the maples across the brook beginning to turn scarlet...the ferns golden brown in the Haunted Wood...and the sunset shadows in Lover's Lane, darling spot. I find it in my heart to wish I were there now with...with...guess whom?

"Do you know, Gilbert, there are times when I strongly suspect that I love you!"

"Windy Poplars,

"Spook's Lane,

"S'side,

"October 10th.

"HONORED AND RESPECTED SIR:—

"That is how a love letter of Aunt Chatty's grandmother began. Isn't it delicious? What a thrill of superiority it must have given the grandfather! Wouldn't you really prefer it to 'Gilbert darling, etc.'? But, on the whole, I think I'm glad you're not the grandfather...or A grandfather. It's wonderful to think we're young and have our whole lives before us...together... isn't it?"

(Several pages omitted. Anne's pen being evidently neither sharp, stub nor rusty.)

"I'm sitting on the window seat in the tower looking out into the trees waving against an amber sky and beyond them to the harbor. Last night I had such a lovely walk with myself. I really had to go somewhere for it was just a trifle dismal at Windy Poplars. Aunt Chatty was crying in the sitting-room because her feelings had been hurt and Aunt Kate was crying in her bedroom because it was the anniversary of Captain Amasa's death and Rebecca Dew was crying in the kitchen for no reason that I could discover. I've never seen Rebecca Dew cry before. But when I tried tactfully to find out what was wrong she pettishly wanted to know if a body couldn't enjoy a cry when she felt like it. So I folded my tent and stole away, leaving her to her enjoyment.

"I went out and down the harbor road. There was such a nice frosty, Octobery smell in the air, blent with the delightful odor of newly plowed fields. I walked on and on until twilight had deepened into a moonlit autumn night. I was alone but not lonely. I held a series of imaginary conversations with imaginary comrades and thought out so many epigrams that I was agreeably surprised at myself. I couldn't help enjoying myself in spite of my Pringle worries.

"The spirit moves me to utter a few yowls regarding the Pringles. I hate to admit it but things are not going any too well in Summerside High. There is no doubt that a cabal has been organized against me.

"For one thing, home work is never done by any of the Pringles or half Pringles. And there is no use in appealing to the parents. They are suave, polite, evasive. I know all the pupils who are not Pringles like me but the Pringle virus of disobedience is undermining the morale of the whole room. One morning I found my desk turned inside out and upside down. Nobody knew who did it, of course. And no one could or would tell who left on it another day the box out of which popped an artificial snake when I opened it. But every Pringle in the school screamed with laughter over my face. I suppose I did look wildly startled.

"Jen Pringle comes late for school half the time, always with some perfectly water-tight excuse, delivered politely, with an insolent tilt to her mouth. She passes notes in class under my very nose. I found a peeled onion in the pocket of my coat when I put it on today. I should love to lock that girl up on bread and water until she learned how to behave herself.

"The worst thing to date was the caricature of myself I found on the blackboard one morning...done in white chalk with scarlet hair. Everybody denied doing it, Jen among the rest, but I knew Jen was the only pupil in the room who could draw like that. It was done well. My nose...which, as you know, has always been my one pride and joy...was humpbacked and my mouth was the mouth of a vinegary spinster who had been teaching a school full of Pringles for thirty years. But it was me. I woke up at three o'clock that night and writhed over the recollection. Isn't it queer that the things we writhe over at night are seldom wicked things? Just humiliating ones.

"All sorts of things are being said. I am accused of 'marking down' Hattie Pringle's examination papers just because she is a Pringle. I am said to 'laugh when the children make mistakes.' (Well, I did laugh when Fred Pringle defined a centurion as 'a man who had lived a hundred years.' I couldn't help it.)

"James Pringle is saying, 'There is no discipline in the school...no discipline whatever.' And a report is being circulated that I am a 'foundling.'

"I am beginning to encounter the Pringle antagonism in other quarters. Socially as well as educationally, Summerside seems to be under the Pringle thumb. No wonder they are called the Royal Family. I wasn't invited to Alice Pringle's walking party last Friday. And when Mrs. Frank Pringle got up a tea in aid of a church project (Rebecca Dew informs me that the ladies are going to 'build' the new spire!), I was the only girl in the Presbyterian church who was not asked to take a table. I have heard that the minister's wife, who is a newcomer in Summerside, suggested asking me to sing in the choir and was informed that all the Pringles would drop out of it if she did. That would leave such a skeleton that the choir simply couldn't carry on.

"Of course I'm not the only one of the teachers who has trouble with pupils. When the other teachers send theirs up to me to be 'disciplined'...how I hate that word!...half of them are Pringles. But there is never any complaint made about them.

"Two evenings ago I kept Jen in after school to do some work she had deliberately left undone. Ten minutes later the carriage from Maplehurst drew up before the school house and Miss Ellen was at the door...a beautifully dressed, sweetly smiling old lady, with elegant black lace mitts and a fine hawk-like nose, looking as if she had just stepped out of an 1840 band-box. She was so sorry but could she have Jen? She was going to visit friends in Lowvale and had promised to take Jen. Jen went off triumphantly and I realized afresh the forces arrayed against me.

"In my pessimistic moods I think the Pringles are a compound of Sloanes and Pyes. But I know they're not. I feel that I could like them if they were not my enemies. They are, for the most part, a frank, jolly, loyal set. I could even like Miss Ellen. I've never seen Miss Sarah. Miss Sarah has not left Maplehurst for ten years.

"'Too delicate...or thinks she is,' says Rebecca Dew with a sniff. 'But there ain't anything the matter with her pride. All the Pringles are proud but those two old girls pass everything. You should hear them talk about their ancestors. Well, their old father, Captain Abraham Pringle, was a fine old fellow. His brother Myrom wasn't quite so fine, but you don't hear the Pringles talking much about him. But I'm desprit afraid you're going to have a hard time with them all. When they make up their mind about anything or anybody they've never been known to change it. But keep your chin up, Miss Shirley...keep your chin up.'

"'I wish I could get Miss Ellen's recipe for pound cake,' sighed Aunt Chatty. 'She's promised it to me time and again but it never comes. It's an old English family recipe. They're so exclusive about their recipes.'

"In wild fantastic dreams I see myself compelling Miss Ellen to hand that recipe over to Aunt Chatty on bended knee and make Jen mind her p's and q's. The maddening thing is that I could easily make Jen do it myself if her whole clan weren't backing her up in her deviltry."

(Two pages omitted.)

"Your obedient servant,

"ANNE SHIRLEY.

"P.S. That was how Aunt Chatty's grandmother signed her love letters."

"October 15th.

"We heard today that there had been a burglary at the other end of the town last night. A house was entered and some money and a dozen silver spoons stolen. So Rebecca Dew has gone up to Mr. Hamilton's to see if she can borrow a dog. She will tie him on the back veranda and she advises me to lock up my engagement ring!

"By the way, I found out why Rebecca Dew cried. It seems there had been a domestic convulsion. Dusty Miller had 'misbehaved again' and Rebecca Dew told Aunt Kate she would really have to do something about That Cat. He was wearing her to a fiddle-string. It was the third time in a year and she knew he did it on purpose. And Aunt Kate said that if Rebecca Dew would always let the cat out when he meowed there would be no danger of his misbehaving.

"'Well, this is the last straw,' said Rebecca Dew.

"Consequently, tears!

"The Pringle situation grows a little more acute every week. Something very impertinent was written across one of my books yesterday and Homer Pringle turned handsprings all the way down the aisle when leaving school. Also, I got an anonymous letter recently full of nasty innuendoes. Somehow, I don't blame Jen for either the book or the letter. Imp as she is, there are things she wouldn't stoop to. Rebecca Dew is furious and I shudder to think what she would do to the Pringles if she had them in her power. Nero's wish isn't to be compared to it. I really don't blame her, for there are times when I feel myself that I could cheerfully hand any and all of the Pringles a poisoned philter of Borgia brewing.

"I don't think I've told you much about the other teachers. There are two, you know...the Vice-principal, Katherine Brooke of the Junior Room, and George MacKay of the Prep. Of George I have little to say. He is a shy, good-natured lad of twenty, with a slight, delicious Highland accent suggestive of low shielings and misty islands...his grandfather 'was Isle of Skye'...and does very well with the Preps. So far as I know him I like him. But I'm afraid I'm going to have a hard time liking Katherine Brooke.

"Katherine is a girl of, I think, about twenty-eight, though she looks thirty-five. I have been told she cherished hopes of promotion to the Principalship and I suppose she resents my getting it, especially when I am considerably her junior. She is a good teacher...a bit of a martinet...but she is not popular with any one. And doesn't worry over it! She doesn't seem to have any friends or relations and boards in a gloomy-looking house on grubby little Temple Street. She dresses very dowdily, never goes out socially and is said to be 'mean.' She is very sarcastic and her pupils dread her biting remarks. I am told that her way of raising her thick black eyebrows and drawling at them reduces them to a pulp. I wish I could work it on the Pringles. But I really shouldn't like to govern by fear as she does. I want my pupils to love me.

"In spite of the fact that she has apparently no trouble in making them toe the line she is constantly sending some of them up to me...especially Pringles. I know she does it purposely and I feel miserably certain that she exults in my difficulties and would be glad to see me worsted.

"Rebecca Dew says that no one can make friends with her. The widows have invited her several times to Sunday supper...the dear souls are always doing that for lonely people, and always have the most delicious chicken salad for them...but she never came. So they have given it up because, as Aunt Kate says, 'there are limits.'

"There are rumors that she is very clever and can sing and recite...'elocute,' a la Rebecca Dew...but will not do either. Aunt Chatty once asked her to recite at a church supper.

"'We thought she refused very ungraciously,' said Aunt Kate.

"'Just growled,' said Rebecca Dew.

"Katherine has a deep throaty voice...almost a man's voice...and it does sound like a growl when she isn't in good humor.

"She isn't pretty but she might make more of herself. She is dark and swarthy, with magnificent black hair always dragged back from her high forehead and coiled in a clumsy knot at the base of her neck. Her eyes don't match her hair, being a clear, light amber under her black brows. She has ears she needn't be ashamed to show and the most beautiful hands I've ever seen. Also, she has a well-cut mouth. But she dresses terribly. Seems to have a positive genius for getting the colors and lines she should not wear. Dull dark greens and drab grays, when she is too sallow for greens and grays, and stripes which make her tall, lean figure even taller and leaner. And her clothes always look as if she'd slept in them.

"Her manner is very repellent...as Rebecca Dew would say, she always has a chip on her shoulder. Every time I pass her on the stairs I feel that she is thinking horrid things about me. Every time I speak to her she makes me feel I've said the wrong thing. And yet I'm very sorry for her...though I know she would resent my pity furiously. And I can't do anything to help her because she doesn't want to be helped. She is really hateful to me. One day, when we three teachers were all in the staff room, I did something which, it seems, transgressed one of the unwritten laws of the school, and Katherine said cuttingly, 'Perhaps you think you are above rules, Miss Shirley.' At another time, when I was suggesting some changes which I thought would be for the good of the school, she said with a scornful smile, 'I'm not interested in fairy tales.' Once, when I said some nice things about her work and methods, she said, 'And what is to be the pill in all this jam?'

"But the thing that annoyed me most...well, one day when I happened to pick up a book of hers in the staff room and glanced at the flyleaf I said,

"'I'm glad you spell your name with a K. Katherine is so much more alluring than Catherine, just as K is ever so much gypsier a letter than smug C.'

"She made no response, but the next note she sent up was signed 'Catherine Brooke'!

"I sneezed all the way home.

"I really would give up trying to be friends with her if I hadn't a queer, unaccountable feeling that under all her bruskness and aloofness she is actually starved for companionship.

"Altogether, what with Katherine's antagonism and the Pringle attitude, I don't know just what I'd do if it wasn't for dear Rebecca Dew and your letters...and little Elizabeth.

"Because I've got acquainted with little Elizabeth. And she

is a darling.

"Three nights ago I took the glass of milk to the wall door and little Elizabeth herself was there to get it instead of the Woman, her head just coming above the solid part of the door, so that her face was framed in the ivy. She is small, pale, golden and wistful. Her eyes, looking at me through the autumn twilight, are large and golden-hazel. Her silver-gold hair was parted in the middle, sleeked plainly down over her head with a circular comb, and fell in waves on her shoulders. She wore a pale blue gingham dress and the expression of a princess of elf-land. She had what Rebecca Dew calls 'a delicate air,' and gave me the impression of a child who was more or less undernourished...not in body, but in soul. More of a moonbeam than a sunbeam.

"'And this is Elizabeth?' I said.

"'Not tonight,' she answered gravely. 'This is my night for being Betty because I love everything in the world tonight. I was Elizabeth last night and tomorrow night I'll prob'ly be Beth. It all depends on how I feel.'

"There was the touch of the kindred spirit for you. I thrilled to it at once.

"'How very nice to have a name you can change so easily and still feel it's your own.'

"Little Elizabeth nodded.

"'I can make so many names out of it. Elsie and Betty and Bess and Elisa and Lisbeth and Beth...but not Lizzie. I never can feel like Lizzie.'

"'Who could?' I said.

"'Do you think it silly of me, Miss Shirley? Grandmother and the Woman do.'

"'Not silly at all...very wise and very delightful,' I said..

"Little Elizabeth made saucer eyes at me over the rim of her glass. I felt that I was being weighed in some secret spiritual balance and presently I realized thankfully that I had not been found wanting. For little Elizabeth asked a favor of me...and little Elizabeth does not ask favors of people she does not like.

"'Would you mind lifting up the cat and letting me pat him?' she asked shyly.

"Dusty Miller was rubbing against my legs. I lifted him and little Elizabeth put out a tiny hand and stroked his head delightedly.

"'I like kittens better than babies,' she said, looking at me with an odd little air of defiance, as if she knew I would be shocked but tell the truth she must.

"'I suppose you've never had much to do with babies, so you don't know how sweet they are,' I said, smiling. 'Have you a kitten of your own?'

"Elizabeth shook her head.

"'Oh, no; Grandmother doesn't like cats. And the Woman hates them. The Woman is out tonight, so that is why I could come for the milk. I love coming for the milk because Rebecca Dew is such an agree'ble person.'

"'Are you sorry she didn't come tonight?' I laughed.

"Little Elizabeth shook her head.

"'No. You are very agree'ble, too. I've been wanting to get 'quainted with you but I was afraid it mightn't happen before Tomorrow comes.'

"We stood there and talked while Elizabeth sipped her milk daintily and she told me all about Tomorrow. The Woman had told her that Tomorrow never comes, but Elizabeth knows better. It will come sometime. Some beautiful morning she will just wake up and find it is Tomorrow. Not Today but Tomorrow. And then things will happen...wonderful things. She may even have a day to do exactly as she likes in, with nobody watching her...though I think Elizabeth feels that is too good to happen even in Tomorrow. Or she may find out what is at the end of the harbor road...that wandering, twisting road like a nice red snake, that leads, so Elizabeth thinks, to the end of the world. Perhaps the Island of Happiness is there. Elizabeth feels sure there is an Island of Happiness somewhere where all the ships that never come back are anchored, and she will find it when Tomorrow comes.

"'And when Tomorrow comes,' said Elizabeth, 'I will have a million dogs and forty-five cats. I told Grandmother that when she wouldn't let me have a kitten, Miss Shirley, and she was angry and said, "I'm not 'customed to be spoken to like that, Miss Impert'nence." I was sent to bed without supper...but I didn't mean to be impert'nent. And I couldn't sleep, Miss Shirley, because the Woman told me that she knew a child once that died in her sleep after being impert'nent.'

"When Elizabeth had finished her milk there came a sharp tapping at some unseen window behind the spruces. I think we had been watched all the time. My elf-maiden ran, her golden head glimmering along the dark spruce aisle until she vanished.

"'She's a fanciful little creature,' said Rebecca Dew when I told her of my adventure...really, it somehow had the quality of an adventure, Gilbert. 'One day she said to me, "Are you scared of lions, Rebecca Dew?" "I never met any so I can't tell you," sez I. "There will be any amount of lions in Tomorrow," sez she, "but they will be nice friendly lions." "Child, you'll turn into eyes if you look like that," sez I. She was looking clean through me at something she saw in that Tomorrow of hers. "I'm thinking deep thoughts, Rebecca Dew," she sez. The trouble with that child is she doesn't laugh enough.'

"I remembered Elizabeth had never laughed once during our talk. I feel that she hasn't learned how. The great house is so still and lonely and laughterless. It looks dull and gloomy even now when the world is a riot of autumn color. Little Elizabeth is doing too much listening to lost whispers.

"I think one of my missions in Summerside will be to teach her how to laugh.

"Your tenderest, most faithful friend,

"ANNE SHIRLEY.

"P.S. More of Aunt Chatty's grandmother!"

3

"Windy Poplars,

"Spook's Lane,

"S'side,

"October 25th.

"GILBERT DEAR:—

"What do you think? I've been to supper at Maplehurst!

"Miss Ellen herself wrote the invitation. Rebecca Dew was really excited...she had never believed they would take any notice of me. And she was quite sure it was not out of friendliness.

"'They have some sinister motive, that I'm certain of!' she exclaimed.

"I really had some such feeling in my own mind.

"'Be sure you put on your best,' ordered Rebecca Dew.

"So I put on my pretty cream challis dress with the purple violets in it and did my hair the new way with the dip in the forehead. It's very becoming.

"The ladies of Maplehurst are positively delightful in their own way, Gilbert. I could love them if they'd let me. Maplehurst is a proud, exclusive house which draws its trees around it and won't associate with common houses. It has a big, white, wooden woman off the bow of old Captain Abraham's famous ship, the Go and Ask Her, in the orchard and billows of southernwood about the front steps, which was brought out from the old country over a hundred years ago by the first emigrating Pringle. They have another ancestor who fought at the battle of Minden and his sword is hanging on the parlor wall beside Captain Abraham's portrait. Captain Abraham was their father and they are evidently tremendously proud of him.

"They have stately mirrors over the old, black, fluted mantels, a glass case with wax flowers in it, pictures full of the beauty of the ships of long ago, a hair-wreath containing the hair of every known Pringle, big conch shells and a quilt on the spare-room bed quilted in infinitesimal fans.

"We sat in the parlor on mahogany Sheraton chairs. It was hung with silver-stripe wallpaper. Heavy brocade curtains at the windows. Marble-topped tables, one bearing a beautiful model of a ship with crimson hull and snow-white sails—the Go and Ask Her. An enormous chandelier, all glass and dingle-dangles, suspended from the ceiling. A round mirror with a clock in the center...something Captain Abraham had brought home from 'foreign parts.' It was wonderful. I'd like something like it in our house of dreams.

"The very shadows were eloquent and traditional. Miss Ellen showed me millions...more or less...of Pringle photographs, many of them daguerreotypes in leather cases. A big tortoise-shell cat came in, jumped on my knee and was at once whisked out to the kitchen by Miss Ellen. She apologized to me. But I expect she had previously apologized to the cat in the kitchen.

"Miss Ellen did most of the talking. Miss Sarah, a tiny thing in a black silk dress and starched petticoat, with snow-white hair and eyes as black as her dress, thin, veined hands folded on her lap amid fine lace ruffles, sad, lovely, gentle, looked almost too fragile to talk. And yet I got the impression, Gilbert, that every Pringle of the clan, including Miss Ellen herself, danced to her piping.

"We had a delicious supper. The water was cold, the linen beautiful, the dishes and glassware thin. We were waited on by a maid, quite as aloof and aristocratic as themselves. But Miss

Sarah pretended to be a little deaf whenever I spoke to her and I thought every mouthful would choke me. All my courage oozed out of me. I felt just like a poor fly caught on fly-paper. Gilbert, I can never, never conquer or win the Royal Family. I can see myself resigning at New Year's. I haven't a chance against a clan like that.

"And yet I couldn't help feeling a little sorry for the old ladies as I looked around their house. It had once lived...people had been born there...died there...exulted there...known sleep, despair, fear, joy, love, hope, hate. And now it has nothing but the memories by which they live...and their pride in them.

"Aunt Chatty is much upset because when she unfolded clean sheets for my bed today she found a diamond-shaped crease in the center. She is sure it foretells a death in the household. Aunt Kate is very much disgusted with such superstition. But I believe I rather like superstitious people. They lend color to life. Wouldn't it be a rather drab world if everybody was wise and sensible...and good? What would we find to talk about?

"We had a catastrophe here two nights ago. Dusty Miller stayed out all night, in spite of Rebecca Dew's stentorian shouts of 'Puss' in the back yard. And when he turned up in the morning...oh, such a looking cat! One eye was closed completely and there was a lump as big as an egg on his jaw. His fur was stiff with mud and one paw was bitten through. But what a triumphant, unrepentant look he had in his one good eye! The widows were horrified but Rebecca Dew said exultantly, 'That Cat has never had a good fight in his life before. And I'll bet the other cat looks far worse than he does!'

"A fog is creeping up the harbor tonight, blotting out the red road that little Elizabeth wants to explore. Weeds and leaves are burning in all the town gardens and the combination of smoke and fog is making Spook's Lane an eerie, fascinating, enchanted place. It is growing late and my bed says, 'I have sleep for you.' I've grown used to climbing a flight of steps into bed...and climbing down them. Oh, Gilbert, I've never told any one this, but it's too funny to keep any longer. The first morning I woke up in Windy Poplars I forgot all about the steps and made a blithe morning-spring out of bed. I came down like a thousand of brick, as Rebecca Dew would say. Luckily I didn't break any bones, but I was black and blue for a week.

"Little Elizabeth and I are very good friends by now. She comes every evening for her milk because the Woman is laid up with what Rebecca Dew calls 'brownkites.' I always find her at the wall gate, waiting for me, her big eyes full of twilight. We talk with the gate, which has never been opened for years, between us. Elizabeth sips the glass of milk as slowly as possible in order to spin our conversation out. Always, when the last drop is drained, comes the tap-tap on the window.

"I have found that one of the things that is going to happen in Tomorrow is that she will get a letter from her father. She had never got one. I wonder what the man can be thinking of.

"'You know, he couldn't bear the sight of me, Miss Shirley,' she told me, 'but he mightn't mind writing to me.'

"'Who told you he couldn't bear the sight of you?' I asked indignantly.

"'The Woman.' (Always when Elizabeth says 'the Woman,' I can see her like a great big forbidding 'W,' all angles and corners.) 'And it must be true or he would come to see me sometimes.'

"She was Beth that night...it is only when she is Beth that she will talk of her father. When she is Betty she makes faces at her grandmother and the Woman behind their backs; but when she turns into Elsie she is sorry for it and thinks she ought to confess, but is scared to. Very rarely she is Elizabeth and then she has the face of one who listens to fairy music and knows what roses and clovers talk about. She's the quaintest thing, Gilbert...as sensitive as one of the leaves of the windy poplars, and I love her. It infuriates me to know that those two terrible old women make her go to bed in the dark.

"'The Woman said I was big enough to sleep without a light. But I feel so small, Miss Shirley, because the night is so big and awful. And there is a stuffed crow in my room and I am afraid of it. The Woman told me it would pick my eyes out if I cried. Of course, Miss Shirley, I don't believe that, but still I'm scared. Things whisper so to each other at night. But in Tomorrow I'll never be scared of anything...not even of being kidnaped!'

"'But there is no danger of your being kidnaped, Elizabeth.'

"'The Woman said there was if I went anywhere alone or talked to strange persons. But you're not a strange person, are you, Miss Shirley?'

"'No, darling. We've always known each other in Tomorrow,' I said."

4

"Windy Poplars,

"Spook's Lane,

"S'side,

"November 10th.

"DEAREST:

"It used to be that the person I hated most in the world was the person who spoiled my pen-nib. But I can't hate Rebecca Dew in spite of her habit of using my pen to copy recipes when

I'm in school. She's been doing it again and as a result you won't get a long or a loving letter this time. (Belovedest.)

"The last cricket song has been sung. The evenings are so chilly now that I have a small chubby, oblong wood-stove in my room. Rebecca Dew put it up...I forgive her the pen for it. There's nothing that woman can't do; and she always has a fire lighted for me in it when I come home from school. It is the tiniest of stoves...I could pick it up in my hands. It looks just like a pert little black dog on its four bandy iron legs. But when you fill it with hardwood sticks it blooms rosy red and throws a wonderful heat and you can't think how cozy it is. I'm sitting before it now, with my feet on its tiny hearth, scribbling to you on my knee.

"Every one else in S'side...more or less...is at the Hardy Pringles' dance. I was not invited. And Rebecca Dew is so cross about it that I'd hate to be Dusty Miller. But when I think of Hardy's daughter Myra, beautiful and brainless, trying to prove in an examination paper that the angels at the base of an isosceles triangle are equal, I forgive the entire Pringle clan. And last week she included 'gallows tree' quite seriously in a list of trees! But, to be just, all the howlers don't originate with the Pringles. Blake Fenton defined an alligator recently as 'a large kind of insect.' Such are the high lights of a teacher's life!

"It feels like snow tonight. I like an evening when it feels like snow. The wind is blowing 'in turret and tree' and making my cozy room seem even cozier. The last golden leaf will be blown from the aspens tonight.

"I think I've been invited to supper everywhere by now...I mean to the homes of all my pupils, both in town and country. And oh, Gilbert darling, I am so sick of pumpkin preserves! Never, never let us have pumpkin preserves in our house of dreams.

"Almost everywhere I've gone for the last month I've had P. P. for supper. The first time I had it I loved it...it was so golden that I felt I was eating preserved sunshine...and I incautiously raved about it. It got bruited about that I was very fond of P. P. and people had it on purpose for me. Last night I was going to Mr. Hamilton's and Rebecca Dew assured me that I wouldn't have to eat P. P. there because none of the Hamiltons liked it. But when we sat down to supper, there on the sideboard was the inevitable cut-glass bowl full of P. P.

"'I hadn't any punkin preserves of my own,' said Mrs. Hamilton, ladling me out a generous dishful, 'but I heard you was terrible partial to it, so when I was to my cousin's in Lowvale last Sunday I sez to her, "I'm having Miss Shirley to supper this week and she's terrible partial to punkin preserves. I wish you'd lend me a jar for her." So she did and here it is and you can take home what's left.'

"You should have seen Rebecca Dew's face when I arrived home from the Hamiltons' bearing a glass jar two-thirds full of P. P.! Nobody likes it here so we buried it darkly at dead of night in the garden.

"'You won't put this in a story, will you?' she asked anxiously. Ever since Rebecca Dew discovered that I do an occasional bit of fiction for the magazines she has lived in the fear...or hope, I don't know which...that I'll put everything that happens at Windy Poplars into a story. She wants me to 'write up the Pringles and blister them.' But alas, it's the Pringles that are doing the blistering and between them and my work in school I have scant time for writing fiction.

"There are only withered leaves and frosted stems in the garden now. Rebecca Dew has done the standard roses up in straw and potato bags, and in the twilight they look exactly like a group of humped-back old men leaning on staffs.

"I got a post-card from Davy today with ten kisses crossed on it and a letter from Priscilla written on some paper that 'a friend of hers in Japan' sent her...silky thin paper with dim cherry blossoms on it like ghosts. I'm beginning to have my suspicions about that friend of hers. But your big fat letter was the purple gift the day gave me. I read it four times over to get every bit of its savor...like a dog polishing off a plate! That certainly isn't a romantic simile, but it's the one that just popped into my head. Still, letters, even the nicest, aren't satisfactory. I want to see you. I'm glad it's only five weeks to Christmas holidays."

5

Anne, sitting at her tower window one late November evening, with her pen at her lip and dreams in her eyes, looked out on a twilight world and suddenly thought she would like a walk to the old graveyard. She had never visited it yet, preferring the birch and maple grove or the harbor road for her evening rambles. But there is always a November space after the leaves have fallen when she felt it was almost indecent to intrude on the woods...for their glory terrestrial had departed and their glory celestial of spirit and purity and whiteness had not yet come upon them. So Anne betook herself to the graveyard instead. She was feeling for the time so dispirited and hopeless that she thought a graveyard would be a comparatively cheerful place. Besides, it was full of Pringles, so Rebecca Dew said. They had buried there for generations, keeping it up in preference to the new graveyard until "no more of them could be squeezed in." Anne felt that it would be positively encouraging to see how many Pringles were where they couldn't annoy anybody any more.

In regard to the Pringles Anne felt that she was at the end of her tether. More and more the whole situation was coming to seem like a nightmare. The subtle campaign of insubordination and disrespect which Jen Pringle had organized had at last come to a head. One day, a week previously, she had asked the Seniors to write a composition on "The Most Important Happenings of the Week." Jen Pringle had written a brilliant one...the little imp was clever...and had inserted in it a sly insult to her teacher...one so pointed that it was impossible to ignore it. Anne had sent her home, telling her that she would have to apologize before she would be allowed to come back. The fat was fairly in the fire. It was open warfare now between her and the Pringles. And poor Anne had no doubt on whose banner victory would perch. The school board would back the Pringles up and she would be given her choice between letting Jen come back or being asked to resign.

She felt very bitter. She had done her best and she knew she could have succeeded if she had had even a fighting chance.

"It's not my fault," she thought miserably. "Who could succeed against such a phalanx and such tactics?"

But to go home to Green Gables defeated! To endure Mrs. Lynde's indignation and the Pyes' exultation! Even the sympathy of friends would be an anguish. And with her Summerside failure bruited abroad she would never be able to get another school.

But at least they had not got the better of her in the matter of the play. Anne laughed a little wickedly and her eyes filled with mischievous delight over the memory.

She had organized a High School Dramatic Club and directed it in a little play hurriedly gotten up to provide some funds for one of her pet schemes...buying some good engravings for the rooms. She had made herself ask Katherine Brooke to help her because Katherine always seemed so left out of everything. She could not help regretting it many times, for Katherine was even more brusk and sarcastic than usual. She seldom let a practice pass without some corrosive remark and she overworked her eyebrows. Worse still, it was Katherine who had insisted on having Jen Pringle take the part of Mary Queen of Scots.

"There's no one else in the school who can play it," she said impatiently. "No one who has the necessary personality."

Anne was not so sure of this. She rather thought that Sophy Sinclair, who was tall and had hazel eyes and rich chestnut hair, would make a far better Queen Mary than Jen. But Sophy was not even a member of the club and had never taken part in a play.

"We don't want absolute greenhorns in this. I'm not going to be associated with anything that is not successful," Katherine had said disagreeably, and Anne had yielded. She could not deny that Jen was very good in the part. She had a natural flair for acting and she apparently threw herself into it wholeheartedly. They practiced four evenings a week and on the surface things went along very smoothly. Jen seemed to be so interested in her part that she behaved herself as far as the play was concerned. Anne did not meddle with her but left her to Katherine's coaching. Once or twice, though, she surprised a certain look of sly triumph on Jen's face that puzzled her. She could not guess just what it meant.

One afternoon, soon after the practices had begun, Anne found Sophy Sinclair in tears in a corner of the girls' coatroom. At first she had blinked her hazel eyes vigorously and denied it...then broke down.

"I did so want to be in the play...to be Queen Mary," she sobbed. "I've never had a chance...father wouldn't let me join the club because there are dues to pay and every cent counts so much. And of course I haven't had any experience. I've always loved Queen Mary...her very name just thrills me to my finger tips. I don't believe...I never will believe she had anything to do with murdering Darnley. It would have been wonderful to fancy I was she for a little while!"

Afterwards Anne concluded that it was her guardian angel

who prompted her reply.

"I'll write the part out for you, Sophy, and coach you in it. It will be good training for you. And, as we plan to give the play in other places if it goes well here, it will be just as well to have an understudy in case Jen shouldn't always be able to go. But we'll say nothing about it to any one."

Sophy had the part memorized by the next day. She went home to Windy Poplars with Anne every afternoon when school came out and rehearsed it in the tower. They had a lot of fun together, for Sophy was full of quiet vivacity. The play was to be put on the last Friday in November in the town hall; it was widely advertised and the reserved seats were sold to the last one. Anne and Katherine spent two evenings decorating the hall, the band was hired, and a noted soprano was coming up from Charlottetown to sing between the acts. The dress rehearsal was a success. Jen was really excellent and the whole cast played up to her. Friday morning Jen was not in school; and in the afternoon her mother sent word that Jen was ill with a very sore throat...they were afraid it was tonsillitis. Everybody concerned was very sorry, but it was out of the question that she should take part in the play that night.

Katherine and Anne stared at each other, drawn together for once in their common dismay.

"We'll have to put it off," said Katherine slowly. "And that means failure. Once we're into December there's so much going on. Well, I always thought it was foolish to try to get up a play this time of the year."

"We are not going to postpone it," said Anne, her eyes as green as Jen's own. She was not going to say it to Katherine Brooke, but she knew as well as she had ever known anything in her life that Jen Pringle was in no more danger of tonsillitis than she was. It was a deliberate device, whether any of the other Pringles were a party to it or not, to ruin the play because she, Anne Shirley, had sponsored it.

"Oh, if you feel that way about it!" said Katherine with a nasty shrug. "But what do you intend to do? Get some one to read the part? That would ruin it...Mary is the whole play."

"Sophy Sinclair can play the part as well as Jen. The costume will fit her and, thanks be, you made it and have it, not Jen."

The play was put on that night before a packed audience. A delighted Sophy played Mary...was Mary, as Jen Pringle could never have been...looked Mary in her velvet robes and ruff and jewels. Students of Summerside High, who had never seen Sophy in anything but her plain, dowdy, dark serge dresses, shapeless coat and shabby hats, stared at her in amazement. It was insisted on the spot that she become a permanent member of the Dramatic Club—Anne herself paid the membership fee—and from then on she was one of the pupils who "counted" in Summerside High. But nobody knew or dreamed, Sophy herself least of all, that she had taken the first step that night on a pathway that was to lead to the stars. Twenty years later Sophy Sinclair was to be one of the leading actresses in America. But probably no plaudits ever sounded so sweet in her ears as the wild applause amid which the curtain fell that night in Summerside town hall.

Mrs. James Pringle took a tale home to her daughter Jen which would have turned that damsel's eyes green if they had not been already so. For once, as Rebecca Dew said feelingly, Jen had got her come-uppance. And the eventual result was the insult in the composition on Important Happenings.

Anne went down to the old graveyard along a deep-rutted lane between high, mossy stone dykes, tasseled with frosted ferns. Slim, pointed lombardies, from which November winds had not yet stripped all the leaves, grew along it at intervals, coming out darkly against the amethyst of the far hills; but the old graveyard, with half its tombstones leaning at a drunken slant, was surrounded by a four-square row of tall, somber fir trees. Anne had not expected to find any one there and was a little taken aback when she met Miss Valentine Courtaloe, with her long delicate nose, her thin delicate mouth, her sloping delicate shoulders and her general air of invincible lady-likeness, just inside the gate. She knew Miss Valentine, of course, as did everyone in Summerside. She was "the" local dressmaker and what she didn't know about people, living or dead, was not worth taking into account. Anne had wanted to wander about by herself, read the odd old epitaphs and puzzle out the names of forgotten lovers under the lichens that were growing over them. But she could not escape when Miss Valentine slipped an arm through hers and proceeded to do the honors of the graveyard, where there were evidently as many Courtaloes buried as Pringles. Miss Valentine had not a drop of Pringle blood in her and one of Anne's favorite pupils was her nephew. So it was no great mental strain to be nice to her, except that one must be very careful never to hint that she "sewed for a living." Miss Valentine was said to be very sensitive on that point.

"I'm glad I happened to be here this evening," said Miss Valentine. "I can tell you all about everybody buried here. I always say you have to know the ins and outs of the corpses to find a graveyard real enjoyable. I like a walk here better than in the new. It's only the old families that are buried here but every Tom, Dick and Harry is being buried in the new. The Courtaloes are buried in this corner. My, we've had a terrible lot of funerals in our family."

"I suppose every old family has," said Anne, because Miss Valentine evidently expected her to say something.

"Don't tell me any family has ever had as many as ours,"

said Miss Valentine jealously. "We're very consumptive. Most of us died of a cough. This is my Aunt Bessie's grave. She was a saint if ever there was one. But there's no doubt her sister, Aunt Cecilia, was the more interesting to talk to. The last time I ever saw her she said to me, 'Sit down, my dear, sit down. I'm going to die tonight at ten minutes past eleven but that's no reason why we shouldn't have a real good gossip for the last.' The strange thing, Miss Shirley, is that she did die that night at ten minutes past eleven. Can you tell me how she knew it?"

Anne couldn't.

"My Great-great-grandfather Courtaloe is buried here. He came out in 1760 and he made spinning-wheels for a living. I've heard he made fourteen hundred in the course of his life. When he died the minister preached from the text, 'Their works do follow them,' and old Myrom Pringle said in that case the road to heaven behind my great-great-grandfather would be choked with spinning-wheels. Do you think such a remark was in good taste, Miss Shirley?"

Had any one but a Pringle said it, Anne might not have remarked so decidedly, "I certainly do not," looking at a gravestone adorned with a skull and cross-bones as if she questioned the good taste of that also.

"My cousin Dora is buried here. She had three husbands but they all died very rapidly. Poor Dora didn't seem to have any luck picking a healthy man. Her last one was Benjamin Banning...not buried here...buried in Lowvale beside his first wife...and he wasn't reconciled to dying. Dora told him he was going to a better world. 'Mebbe, mebbe,' says poor Ben, 'but I'm sorter used to the imperfections of this one.' He took sixty-one different kinds of medicine but in spite of that he lingered for a good while. All Uncle David Courtaloe's family are here. There's a cabbage rose planted at the foot of every grave and, my, don't they bloom! I come here every summer and gather them for my rose-jar. It would be a pity to let them go to waste, don't you think?"

"I...I suppose so."

"My poor young sister Harriet lies here," sighed Miss Valentine. "She had magnificent hair...about the color of yours...not so red perhaps. It reached to her knees. She was engaged when she died. They tell me you're engaged. I never much wanted to be married but I think it would have been nice to be engaged. Oh, I've had some chances of course...perhaps I was too fastidious...but a Courtaloe couldn't marry everybody, could she?"

It did not seem likely she could.

"Frank Digby...over in that corner under the sumacs...wanted me. I did feel a little regretful over refusing him...but a Digby, my dear! He married Georgina Troop. She always went to church a little late to show off her clothes. My, she was fond of clothes. She was buried in such a pretty blue dress...I made it for her to wear to a wedding but in the end she wore it to her own funeral. She had three darling little children. They used to sit in front of me at church and I always gave them candy. Do you think it wrong to give children candy in church, Miss Shirley? Not peppermints...that would be all right...there's something religious about peppermints, don't you think? But the poor things don't like them."

When the Courtaloe's plots were exhausted Miss Valentine's reminiscences became a bit spicier. It did not make so much difference if you weren't a Courtaloe.

"Old Mrs. Russell Pringle is here. I often wonder if she's in heaven or not."

"But why?" gasped a rather shocked Anne.

"Well, she always hated her sister, Mary Ann, who had died a few months before. 'If Mary Ann is in heaven I won't stay there,' says she. And she was a woman who always kept her word, my dear...Pringle-like. She was born a Pringle and married her cousin Russell. This is Mrs. Dan Pringle...Janetta Bird. Seventy to a day when she died. Folks say she would have thought it wrong to die a day older than three-score and ten because that is the Bible limit. People do say such funny things, don't they? I've heard that dying was the only thing she ever dared do without asking her husband. Do you know, my dear, what he did once when she bought a hat he didn't like?"

"I can't imagine."

"He et it," said Miss Valentine solemnly. "Of course it was only a small hat...lace and flowers...no feathers. Still, it must have been rather indigestible. I understand he had gnawing pains in his stomach for quite a time. Of course I didn't see him eat it, but I've always been assured the story was true. Do you suppose it was?"

"I'd believe anything of a Pringle," said Anne bitterly.

Miss Valentine pressed her arm sympathetically.

"I feel for you...indeed I do. It's terrible the way they're treating you. But Summerside isn't all Pringle, Miss Shirley."

"Sometimes I think it is," said Anne with a rueful smile.

"No, it isn't. And there are plenty of people would like to see you get the better of them. Don't you give in to them no matter what they do. It's just the old Satan that's got into them. But they hang together so and Miss Sarah did want that cousin of theirs to get the school.

"The Nathan Pringles are here. Nathan always believed his wife was trying to poison him but he didn't seem to mind. He said it made life kind of exciting. Once he kind of suspected she'd put arsenic in his porridge. He went out and fed it to a pig. The pig died three weeks afterwards. But he said maybe it was only a coincidence and anyway he couldn't be sure it was the same pig. In the end she died before him and he said she'd always been a real good wife to him except for that one thing. I think it would be charitable to believe that he was mistaken about it."

"'Sacred to the memory of Miss Kinsey,'" read Anne in amazement. "What an extraordinary inscription! Had she no other name?"

"If she had, nobody ever knew it," said Miss Valentine. "She came from Nova Scotia and worked for the George Pringles for forty years. She gave her name as Miss Kinsey and everybody called her that. She died suddenly and then it was discovered that nobody knew her first name and she had no relations that anybody could find. So they put that on her stone...the George Pringles buried her very nicely and paid for the monument. She was a faithful, hard-working creature but if you'd ever seen her you'd have thought she was born Miss Kinsey. The James Morleys are here. I was at their golden wedding. Such a to-do... gifts and speeches and flowers...and their children all home and them smiling and bowing and just hating each other as hard as they could."

"Hating each other?"

"Bitterly, my dear. Every one knew it. They had for years and years...almost all their married life in fact. They quarreled on the way home from church after the wedding. I often wonder how they manage to lie here so peaceably side by side."

Again Anne shivered. How terrible...sitting opposite each other at table...lying down beside each other at night...going to church with their babies to be christened...and hating each other through it all! Yet they must have loved to begin with. Was it possible she and Gilbert could ever...nonsense! The Pringles were getting on her nerves.

"Handsome John MacTabb is buried here. He was always suspected of being the reason why Annetta Kennedy drowned herself. The MacTabbs were all handsome but you could never believe a word they said. There used to be a stone here for his Uncle Samuel, who was reported drowned at sea fifty years ago. When he turned up alive the family took the stone down. The man they bought it from wouldn't take it back so Mrs. Samuel used it for a baking-board. Talk about a marble slab for mixing on! That old tombstone was just fine, she said. The MacTabb children were always bringing cookies to school with raised letters and figures on them...scraps of the epitaph. They gave them away real generous, but I never could bring myself to eat one. I'm peculiar that way. Mr. Harley Pringle is here. He had to wheel Peter MacTabb down Main Street once, in a wheelbarrow, wearing a bonnet, for an election bet. All Summerside turned out to see it...except the Pringles, of course. They nearly died of shame. Milly Pringle is here. I was very fond of Milly, even if she was a Pringle. She was so pretty and as light-footed as a fairy. Sometimes I think, my dear, on nights like this she must slip out of her grave and dance like she used to do. But I suppose a Christian shouldn't be harboring such thoughts. This is Herb Pringle's grave. He was one of the jolly Pringles. He always made you laugh. He laughed right out in church once...when the mouse dropped out of the flowers on Meta Pringle's hat when she bowed in prayer. I didn't feel much like laughing. I didn't know where the mouse had gone. I pulled my skirts tight about my ankles and held them there till church was out, but it spoiled the sermon for me. Herb sat behind me and such a shout as he gave. People who couldn't see the mouse thought he'd gone crazy. It seemed to me that laugh of his couldn't die. If he was alive he'd stand up for you, Sarah or no Sarah. This, of course, is Captain Abraham Pringle's monument."

It dominated the whole graveyard. Four receding platforms of stone formed a square pedestal on which rose a huge pillar of marble topped with a ridiculous draped urn beneath which a fat cherub was blowing a horn.

"How ugly!" said Anne candidly.

"Oh, do you think so?" Miss Valentine seemed rather shocked. "It was thought very handsome when it was erected. That is supposed to be Gabriel blowing his trumpet. I think it gives quite a touch of elegance to the graveyard. It cost nine hundred dollars. Captain Abraham was a very fine old man. It is a great pity he is dead. If he was living they wouldn't be persecuting you the way they are. I don't wonder Sarah and Ellen are proud of him, though I think they carry it a bit too far."

At the graveyard gate Anne turned and looked back. A strange, peaceful hush lay over the windless land. Long fingers of moonlight were beginning to pierce the darkling firs, touching a gravestone here and there, and making strange shadows among them. But the graveyard wasn't a sad place after all. Really, the people in it seemed alive after Miss Valentine's tales.

"I've heard you write," said Miss Valentine anxiously, as they went down the lane. "You won't put the things I've told you in your stories, will you?"

"You may be sure I won't," promised Anne.

"Do you think it is really wrong...or dangerous...to speak ill of the dead?" whispered Miss Valentine a bit anxiously.

"I don't suppose it's exactly either," said Anne. "Only...rather unfair...like hitting those who can't defend themselves. But you didn't say anything very dreadful of anybody, Miss Courtaloe."

"I told you Nathan Pringle thought his wife was trying to poison him..."

"But you give her the benefit of the doubt..." and Miss Valentine went her way reassured.

6

"I wended my way to the graveyard this evening," wrote Anne to Gilbert after she got home. "I think 'wend your way' is a lovely phrase and I work it in whenever I can. It sounds funny to say I enjoyed my stroll in the graveyard but I really did. Miss Courtaloe's stories were so funny. Comedy and tragedy are so mixed up in life, Gilbert. The only thing that haunts me is that tale of the two who lived together fifty years and hated each other all that time. I can't believe they really did. Somebody has said that 'hate is only love that has missed its way.' I feel sure that under the hatred they really loved each other...just as I really loved you all those years I thought I hated you...and I think death would show it to them. I'm glad I found out in life. And I have found out there are some decent Pringles...dead ones.

"Last night when I went down late for a drink of water I found Aunt Kate buttermilking her face in the pantry. She asked me not to tell Chatty...she would think it so silly. I promised I wouldn't.

"Elizabeth still comes for the milk, though the Woman is pretty well over her bronchitis. I wonder they let her, especially since old Mrs. Campbell is a Pringle. Last Saturday night Elizabeth...she was Betty that night I think...ran in singing when she left me and I distinctly heard the Woman say to her at the porch door, 'It's too near the Sabbath for you to be singing that song.' I am sure that Woman would prevent Elizabeth from singing on any day if she could!

"Elizabeth had on a new dress that night, a dark wine color...they do dress her nicely...and she said wistfully, 'I thought I looked a little bit pretty when I put it on tonight, Miss Shirley, and I wished father could see me. Of course he will see me in Tomorrow...but it sometimes seems so slow in coming. I wish we could hurry time a bit, Miss Shirley.'

"Now, dearest, I must work out some geometrical exercises. Geometry exercises have taken the place of what Rebecca calls my 'literary efforts.' The specter that haunts my daily path now is the dread of an exercise popping up in class that I can't do. And what would the Pringles say then, oh, then...oh, what would the Pringles say then!

"Meanwhile, as you love me and the cat tribe, pray for a poor broken-hearted, ill-used Thomas cat. A mouse ran over Rebecca Dew's foot in the pantry the other day and she has fumed ever since. 'That Cat does nothing but eat and sleep and let mice overrun everything. This is the last straw.' So she chivies him from pillar to post, routs him off his favorite cushion and...I know, for I caught her at it...assists him none too gently with her foot when she lets him out."

7

One Friday evening, at the end of a mild, sunny December day Anne went out to Lowvale to attend a turkey supper. Wilfred Bryce's home was in Lowvale, where he lived with an uncle, and he had asked her shyly if she would go out with him after school, go to the turkey supper in the church and spend Saturday at his home. Anne agreed, hoping that she might be able to influence the uncle to let Wilfred keep on going to High School. Wilfred was afraid that he would not be able to go back after New Year. He was a clever, ambitious boy and Anne felt a special interest in him.

It could not be said that she enjoyed her visit overmuch, except in the pleasure it gave Wilfred. His uncle and aunt were a rather odd and uncouth pair. Saturday morning was windy and dark, with showers of snow, and at first Anne wondered how she was going to put in the day. She felt tired and sleepy after the late hours of the turkey supper; Wilfred had to help thrash; and there was not even a book in sight. Then she thought of the battered old seaman's chest she had seen in the back of the hall upstairs and recalled Mrs. Stanton's request. Mrs. Stanton was writing a history of Prince County and had asked Anne if she knew of, or could find, any old diaries or documents that might be helpful.

"The Pringles, of course, have lots that I could use," she told Anne. "But I can't ask them. You know the Pringles and Stantons have never been friends."

"I can't ask them either, unfortunately," said Anne.

"Oh, I'm not expecting you to. All I want is for you to keep your eyes open when you are visiting round in other people's homes and if you find or hear of any old diaries or maps or anything like that, try to get the loan of them for me. You've no idea what interesting things I've found in old diaries...little bits of real life that make the old pioneers live again. I want to get things like that for my book as well as statistics and genealogical tables."

Anne asked Mrs. Bryce if they had any such old records. Mrs. Bryce shook her head.

"Not as I knows on. In course..." brightening up..."there's old Uncle Andy's chist up there. There might be something in it. He used to sail with old Captain Abraham Pringle. I'll go out and ask Duncan if ye kin root in it."

Duncan sent word back that she could "root" in it all she liked and if she found any "dockymints" she could have them. He'd been meaning to burn the hull contents anyway and take the chest for a tool-box. Anne accordingly rooted, but all she found was an old yellowed diary or "log" which Andy Bryce seemed to have kept all through his years at sea. Anne beguiled the stormy forenoon away by reading it with interest and amusement. Andy was learned in sea lore and had gone on many voyages with Captain Abraham Pringle, whom he evidently admired immensely. The diary was full of ill-spelled, ungrammatical tributes to the Captain's courage and resourcefulness, especially in one wild enterprise of beating round the Horn. But his admiration had not, it seemed, extended to Abraham's brother Myrom, who was also a captain but of a different ship.

"Up to Myrom Pringle's tonight. His wife made him mad and he up and throwed a glass of water in her face."

"Myrom is home. His ship was burned and they took to the boats. Nearly starved. In the end they et up Jonas Selkirk, who had shot himself. They lived on him till the Mary G. picked them up. Myrom told me this himself. Seemed to think it a good joke."

Anne shivered over this last entry, which seemed all the more horrifying for Andy's unimpassioned statement of the grim facts. Then she fell into a reverie. There was nothing in the book that could be of any use to Mrs. Stanton, but wouldn't Miss Sarah and Miss Ellen be interested in it since it contained so much about their adored old father? Suppose she sent it to them? Duncan Bryce had said she could do as she liked with it.

No, she wouldn't. Why should she try to please them or cater to their absurd pride, which was great enough now without any more food? They had set themselves to drive her out of the school and they were succeeding. They and their clan had beaten her.

Wilfred took her back to Windy Poplars that evening, both of them feeling happy. Anne had talked Duncan Bryce into letting Wilfred finish out his year in High School.

"Then I'll manage Queen's for a year and after that teach and educate myself," said Wilfred. "How can I ever repay you, Miss Shirley? Uncle wouldn't have listened to any one else, but he likes you. He said to me out in the barn, 'Red-haired women could always do what they liked with me.' But I don't think it was your hair, Miss Shirley, although it is so beautiful. It was just...you."

At two o'clock that night Anne woke up and decided that she would send Andy Bryce's diary to Maplehurst. After all, she had a bit of liking for the old ladies. And they had so little to make life warm...only their pride in their father. At three she woke again and decided she wouldn't. Miss Sarah pretending to be deaf, indeed! At four she was in the swithers again. Finally she determined she would send it to them. She wouldn't be petty. Anne had a horror of being petty...like the Pyes.

Having settled this, Anne went to sleep for keeps, thinking how lovely it was to wake up in the night and hear the first snowstorm of the winter around your tower and then snuggle down in your blankets and drift into dreamland again.

Monday morning she wrapped up the old diary carefully and sent it to Miss Sarah with a little note.

"DEAR MISS PRINGLE:

"I wonder if you would be interested in this old diary. Mr. Bryce gave it to me for Mrs. Stanton, who is writing a history of the county, but I don't think it would be of any use to her and I thought you might like to have it.

"Yours sincerely,

"ANNE SHIRLEY."

"That's a horribly stiff note," thought Anne, "but I can't write naturally to them. And I wouldn't be a bit surprised if they sent it haughtily back to me."

In the fine blue of the early winter evening Rebecca Dew got the shock of her life. The Maplehurst carriage drove along Spook's Lane, over the powdery snow, and stopped at the front gate. Miss Ellen got out of it and then...to every one's amazement...Miss Sarah, who had not left Maplehurst for ten years.

"They're coming to the front door," gasped Rebecca Dew, panic-stricken.

"Where else would a Pringle come to?" asked Aunt Kate.

"Of course...of course...but it sticks," said Rebecca tragically. "It does stick...you know it does. And it hasn't been opened since we house-cleaned last spring. This is the last straw."

The front door did stick...but Rebecca Dew wrenched it open with desperate violence and showed the Maplehurst ladies into the parlor.

"Thank heaven, we've had a fire in it today," she thought, "and all I hope is That Cat hasn't haired up the sofa. If Sarah Pringle got cat hairs on her dress in our parlor..."

Rebecca Dew dared not imagine the consequences. She called Anne from the tower room, Miss Sarah having asked if Miss Shirley were in, and then betook herself to the kitchen, half mad with curiosity as to what on earth was bringing the old Pringle girls to see Miss Shirley.

"If there's any more persecution in the wind..." said Rebecca Dew darkly.

Anne herself descended with considerable trepidation. Had they come to return the diary with icy scorn?

It was little, wrinkled, inflexible Miss Sarah who rose and spoke without preamble when Anne entered the room.

"We have come to capitulate," she said bitterly. "We can do nothing else...of course you knew that when you found that scandalous entry about poor Uncle Myrom. It wasn't true...it couldn't be true. Uncle Myrom was just taking a rise out of Andy Bryce...Andy was so credulous. But everybody outside of our family will be glad to believe it. You knew it would make us all a laughing stock...and worse. Oh, you are very clever. We admit that. Jen will apologize and behave herself in future...I, Sarah Pringle, assure you of that. If you will only promise not to tell Mrs. Stanton...not to tell any one...we will do anything...anything."

Miss Sarah wrung her fine lace handkerchief in her little blue-veined hands. She was literally trembling.

Anne stared in amazement...and horror. The poor old darlings! They thought she had been threatening them!

"Oh, you've misunderstood me dreadfully," she exclaimed, taking Miss Sarah's poor, piteous hands. "I...I never dreamed you would think I was trying to...oh, it was just because I thought you would like to have all those interesting details about your splendid father. I never dreamed of showing or telling that other little item to any one. I didn't think it was of the least importance. And I never will."

There was a moment's silence. Then Miss Sarah freed her hands gently, put her handkerchief to her eyes and sat down, with a faint blush on her fine wrinkled face.

"We...we have misunderstood you, my dear. And we've...we've been abominable to you. Will you forgive us?"

Half an hour later...a half hour which nearly was the death of Rebecca Dew...the Misses Pringle went away. It had been a half hour of friendly chat and discussion about the non-combustible items of Andy's diary. At the front door Miss Sarah...who had not had the least trouble with her hearing during the interview...turned back for a moment and took a bit of paper, covered with very fine, sharp writing, from her reticule.

"I had almost forgotten...we promised Mrs. MacLean our recipe for pound cake some time ago. Perhaps you won't mind handing it to her? And tell her the sweating process is very important...quite indispensable, indeed. Ellen, your bonnet is slightly over one ear. You had better adjust it before we leave. We...we were somewhat agitated while dressing."

Anne told the widows and Rebecca Dew that she had given Andy Bryce's old diary to the ladies of Maplehurst and that they had come to thank her for it. With this explanation they had to be contented, although Rebecca Dew always felt that there was more behind it than that...much more. Gratitude for an old faded, tobacco-stained diary would never have brought Sarah Pringle to the front door of Windy Poplars. Miss Shirley was deep...very deep!

"I'm going to open that front door once a day after this," vowed Rebecca. "Just to keep it in practice. I all but went over flat when it did give way. Well, we've got the recipe for the pound cake anyway. Thirty-six eggs! If you'd dispose of That Cat and let me keep hens we might be able to afford it once a year."

Whereupon Rebecca Dew marched to the kitchen and got square with fate by giving That Cat milk when she knew he wanted liver.

The Shirley-Pringle feud was over. Nobody outside of the Pringles ever knew why, but Summerside people understood that Miss Shirley, single-handed, had, in some mysterious way, routed the whole clan, who ate out of her hand from then on. Jen came back to school the next day and apologized meekly to Anne before the whole room. She was a model pupil thereafter and every Pringle student followed her lead. As for the adult Pringles, their antagonism vanished like mist before the sun. There were no more complaints regarding "discipline" or home work. No more of the fine, subtle snubs characteristic of the ilk. They fairly fell over one another trying to be nice to Anne. No dance or skating party was complete without her. For, although the fatal diary had been committed to the flames by Miss Sarah herself, memory was memory and Miss Shirley had a tale to tell if she chose to tell it. It would never do to have that nosey Mrs. Stanton know that Captain Myrom Pringle had been a cannibal!

8

(Extract from letter to Gilbert)

"I am in my tower and Rebecca Dew is caroling Could I but climb? in the kitchen. Which reminds me that the minister's wife has asked me to sing in the choir! Of course the Pringles have told her to do it. I may do it on the Sundays I don't spend at Green Gables. The Pringles have held out the right hand of fellowship with a vengeance...accepted me lock, stock and barrel. What a clan!

"I've been to three Pringle parties. I set nothing down in malice but I think all the Pringle girls are imitating my style of hair-dressing. Well, 'imitation is the sincerest flattery.' And, Gilbert, I'm really liking them...as I always knew I would if they would give me a chance. I'm even beginning to suspect that sooner or later I'll find myself liking Jen. She can be charming when she wants to be and it is very evident she wants to be.

"Last night I bearded the lion in his den...in other words, I went boldly up the front steps of The Evergreens to the square porch with the four whitewashed iron urns in its corners, and rang the bell. When Miss Monkman came to the door I asked her if she would lend little Elizabeth to me for a walk. I expected a refusal, but after the Woman had gone in and conferred with Mrs. Campbell, she came back and said dourly that Elizabeth could go but, please, I wasn't to keep her out late. I wonder if even Mrs. Campbell has got her orders from Miss Sarah.

"Elizabeth came dancing down the dark stairway, looking like a pixy in a red coat and little green cap, and almost speechless for joy.

"'I feel all squirmy and excited, Miss Shirley,' she whispered as soon as we got away. 'I'm Betty...I'm always Betty when I feel like that.'

"We went as far down the Road that Leads to the End of the World as we dared and then back. Tonight the harbor, lying dark under a crimson sunset, seemed full of implications of 'fairylands forlorn' and mysterious isles in uncharted seas. I thrilled to it and so did the mite I held by the hand.

"'If we ran hard, Miss Shirley, could we get into the sunset?' she wanted to know. I remembered Paul and his fancies about the 'sunset land.'

"'We must wait for Tomorrow before we can do that,' I said. 'Look, Elizabeth, at that golden island of cloud just over the harbor mouth. Let's pretend that's your island of Happiness.'

"'There is an island down there somewhere,' said Elizabeth dreamily. 'Its name is Flying Cloud. Isn't that a lovely name...a name just out of Tomorrow? I can see it from the garret windows. It belongs to a gentleman from Boston and he has a summer home there. But I pretend it's mine.'

"At the door I stooped and kissed Elizabeth's cheek before she went in. I shall never forget her eyes. Gilbert, that child is just starved for love.

"Tonight, when she came over for her milk, I saw that she had been crying.

"'They...they made me wash your kiss off, Miss Shirley,' she sobbed. 'I didn't want ever to wash my face again. I vowed I wouldn't. Because, you see, I didn't want to wash your kiss off. I got away to school this morning without doing it, but tonight the Woman just took me and scrubbed it off.'

"I kept a straight face.

"'You couldn't go through life without washing your face occasionally, darling. But never mind about the kiss. I'll kiss you every night when you come for the milk and then it won't matter if it is washed off the next morning.'

"'You are the only person who loves me in the world,' said Elizabeth. 'When you talk to me I smell violets.'

"Was anybody ever paid a prettier compliment? But I couldn't quite let the first sentence pass.

"'Your grandmother loves you, Elizabeth.'

"'She doesn't...she hates me.'

"'You're just a wee bit foolish, darling. Your grandmother

and Miss Monkman are both old people and old people are easily disturbed and worried. Of course you annoy them sometimes. And...of course...when they were young, children were brought up much more strictly than they are now. They cling to the old way.'

"But I felt I was not convincing Elizabeth. After all, they don't love her and she knows it. She looked carefully back at the house to see if the door was shut. Then she said deliberately:

"'Grandmother and the Woman are just two old tyrants and when Tomorrow comes I'm going to escape them forever.'

"I think she expected I'd die of horror...I really suspect Elizabeth said it just to make a sensation. I merely laughed and kissed her. I hope Martha Monkman saw it from the kitchen window.

"I can see over Summerside from the left window in the tower. Just now it is a huddle of friendly white roofs...friendly at last since the Pringles are my friends. Here and there a light is gleaming in gable and dormer. Here and there is a suggestion of gray-ghost smoke. Thick stars are low over it all. It is 'a dreaming town.' Isn't that a lovely phrase? You remember...'Galahad through dreaming towns did go'?

"I feel so happy, Gilbert. I won't have to go home to Green Gables at Christmas, defeated and discredited. Life is good...

good!

"So is Miss Sarah's pound cake. Rebecca Dew made one and 'sweated' it according to directions...which simply means that she wrapped it in several thicknesses of brown paper and several more towels and left it for three days. I can recommend it.

"(Are there, or are there not, two 'c's' in recommend'? In spite of the fact that I am a B.A. I can never be certain. Fancy if the Pringles had discovered that before I found Andy's diary!)"

9

Trix Taylor was curled up in the tower one night in February, while little flurries of snow hissed against the windows and that absurdly tiny stove purred like a red-hot black cat. Trix was pouring out her woes to Anne. Anne was beginning to find herself the recipient of confidences on all sides. She was known to be engaged, so that none of the Summerside girls feared her as a possible rival, and there was something about her that made you feel it was safe to tell her secrets.

Trix had come up to ask Anne to dinner the next evening. She was a jolly, plump little creature, with twinkling brown eyes and rosy cheeks, and did not look as if life weighed too heavily on her twenty years. But it appeared that she had troubles of her own.

"Dr. Lennox Carter is coming to dinner tomorrow night. That is why we want you especially. He is the new Head of the Modern Languages Department at Redmond and dreadfully clever, so we want somebody with brains to talk to him. You know I haven't any to boast of, nor Pringle either. As for Esme...well, you know, Anne, Esme is the sweetest thing and she's really clever, but she's so shy and timid she can't even make use of what brains she has when Dr. Carter is around. She's so terribly in love with him. It's pitiful. I'm very fond of Johnny...but before I'd dissolve into such a liquid state for him!"

"Are Esme and Dr. Carter engaged?"

"Not yet"...significantly. "But, oh, Anne, she's hoping he means to ask her this time. Would he come over to the Island to visit his cousin right in the middle of the term if he didn't intend to? I hope he will for Esme's sake, because she'll just die if he doesn't. But between you and me and the bed-post I'm not terribly struck on him for a brother-in-law. He's awfully fastidious, Esme says, and she's desperately afraid he won't approve of us. If he doesn't, she thinks he'll never ask her to marry him. So you can't imagine how she's hoping everything will go well at the dinner tomorrow night. I don't see why it shouldn't...Mamma is the most wonderful cook...and we have a good maid and I've bribed Pringle with half my week's allowance to behave himself. Of course he doesn't like Dr. Carter either...says he's got swelled head...but he's fond of Esme. If only Papa won't have a sulky fit on!"

"Have you any reason to fear it?" asked Anne. Every one in Summerside knew about Cyrus Taylor's sulky fits.

"You never can tell when he'll take one," said Trix dolefully. "He was frightfully upset tonight because he couldn't find his new flannel nightshirt. Esme had put it in the wrong drawer. He may be over it by tomorrow night or he may not. If he's not, he'll disgrace us all and Dr. Carter will conclude he can't marry into such a family. At least, that is what Esme says and I'm afraid she may be right. I think, Anne, that Lennox Carter is very fond of Esme...thinks she would make a 'very suitable wife' for him...but doesn't want to do anything rash or throw his wonderful self away. I've heard that he told his cousin a man couldn't be too careful what kind of family he married into. He's just at the point where he might be turned either way by a trifle. And, if it comes to that, one of Papa's sulky fits isn't any trifle."

"Doesn't he like Dr. Carter?"

"Oh, he does. He thinks it would be a wonderful match for Esme. But when Father has one of his spells on, nothing has any influence over him while it lasts. That's the Pringle for you, Anne. Grandmother Taylor was a Pringle, you know. You just can't imagine what we've gone through as a family. He never goes into rages, you know...like Uncle George. Uncle George's family don't mind his rages. When he goes into a temper he blows off...you can hear him roaring three blocks away...and then he's like a lamb and brings every one a new dress for a peace-offering. But Father just sulks and glowers, and won't say a word to anybody at meal times. Esme says that, after all, that's better than cousin Richard Taylor, who is always saying sarcastic things at the table and insulting his wife; but it seems to me nothing could be worse than those awful silences of Papa's. They rattle us and we're terrified to open our mouths. It wouldn't be so bad, of course, if it was only when we are alone. But it's just as apt to be where we have company. Esme and I are simply tired of trying to explain away Papa's insulting silences. She's just sick with fear that he won't have got over the nightshirt before tomorrow night...and what will Lennox think? And she wants you to wear your blue dress. Her new dress is blue, because Lennox likes blue. But Papa hates it. Yours may reconcile him to hers."

"Wouldn't it be better for her to wear something else?"

"She hasn't anything else fit to wear at a company dinner except the green poplin Father gave her at Christmas. It's a lovely dress in itself...Father likes us to have pretty dresses...but you can't think of anything as awful as Esme in green. Pringle says it makes her look as if she was in the last stages of consumption. And Lennox Carter's cousin told Esme he would never marry a delicate person. I'm more than glad Johnny isn't so 'fastidious.'"

"Have you told your father about your engagement to Johnny yet?" asked Anne, who knew all about Trix's love affair.

"No," poor Trix groaned. "I can't summon up the courage, Anne. I know he'll make a frightful scene. Papa has always been so down on Johnny because he's poor. Papa forgets that he was poorer than Johnny when he started out in the hardware business. Of course he'll have to be told soon...but I want to wait until Esme's affair is settled. I know Papa won't speak to any of us for weeks after I tell him, and Mamma will worry so...she can't bear Father's sulky fits. We're all such cowards before Papa. Of course, Mamma and Esme are naturally timid with every one, but Pringle and I have lots of ginger. It's only Papa who can cow us. Sometimes I think if we had any one to back us up...but we haven't, and we just feel paralyzed. You can't imagine, Anne darling, what a company dinner is like at our place when Papa is sulking. But if he only behaves tomorrow night I'll forgive him for everything. He can be very agreeable when he wants to be...Papa is really just like Longfellow's little girl...'when he's good he's very, very good and when he's bad he's horrid.' I've seen him the life of the party."

"He was very nice the night I had dinner with you last month."

"Oh, he likes you, as I've said. That's one of the reasons why we want you so much. It may have a good influence on him. We're not neglecting anything that may please him. But when he has a really bad fit of sulks on he seems to hate everything and everybody. Anyhow, we've got a bang-up dinner planned, with an elegant orange-custard dessert. Mamma wanted pie because she says every man in the world but Papa likes pie for dessert better than anything else...even Professors of Modern Languages. But Papa doesn't, so it would never do to take a chance on it tomorrow night, when so much depends on it. Orange custard is Papa's favorite dessert. As for poor Johnny and me, I suppose I'll just have to elope with him some day and Papa will never forgive me.

"I believe if you'd just get up enough spunk to tell him and endure his resulting sulks you'd find he'd come round to it beautifully and you'd be saved months of anguish."

"You don't know Papa," said Trix darkly.

"Perhaps I know him better than you do. You've lost your perspective."

"Lost my...what? Anne darling, remember I'm not a B.A. I only went through the High. I'd have loved to go to college, but Papa doesn't believe in the Higher Education of women."

"I only meant that you're too close to him to understand him. A stranger could very well see him more clearly...understand him better."

"I understand that nothing can induce Papa to speak if he has made up his mind not to...nothing. He prides himself on that."

"Then why don't the rest of you just go on and talk as if nothing was the matter?"

"We can't...I've told you he paralyzes us. You'll find it out for yourself tomorrow night if he hasn't got over the nightshirt. I don't know how he does it but he does. I don't believe we'd mind so much how cranky he was if he would only talk. It's the silence that shatters us. I'll never forgive Papa if he acts up tomorrow night when so much is at stake."

"Let's hope for the best, dear."

"I'm trying to. And I know it will help to have you there. Mamma thought we ought to have Katherine Brooke too, but I knew it wouldn't have a good effect on Papa. He hates her. I don't blame him for that, I must say. I haven't any use for her myself. I don't see how you can be as nice to her as you are."

"I'm sorry for her, Trix."

"Sorry for her! But it's all her own fault she isn't liked. Oh, well, it takes all kinds of people to make a world...but Summerside could spare Katherine Brooke...glum old cat!"

"She's an excellent teacher, Trix..."

"Oh, do I know it? I was in her class. She did hammer things into my head...and flayed the flesh off my bones with sarcasm as well. And the way she dresses! Papa can't bear to see a woman badly dressed. He says he has no use for dowds and he's sure God hasn't either. Mamma would be horrified if she knew I told you that, Anne. She excused it in Papa because he is a man. If that was all we had to excuse in him! And poor Johnny hardly daring to come to the house now because Papa is so rude to him. I slip out on fine nights and we walk round and round the square and get half frozen."

Anne drew what was something like a breath of relief when Trix had gone, and slipped down to coax a snack out of Rebecca Dew.

"Going to the Taylors for dinner, are you? Well, I hope old Cyrus will be decent. If his family weren't all so afraid of him in his sulky fits he wouldn't indulge in them so often, of that I feel certain. I tell you, Miss Shirley, he enjoys his sulks. And now I suppose I must warm That Cat's milk. Pampered animal!"

10

When Anne arrived at the Cyrus Taylor house the next evening she felt the chill in the atmosphere as soon as she entered the door. A trim maid showed her up to the guest room but as Anne went up the stairs she caught sight of Mrs. Cyrus Taylor scuttling from the dining-room to the kitchen and Mrs. Cyrus was wiping tears away from her pale, careworn, but still rather sweet face. It was all too clear that Cyrus had not yet "got over" the nightshirt.

This was confirmed by a distressed Trix creeping into the room and whispering nervously,

"Oh, Anne, he's in a dreadful humor. He seemed pretty amiable this morning and our hopes rose. But Hugh Pringle beat him at a game of checkers this afternoon and Papa can't bear to lose a checker game. And it had to happen today, of course. He found Esme 'admiring herself in the mirror,' as he put it, and just walked her out of her room and locked the door. The poor darling was only wondering if he looked nice enough to please Lennox Carter, Ph.D. She hadn't even a chance to put her pearl string on. And look at me. I didn't dare curl my hair...Papa doesn't like curls that are not natural...and I look like a fright. Not that it matters about me...only it just shows you. Papa threw out the flowers Mamma put on the dining-room table and she feels it so...she took such trouble with them...and he wouldn't let her put on her garnet earrings. He hasn't had such a bad spell since he came home from the west last spring and found Mamma had put red curtains in the sitting-room, when he preferred mulberry. Oh, Anne, do talk as hard as you can at dinner, if he won't. If you don't, it will be too dreadful."

"I'll do my best," promised Anne, who certainly had never found herself at a loss for something to say. But then never had she found herself in such a situation as presently confronted her.

They were all gathered around the table...a very pretty and well appointed table in spite of the missing flowers. Timid Mrs. Cyrus, in a gray silk dress, had a face that was grayer than her dress. Esme, the beauty of the family...a very pale beauty, pale gold hair, pale pink lips, pale forget-me-not eyes...was so much paler than usual that she looked as if she were going to faint. Pringle, ordinarily a fat, cheerful urchin of fourteen, with round eyes and glasses and hair so fair it looked almost white, looked like a tied dog, and Trix had the air of a terrified schoolgirl.

Dr. Carter, who was undeniably handsome and distinguished-looking, with crisp dark hair, brilliant dark eyes and silver-rimmed glasses, but whom Anne, in the days of his Assistant Professorship at Redmond, had thought a rather pompous young bore, looked ill at ease. Evidently he felt that something was wrong somewhere...a reasonable conclusion when your host simply stalks to the head of the table and drops into his chair without a word to you or anybody.

Cyrus would not say grace. Mrs. Cyrus, blushing beet-red, murmured almost inaudibly, "For what we are about to receive the Lord make us truly thankful." The meal started badly by nervous Esme dropping her fork on the floor. Everybody except Cyrus jumped, because their nerves were likewise keyed up to the highest pitch. Cyrus glared at Esme out of his bulging blue eyes in a kind of enraged stillness. Then he glared at everybody and froze them into dumbness. He glared at poor Mrs. Cyrus, when she took a helping of horseradish sauce, with a glare that reminded her of her weak stomach. She couldn't eat any of it after that...and she was so fond of it. She didn't believe it would hurt her. But for that matter she couldn't eat anything, nor could Esme. They only pretended. The meal proceeded in a ghastly silence, broken by spasmodic speeches about the weather from Trix and Anne. Trix implored Anne with her eyes to talk, but Anne found herself for once in her life with absolutely nothing to say. She felt desperately that she must talk, but only the most idiotic things came into her head...things it would be impossible to utter aloud. Was everyone bewitched? It was curious, the effect one sulky, stubborn man had on you. Anne couldn't have believed it possible. And there was no doubt that he was really quite happy in the knowledge that he had made everybody at his table horribly uncomfortable. What on earth was going on in his mind? Would he jump if any one stuck a pin in him? Anne wanted to slap him...rap his knuckles...stand him in a corner...treat him like the spoiled child he really was, in spite of his spiky gray hair and truculent mustache.

Above all she wanted to make him speak. She felt instinctively that nothing in the world would punish him so much as to be tricked into speaking when he was determined not to.

Suppose she got up and deliberately smashed that huge, hideous, old-fashioned vase on the table in the corner...an ornate thing covered with wreaths of roses and leaves which it was most difficult to dust but which must be kept immaculately clean. Anne knew that the whole family hated it, but Cyrus Taylor would not hear of having it banished to the attic, because it had been his mother's. Anne thought she would do it fearlessly if she really believed that it would make Cyrus explode into vocal anger.

Why didn't Lennox Carter talk? If he would, she, Anne, could talk, too, and perhaps Trix and Pringle would escape from the spell that bound them and some kind of conversation would be possible. But he simply sat there and ate. Perhaps he thought it was really the best thing to do...perhaps he was afraid of saying something that would still further enrage the evidently already enraged parent of his lady.

"Will you please start the pickles, Miss Shirley?" said Mrs. Taylor faintly.

Something wicked stirred in Anne. She started the pickles...and something else. Without letting herself stop to think she bent forward, her great, gray-green eyes glimmering limpidly, and said gently,

"Perhaps you would be surprised to hear, Dr. Carter, that Mr. Taylor went deaf very suddenly last week?"

Anne sat back, having thrown her bomb. She could not tell precisely what she expected or hoped. If Dr. Carter got the impression that his host was deaf instead of in a towering rage of silence, it might loosen his tongue. She had not told a falsehood...she had not said Cyrus Taylor was deaf. As for Cyrus Taylor, if she had hoped to make him speak she had failed. He merely glared at her, still in silence.

But Anne's remark had an effect on Trix and Pringle that she had never dreamed of. Trix was in a silent rage herself. She had, the moment before Anne had hurled her rhetorical question, seen Esme furtively wipe away a tear that had escaped from one of her despairing blue eyes. Everything was hopeless...Lennox Carter would never ask Esme to marry him now...it didn't matter any more what any one said or did. Trix was suddenly possessed with a burning desire to get square with her brutal father. Anne's speech gave her a weird inspiration, and Pringle, a volcano of suppressed impishness, blinked his white eyelashes for a dazed moment and then promptly followed her lead. Never, as long as they might live, would Anne, Esme or Mrs. Cyrus forget the dreadful quarter of an hour that followed.

"Such an affliction for poor papa," said Trix, addressing Dr. Carter across the table. "And him only sixty-eight."

Two little white dents appeared at the corners of Cyrus Taylor's nostrils when he heard his age advanced six years. But he remained silent.

"It's such a treat to have a decent meal," said Pringle, clearly and distinctly. "What would you think, Dr. Carter, of a man who makes his family live on fruit and eggs...nothing but fruit and eggs...just for a fad?"

"Does your father...?" began Dr. Carter bewilderedly.

"What would you think of a husband who bit his wife when she put up curtains he didn't like...deliberately bit her?" demanded Trix.

"Till the blood came," added Pringle solemnly.

"Do you mean to say your father...?"

"What would you think of a man who would cut up a silk dress of his wife's just because the way it was made didn't suit him?" said Trix.

"What would you think," said Pringle, "of a man who refuses to let his wife have a dog?"

"When she would so love to have one," sighed Trix.

"What would you think of a man," continued Pringle, who was beginning to enjoy himself hugely, "who would give his wife a pair of goloshes for a Christmas present...nothing but a pair of goloshes?"

"Goloshes don't exactly warm the heart," admitted Dr. Carter. His eyes met Anne's and he smiled. Anne reflected that she had never seen him smile before. It changed his face wonderfully for the better. What was Trix saying? Who would have thought she could be such a demon?

"Have you ever wondered, Dr. Carter, how awful it must be to live with a man who thinks nothing...nothing—of picking up the roast, if it isn't perfectly done, and hurling it at the maid?"

Dr. Carter glanced apprehensively at Cyrus Taylor, as if he feared Cyrus might throw the skeletons of the chickens at somebody. Then he seemed to remember comfortingly that his host was deaf.

"What would you think of a man who believed the earth was flat?" asked Pringle.

Anne thought Cyrus would speak then. A tremor seemed to pass over his rubicund face, but no words came. Still, she was sure his mustaches were a little less defiant.

"What would you think of a man who let his aunt...his only

aunt...go to the poorhouse?" asked Trix.

"And pastured his cow in the graveyard?" said Pringle. "Summerside hasn't got over that sight yet."

"What would you think of a man who would write down in his diary every day what he had for dinner?" asked Trix.

"The great Pepys did that," said Dr. Carter with another smile. His voice sounded as if he would like to laugh. Perhaps after all he was not pompous, thought Anne...only young and shy and overserious. But she was feeling positively aghast. She had never meant things to go as far as this. She was finding out that it is much easier to start things than finish them. Trix and Pringle were being diabolically clever. They had not said that their father did a single one of these things. Anne could fancy Pringle saying, his round eyes rounder still with pretended innocence, "I just asked those questions of Dr. Carter for information."

"What would you think," kept on Trix, "of a man who opens and reads his wife's letters?"

"What would you think of a man who would go to a funeral...his father's funeral...in overalls?" asked Pringle.

What would they think of next? Mrs. Cyrus was crying openly and Esme was quite calm with despair. Nothing mattered any more. She turned and looked squarely at Dr. Carter, whom she had lost forever. For once in her life she was stung into saying a really clever thing.

"What," she asked quietly, "would you think of a man who spent a whole day hunting for the kittens of a poor cat who had been shot, because he couldn't bear to think of them starving to death?"

A strange silence descended on the room. Trix and Pringle looked suddenly ashamed of themselves. And then Mrs. Cyrus piped up, feeling it her wifely duty to back up Esme's unexpected defense of her father.

"And he can crochet so beautifully...he made the loveliest centerpiece for the parlor table last winter when he was laid up with lumbago."

Every one has some limit of endurance and Cyrus Taylor had reached his. He gave his chair such a furious backward push that it shot instantly across the polished floor and struck the table on which the vase stood. The table went over and the vase broke in the traditional thousand pieces. Cyrus, his bushy white eyebrows fairly bristling with wrath, stood up and exploded at last.

"I don't crochet, woman! Is one contemptible doily going to blast a man's reputation forever? I was so bad with that blamed lumbago I didn't know what I was doing. And I'm deaf, am I, Miss Shirley? I'm deaf?"

"She didn't say you were, Papa," cried Trix, who was never

afraid of her father when his temper was vocal.

"Oh, no, she didn't say it. None of you said anything! You didn't say I was sixty-eight when I'm only sixty-two, did you? You didn't say I wouldn't let your mother have a dog! Good Lord, woman, you can have forty thousand dogs if you want to and you know it! When did I ever deny you anything you wanted...when?"

"Never, Poppa, never," sobbed Mrs. Cyrus brokenly. "And I never wanted a dog. I never even thought of wanting a dog, Poppa."

"When did I open your letters? When have I ever kept a diary? A diary! When did I ever wear overalls to anybody's funeral? When did I pasture a cow in the graveyard? What aunt of mine is in the poorhouse? Did I ever throw a roast at anybody? Did I ever make you live on fruit and eggs?"

"Never, Poppa, never," wept Mrs. Cyrus. "You've always been a good provider...the best."

"Didn't you tell me you wanted goloshes last Christmas?"

"Yes, oh, yes; of course I did, Poppa. And my feet have been so nice and warm all winter."

"Well, then!" Cyrus threw a triumphant glance around the room. His eyes encountered Anne's. Suddenly the unexpected happened. Cyrus chuckled. His cheeks actually dimpled. Those dimples worked a miracle with his whole expression. He brought his chair back to the table and sat down.

"I've got a very bad habit of sulking, Dr. Carter. Every one has some bad habit...that's mine. The only one. Come, come, Momma, stop crying. I admit I deserved all I got except that crack of yours about crocheting. Esme, my girl, I won't forget that you were the only one who stood up for me. Tell Maggie to come and clear up that mess...I know you're all glad the darn thing is smashed...and bring on the pudding."

Anne could never have believed that an evening which began so terribly could end up so pleasantly. Nobody could have been more genial or better company than Cyrus: and there was evidently no aftermath of reckoning, for when Trix came down a few evenings later it was to tell Anne that she had at last scraped up enough courage to tell her father about Johnny.

"Was he very dreadful, Trix?"

"He...he wasn't dreadful at all," admitted Trix sheepishly. "He just snorted and said it was about time Johnny came to the point after hanging around for two years and keeping every one else away. I think he felt he couldn't go into another spell of sulks so soon after the last one. And you know, Anne, between sulks Papa really is an old duck."

"I think he is a great deal better father to you than you deserve," said Anne, quite in Rebecca Dew's manner. "You were simply outrageous at that dinner, Trix."

"Well, you know you started it," said Trix. "And good old Pringle helped a bit. All's well that ends well...and thank goodness I'll never have to dust that vase again."

11

(Extract from letter to Gilbert two weeks later.)

"Esme Taylor's engagement to Dr. Lennox Carter is announced. By all I can gather from various bits of local gossip I think he decided that fatal Friday night that he wanted to protect her, and save her from her father and her family...and perhaps from her friends! Her plight evidently appealed to his sense of chivalry. Trix persists in thinking I was the means of bringing it about and perhaps I did take a hand, but I don't think I'll ever try an experiment like that again. It's too much like picking up a lightning flash by the tail.

"I really don't know what got into me, Gilbert. It must have been a hangover from my old detestation of anything savoring of Pringleism. It does seem old now. I've almost forgotten it. But other folks are still wondering. I hear Miss Valentine Courtaloe says she isn't at all surprised I have won the Pringles over, because I have 'such a way with me'; and the minister's wife thinks it is an answer to the prayer she put up. Well, who knows but that it was?

"Jen Pringle and I walked part of the way home from school yesterday and talked of 'ships and shoes and sealing wax'...of almost everything but geometry. We avoid that subject. Jen knows I don't know too much about geometry, but my own wee bit of knowledge about Captain Myrom balances that. I lent Jen my Foxe's Book of Martyrs. I hate to lend a book I love...it never seems quite the same when it comes back to me...but I love Foxe's Martyrs only because dear Mrs. Allan gave it to me for a Sunday-school prize years ago. I don't like reading about martyrs because they always make me feel petty and ashamed...ashamed to admit I hate to get out of bed on frosty mornings and shrink from a visit to the dentist!

"Well, I'm glad Esme and Trix are both happy. Since my own little romance is in flower I am all the more interested in other people's. A nice interest, you know. Not curious or malicious but just glad there's such a lot of happiness spread about.

"It's still February and 'on the convent roof the snows are sparkling to the moon'...only it isn't a convent...just the roof of Mr. Hamilton's barn. But I'm beginning to think, 'Only a few more weeks till spring...and a few more weeks then till summer...and holidays...and Green Gables...and golden sunlight on Avonlea meadows...and a gulf that will be silver at dawn and sapphire at noon and crimson at sunset...and you.'

"Little Elizabeth and I have no end of plans for spring. We are such good friends. I take her milk every evening and once in so long she is allowed to go for a walk with me. We have discovered that our birthdays are on the same day and Elizabeth flushed 'divinest rosy red' with the excitement of it. She is so sweet when she blushes. Ordinarily she is far too pale and doesn't get any pinker because of the new milk. Only when we come back from our twilight trysts with evening winds does she have a lovely rose color in her little cheeks. Once she asked me gravely, 'Will I have a lovely creamy skin like yours when I grow up, Miss Shirley, if I put buttermilk on my face every night?' Buttermilk seems to be the preferred cosmetic in Spook's Lane. I have discovered that Rebecca Dew uses it. She has bound me over to keep it secret from the widows because they would think it too frivolous for her age. The number of secrets I have to keep at Windy Poplars is aging me before my time. I wonder if I buttermilked my nose if it would banish those seven freckles. By the way, did it ever occur to you, sir, that I had a 'lovely creamy skin'? If it did, you never told me so. And have you realized to the full that I am 'comparatively beautiful'? Because I have discovered that I am.

"'What is it like to be beautiful, Miss Shirley?' asked Rebecca Dew gravely the other day...when I was wearing my new biscuit-colored voile.

"'I've often wondered,' said I.

"'But you are beautiful,' said Rebecca Dew.

"'I never thought you could be sarcastic, Rebecca,' I said reproachfully.

"'I did not mean to be sarcastic, Miss Shirley. You are beautiful...comparatively.'

"'Oh! Comparatively!' said I.

"'Look in the sideboard glass,' said Rebecca Dew, pointing. 'Compared to me, you are.'

"Well, I was!

"But I hadn't finished with Elizabeth. One stormy evening when the wind was howling along Spook's Lane, we couldn't go for a walk, so we came up to my room and drew a map of fairyland. Elizabeth sat on my blue doughnut cushion to make her higher, and looked like a serious little gnome as she bent over the map. (By the way, no phonetic spelling for me! 'Gnome' is far eerier and fairy-er than 'nome.')

"Our map isn't completed yet...every day we think of something more to go in it. Last night we located the house of the Witch of the Snow and drew a triple hill, covered completely with wild cherry trees in bloom, behind it. (By the way, I want some wild cherry trees near our house of dreams, Gilbert.) Of course we have a Tomorrow on the map...located east of Today and west of Yesterday...and we have no end of 'times' in fairyland. Spring-time, long time, short time, new-moon time, good-night time, next time...but no last time, because that is too sad a time for fairyland; old time, young time...because if there is an old time there ought to be a young time, too; mountain time...because that has such a fascinating sound; night-time and day-time...but no bed-time or school-time; Christmas-time; no only time, because that also is too sad...but lost time, because it is so nice to find it; some time, good time, fast time, slow time, half-past kissing-time, going-home time, and time immemorial...which is one of the most beautiful phrases in the world. And we have cunning little red arrows everywhere, pointing to the different 'times.' I know Rebecca Dew thinks I'm quite childish. But, oh, Gilbert, don't let's ever grow too old and wise...no, not too old and silly for fairyland.

"Rebecca Dew, I feel sure, is not quite certain that I am an influence for good in Elizabeth's life. She thinks I encourage her in being 'fanciful.' One evening when I was away Rebecca Dew took the milk to her and found her already at the gate, looking at the sky so intently that she never heard Rebecca's (anything but) fairy footfalls.

"'I was listening, Rebecca,' she explained.

"'You do too much listening,' said Rebecca disapprovingly.

"Elizabeth smiled, remotely, austerely. (Rebecca Dew didn't use those words but I know exactly how Elizabeth smiled.)

"'You would be surprised, Rebecca, if you knew what I hear sometimes,' she said, in a way that made Rebecca Dew's flesh creep on her bones...or so she avers.

"But Elizabeth is always touched with faery and what can be done about it?

"Your Very Anne-est ANNE.

"P.S.1. Never, never, never shall I forget Cyrus Taylor's face when his wife accused him of crocheting. But I shall always like him because he hunted for those kittens. And I like Esme for standing up for her father under the supposed wreck of all her hopes.

"P.S.2. I have put in a new pen. And I love you because you aren't pompous like Dr. Carter...and I love you because you haven't got sticky-out ears like Johnny. And...the very best reason of all...I love you for just being Gilbert!"

12

"Windy Poplars,

"Spook's Lane,

"May 30th.

"DEAREST-AND-THEN-MORE-DEAR:

"It's spring!

"Perhaps you, up to your eyes in a welter of exams in Kingsport, don't know it. But I am aware of it from the crown of my head to the tips of my toes. Summerside is aware of it. Even the most unlovely streets are transfigured by arms of bloom reaching over old board fences and a ribbon of dandelions in the grass that borders the sidewalks. Even the china lady on my shelf is aware of it and I know if I could only wake up suddenly enough some night I'd catch her dancing a pas seul in her pink, gilt-heeled shoes.

"Everything is calling 'spring' to me...the little laughing brooks, the blue hazes on the Storm King, the maples in the grove when I go to read your letters, the white cherry trees along Spook's Lane, the sleek and saucy robins hopping defiance to Dusty Miller in the back yard, the creeper hanging greenly down over the half-door to which little Elizabeth comes for milk, the fir trees preening in new tassel tips around the old graveyard...even the old graveyard itself, where all sorts of flowers planted at the heads of the graves are budding into leaf and bloom, as if to say, 'Even here life is triumphant over death.' I had a really lovely prowl about the graveyard the other night. (I'm sure Rebecca Dew thinks my taste in walks frightfully morbid. 'I can't think why you have such a hankering after that unchancy place,' she says.) I roamed over it in the scented green cat's light and wondered if Nathan Pringle's wife really had tried to poison him. Her grave looked so innocent with its new grass and its June lilies that I concluded she had been entirely maligned.

"Just another month and I'll be home for vacation! I keep thinking of the old orchard at Green Gables with its trees now in full snow...the old bridge over the Lake of Shining Waters...the murmur of the sea in your ears...a summer afternoon in Lover's Lane...and you!

"I have just the right kind of pen tonight, Gilbert, and so...

(Two pages omitted.)

"I was around at the Gibsons' this evening for a call. Marilla asked me some time ago to look them up because she once knew them when they lived in White Sands. Accordingly I looked them up and have been looking them up weekly ever since because Pauline seems to enjoy my visits and I'm so sorry for her. She is simply a slave to her mother...who is a terrible old woman.

"Mrs. Adoniram Gibson is eighty and spends her days in a wheel-chair. They moved to Summerside fifteen years ago. Pauline, who is forty-five, is the youngest of the family, all her brothers and sisters being married and all of them determined not to have Mrs. Adoniram in their homes. She keeps the house and waits on her mother hand and foot. She is a little pale, fawn-eyed thing with golden-brown hair that is still glossy and pretty. They are quite comfortably off and if it were not for her mother Pauline could have a very pleasant easy life. She just loves church work and would be perfectly happy attending Ladies' Aids and Missionary Societies, planning for church suppers and Welcome socials, not to speak of exulting proudly in being the possessor of the finest wandering-jew in town. But she can hardly ever get away from the house, even to go to church on Sundays. I can't see any way of escape for her, for old Mrs. Gibson will probably live to be a hundred. And, while she may not have the use of her legs, there is certainly nothing the matter with her tongue. It always fills me with helpless rage to sit there and hear her making poor Pauline the target for her sarcasm. And yet Pauline has told me that her mother 'thinks quite highly' of me and is much nicer to her when I am around. If this be so I shiver to think what she must be when I am not around.

"Pauline dares not do anything without asking her mother. She can't even buy her own clothes...not so much as a pair of stockings. Everything has to be sent up for Mrs. Gibson's approval; everything has to be worn until it has been turned twice. Pauline has worn the same hat for four years.

"Mrs. Gibson can't bear any noise in the house or a breath

of fresh air. It is said she never smiled in her life...I've never caught her at it, anyway, and when I look at her I find myself wondering what would happen to her face if she did smile. Pauline can't even have a room to herself. She has to sleep in the same room with her mother and be up almost every hour of the night rubbing Mrs. Gibson's back or giving her a pill or getting a hot-water bottle for her...hot, not lukewarm!...or changing her pillows or seeing what that mysterious noise is in the back yard. Mrs. Gibson does her sleeping in the afternoons and spends her nights devising tasks for Pauline.

"Yet nothing has ever made Pauline bitter. She is sweet and unselfish and patient and I am glad she has a dog to love. The only thing she has ever had her own way about is keeping that dog...and then only because there was a burglary somewhere in town and Mrs. Gibson thought it would be a protection. Pauline never dares to let her mother see how much she loves the dog. Mrs. Gibson hates him and complains of his bringing bones in but she never actually says he must go, for her own selfish reason.

"But at last I have a chance to give Pauline something and I'm going to do it. I'm going to give her a day, though it will mean giving up my next week-end at Green Gables.

"Tonight when I went in I could see that Pauline had been crying. Mrs. Gibson did not long leave me in doubt why.

"'Pauline wants to go and leave me, Miss Shirley,' she said. 'Nice, grateful daughter I've got, haven't I?'

"'Only for a day, Ma,' said Pauline, swallowing a sob and trying to smile.

"'Only for a day,' says she! 'Well, you know what my days are like, Miss Shirley...every one knows what my days are like. But you don't know...yet...Miss Shirley, and I hope you never will, how long a day can be when you are suffering.'

"I knew Mrs. Gibson didn't suffer at all now, so I didn't try to be sympathetic.

"'I'd get some one to stay with you, of course, Ma,' said Pauline. 'You see,' she explained to me, 'my cousin Louisa is going to celebrate her silver wedding at White Sands next Saturday week and she wants me to go. I was her bridesmaid when she was married to Maurice Hilton. I would like to go so much if Ma would give her consent.'

"'If I must die alone I must,' said Mrs. Gibson. 'I leave it to your conscience, Pauline.'

"I knew Pauline's battle was lost the moment Mrs. Gibson left it to her conscience. Mrs. Gibson has got her way all her life by leaving things to people's consciences. I've heard that years ago somebody wanted to marry Pauline and Mrs. Gibson prevented it by leaving it to her conscience.

"Pauline wiped her eyes, summoned up a piteous smile and

picked up a dress she was making over...a hideous green and black plaid.

"'Now don't sulk, Pauline,' said Mrs. Gibson. 'I can't abide people who sulk. And mind you put a collar on that dress. Would you believe it, Miss Shirley, she actually wanted to make the dress without a collar? She'd wear a low-necked dress, that one, if I'd let her.'

"I looked at poor Pauline with her slender little throat...which is rather plump and pretty yet...enclosed in a high, stiff-boned net collar.

"'Collarless dresses are coming in,' I said.

"'Collarless dresses,' said Mrs. Gibson, 'are indecent.'

"(Item:—I was wearing a collarless dress.)

"'Moreover,' went on Mrs. Gibson, as if it were all of a piece. 'I never liked Maurice Hilton. His mother was a Crockett. He never had any sense of decorum...always kissing his wife in the most unsuitable places!'

"(Are you sure you kiss me in suitable places, Gilbert? I'm afraid Mrs. Gibson would think the nape of the neck, for instance, most unsuitable.)

"'But, Ma, you know that was the day she nearly escaped being trampled by Harvey Wither's horse running amuck on the church green. It was only natural Maurice should feel a little excited.'

"'Pauline, please don't contradict me. I still think the church steps were an unsuitable place for any one to be kissed. But of course my opinions don't matter to any one any longer. Of course every one wishes I was dead. Well, there'll be room for me in the grave. I know what a burden I am to you. I might as well die. Nobody wants me.'

"'Don't say that, Ma,' begged Pauline.

"'I will say it. Here you are, determined to go to that silver wedding although you know I'm not willing.'

"'Ma dear. I'm not going...I'd never think of going if you weren't willing. Don't excite yourself so...'

"'Oh, I can't even have a little excitement, can't I, to brighten my dull life? Surely you're not going so soon, Miss Shirley?'

"I felt that if I stayed any longer I'd either go crazy or slap Mrs. Gibson's nut-cracker face. So I said I had exam papers to correct.

"'Ah well, I suppose two old women like us are very poor company for a young girl,' sighed Mrs. Gibson. 'Pauline isn't very cheerful...are you, Pauline? Not very cheerful. I don't wonder Miss Shirley doesn't want to stay long.'

"Pauline came out to the porch with me. The moon was shining down on her little garden and sparkling on the harbor. A soft, delightful wind was talking to a white apple tree. It was spring...spring...spring! Even Mrs. Gibson can't stop plum trees from blooming. And Pauline's soft gray-blue eyes were full of tears.

"'I would like to go to Louie's wedding so much,' she said, with a long sigh of despairing resignation.

"'You are going,' I said.

"'Oh, no, dear, I can't go. Poor Ma will never consent. I'll just put it out of my mind. Isn't the moon beautiful tonight?' she added, in a loud, cheerful tone.

"'I've never heard of any good that came from moon gazing,' called out Mrs. Gibson from the sitting-room. 'Stop chirruping there, Pauline, and come in and get my red bedroom slippers with the fur round the tops for me. These shoes pinch my feet something terrible. But nobody cares how I suffer.'

"I felt that I didn't care how much she suffered. Poor darling Pauline! But a day off is certainly coming to Pauline and she is going to have her silver wedding. I, Anne Shirley, have spoken it.

"I told Rebecca Dew and the widows all about it when I came home and we had such fun, thinking up all the lovely, insulting things I might have said to Mrs. Gibson. Aunt Kate does not think I will succeed in getting Mrs. Gibson to let Pauline go but Rebecca Dew has faith in me. 'Anyhow, if you can't, nobody can,' she said.

"I was at supper recently with Mrs. Tom Pringle who wouldn't take me to board. (Rebecca says I am the best paying boarder she ever heard of because I am invited out to supper so often.) I'm very glad she didn't. She's nice and purry and her pies praise her in the gates, but her home isn't Windy Poplars and she doesn't live in Spook's Lane and she isn't Aunt Kate and Aunt Chatty and Rebecca Dew. I love them all three and I'm going to board here next year and the year after. My chair is always called 'Miss Shirley's chair' and Aunt Chatty tells me that when I'm not here Rebecca Dew sets my place at the table just the same, so it won't seem so lonesome.' Sometimes Aunt Chatty's feelings have complicated matters a bit but she says she understands me now and knows I would never hurt her intentionally.

"Little Elizabeth and I go out for a walk twice a week now. Mrs. Campbell has agreed to that, but it must not be oftener and never on Sundays. Things are better for little Elizabeth in spring. Some sunshine gets into even that grim old house and outwardly it is even beautiful because of the dancing shadows of tree tops. Still, Elizabeth likes to escape from it whenever she can. Once in a while we go up-town so that Elizabeth can see the lighted shop windows. But mostly we go as far as we dare down the Road that Leads to the End of the World, rounding every corner adventurously and expectantly, as if we were going to find Tomorrow behind it, while all the little green evening hills neatly nestle together in the distance. One of the things Elizabeth is going to do in Tomorrow is 'go to Philadelphia and see the angel in the church.' I haven't told her...I never will tell her...that the Philadelphia St. John was writing about was not Phila., Pa. We lose our illusions soon enough. And anyhow, if we could get into Tomorrow, who knows what we might find there? Angels everywhere, perhaps.

"Sometimes we watch the ships coming up the harbor before a fair wind, over a glistening pathway, through the transparent spring air, and Elizabeth wonders if her father may be on board one of them. She clings to the hope that he may come some day. I can't imagine why he doesn't. I'm sure he would if he knew what a darling little daughter he has here longing for him. I suppose he never realizes she is quite a girl now...I suppose he still thinks of her as the little baby who cost his wife her life.

"I'll soon have finished my first year in Summerside High. The first term was a nightmare, but the last two have been very pleasant. The Pringles are delightful people. How could I ever have compared them to the Pyes? Sid Pringle brought me a bunch of trilliums today. Jen is going to lead her class and Miss Ellen is reported to have said that I am the only teacher who ever really understood the child! The only fly in my ointment is Katherine Brooke, who continues unfriendly and distant. I'm going to give up trying to be friends with her. After all, as Rebecca Dew says, there are limits.

"Oh, I nearly forgot to tell you...Sally Nelson has asked me to be one of her bridesmaids. She is going to be married the last of June at Bonnyview, Dr. Nelson's summer home down at the jumping-off place. She is marrying Gordon Hill. Then Nora Nelson will be the only one of Dr. Nelson's six girls left unmarried. Jim Wilcox has been going with her for years...'off and on' as Rebecca Dew says...but it never seems to come to anything and nobody thinks it will now. I'm very fond of Sally, but I've never made much headway getting acquainted with Nora. She's a good deal older than I am, of course, and rather reserved and proud. Yet I'd like to be friends with her. She isn't pretty or clever or charming but somehow she's got a tang. I've a feeling she'd be worth while.

"Speaking of weddings, Esme Taylor was married to her Ph.D. last month. As it was on Wednesday afternoon I couldn't go to the church to see her, but every one says she looked very beautiful and happy and Lennox looked as if he knew he had done the right thing and had the approval of his conscience. Cyrus Taylor and I are great friends. He often refers to the dinner which he has come to consider a great joke on everybody. 'I've never dared sulk since,' he told me. 'Momma might accuse me of sewing patchwork next time.' And then he tells me to be sure and give his love to 'the widows.' Gilbert, people are delicious and life is delicious and I am

"Forevermore

"Yours!

"P.S. Our old red cow down at Mr. Hamilton's has a spotted calf. We've been buying our milk for three months from Lew Hunt. Rebecca says we'll have cream again now...and that she has always heard the Hunt well was inexhaustible and now she believes it. Rebecca didn't want that calf to be born at all. Aunt Kate had to get Mr. Hamilton to tell her that the cow was really too old to have a calf before she would consent."

13

"Ah, when you've been old and bed-rid as long as me you'll have more sympathy," whined Mrs. Gibson.

"Please don't think I'm lacking in sympathy, Mrs. Gibson," said Anne, who, after half an hour's vain effort, felt like wringing Mrs. Gibson's neck. Nothing but poor Pauline's pleading eyes in the background kept her from giving up in despair and going home. "I assure you, you won't be lonely and neglected. I will be here all day and see that you lack nothing in any way."

"Oh, I know I'm of no use to any one," said Mrs. Gibson,

apropos of nothing that had been said. "You don't need to rub that in, Miss Shirley. I'm ready to go any time...any time. Pauline can gad round all she wants to then. I won't be here to feel neglected. None of the young people of today have any sense. Giddy...very giddy."

Anne didn't know whether it was Pauline or herself who was the giddy young person without sense, but she tried the last shot in her locker.

"Well, you know, Mrs. Gibson, people will talk so terribly if Pauline doesn't go to her cousin's silver wedding."

"Talk!" said Mrs. Gibson sharply. "What will they talk about?"

"Dear Mrs. Gibson..." ('May I be forgiven the adjective!' thought Anne) "in your long life you have learned, I know, just what idle tongues can say."

"You needn't be casting my age up to me," snapped Mrs. Gibson. "And I don't need to be told it's a censorious world. Too well...too well I know it. And I don't need to be told that this town is full of tattling toads neither. But I dunno's I fancy them jabbering about me...saying, I s'pose, that I'm an old tyrant. I ain't stopping Pauline from going. Didn't I leave it to her conscience?"

"So few people will believe that," said Anne, carefully sorrowful.

Mrs. Gibson sucked a peppermint lozenge fiercely for a minute or two. Then she said,

"I hear there's mumps at White Sands."

"Ma, dear, you know I've had the mumps."

"There's folks as takes them twice. You'd be just the one to take them twice, Pauline. You always took everything that come round. The nights I've set up with you, not expecting you'd see the morning! Ah me, a mother's sacrifices ain't long remembered. Besides, how would you get to White Sands? You ain't been on a train for years. And there ain't any train back Saturday night."

"She could go on the Saturday morning train," said Anne. "And I'm sure Mr. James Gregor will bring her back."

"I never liked Jim Gregor. His mother was a Tarbush."

"He is taking his double-seated buggy and going down Friday, or else he would take her down, too. But she'll be quite safe on the train, Mrs. Gibson. Just step on at Summerside... step off at White Sands...no changing."

"There's something behind all this," said Mrs. Gibson suspiciously. "Why are you so set on her going, Miss Shirley? Just tell me that."

Anne smiled into the beady-eyed face.

"Because I think Pauline is a good, kind daughter to you, Mrs. Gibson, and needs a day off now and then, just as everybody does."

Most people found it hard to resist Anne's smile. Either that, or the fear of gossip vanquished Mrs. Gibson.

"I s'pose it never occurs to any one I'd like a day off from this wheel-chair if I could get it. But I can't...I just have to bear my affliction patiently. Well, if she must go she must. She's always been one to get her own way. If she catches mumps or gets poisoned by strange mosquitoes, don't blame me for it. I'll have to get along as best I can. Oh, I s'pose you'll be here, but you ain't used to my ways as Pauline is. I s'pose I can stand it for one day. If I can't...well, I've been living on borrowed time many's the year now so what's the difference?" Not a gracious assent by any means but still an assent. Anne in her relief and gratitude found herself doing something she could never have imagined herself doing...she bent over and kissed Mrs. Gibson's leathery cheek. "Thank you," she said.

"Never mind your wheedling ways," said Mrs. Gibson. "Have a peppermint."

"How can I ever thank you, Miss Shirley?" said Pauline, as she went a little way down the street with Anne.

"By going to White Sands with a light heart and enjoying every minute of the time."

"Oh, I'll do that. You don't know what this means to me, Miss Shirley. It's not only Louisa I want to see. The old Luckley place next to her home is going to be sold and I did so want to see it once more before it passed into the hands of strangers. Mary Luckley...she's Mrs. Howard Flemming now and lives out west...was my dearest friend when I was a girl. We were like sisters. I used to be at the Luckley place so much and I loved it so. I've often dreamed of going back. Ma says I'm getting too old to dream. Do you think I am, Miss Shirley?"

"Nobody is ever too old to dream. And dreams never grow old."

"I'm so glad to hear you say that. Oh, Miss Shirley, to think of seeing the gulf again. I haven't seen it for fifteen years. The harbor is beautiful, but it isn't the gulf. I feel as if I was walking on air. And I owe it all to you. It was just because Ma likes you she let me go. You've made me happy...you are always making people happy. Why, whenever you come into a room, Miss Shirley, the people in it feel happier."

"That's the very nicest compliment I've ever had paid me, Pauline."

"There's just one thing, Miss Shirley...I've nothing to wear but my old black taffeta. It's too gloomy for a wedding, isn't it? And it's too big for me since I got thin. You see it's six years since I got it."

"We must try to induce your mother to let you have a new dress," said Anne hopefully.

But that proved to be beyond her powers. Mrs. Gibson was adamant. Pauline's black taffeta was plenty good for Louisa Hilton's wedding.

"I paid two dollars a yard for it six years ago and three to Jane Sharp for making it. Jane was a good dressmaker. Her mother was a Smiley. The idea of you wanting something 'light,' Pauline Gibson! She'd go dressed in scarlet from head to foot, that one, if she was let, Miss Shirley. She's just waiting till I'm dead to do it. Ah, well, you'll soon be shet of all the trouble I am to you, Pauline. Then you can dress as gay and giddy as you like, but as long as I'm alive you'll be decent. And what's the matter with your hat? It's time you wore a bonnet, anyhow."

Poor Pauline had a lively horror of having to wear a bonnet. She would wear her old hat for the rest of her life before she would do that.

"I'm just going to be glad inside and forget all about my clothes," she told Anne, when they went out to the garden to pick a bouquet of June lilies and bleeding-heart for the widows.

"I've a plan," said Anne, with a cautious glance to make sure Mrs. Gibson couldn't hear her, though she was watching from the sitting-room window. "You know that silver-gray poplin of mine? I'm going to lend you that for the wedding."

Pauline dropped the basket of flowers in her agitation, making a pool of pink and white sweetness at Anne's feet.

"Oh, my dear, I couldn't...Ma wouldn't let me."

"She won't know a thing about it. Listen. Saturday morning you'll put it on under your black taffeta. I know it will fit you. It's a little long, but I'll run some tucks in it tomorrow...tucks are fashionable now. It's collarless, with elbow sleeves so no one will suspect. As soon as you get to Gull Cove, take off the taffeta. When the day is over you can leave the poplin at Gull Cove and I can get it the next week-end I'm home."

"But wouldn't it be too young for me?"

"Not a bit of it. Any age can wear gray."

"Do you think it would be...right...to deceive Ma?" faltered Pauline.

"In this case entirely right," said Anne shamelessly. "You know, Pauline, it would never do to wear a black dress to a wedding. It might bring the bride bad luck."

"Oh, I wouldn't do that for anything. And of course it won't hurt Ma. I do hope she'll get through Saturday all right. I'm afraid she won't eat a bite when I'm away...she didn't the time I went to Cousin Matilda's funeral. Miss Prouty told me she didn't...Miss Prouty stayed with her. She was so provoked at Cousin Matilda for dying...Ma was, I mean."

"She'll eat...I'll see to that."

"I know you've a great knack of managing her," conceded Pauline. "And you won't forget to give her her medicine at the regular times, will you, dear? Oh, perhaps I oughtn't to go after all."

"You've been out there long enough to pick forty bokays," called Mrs. Gibson irately. "I dunno what the widows want of your flowers. They've plenty of their own. I'd go a long time without flowers if I waited for Rebecca Dew to send me any. I'm dying for a drink of water. But then I'm of no consequence."

Friday night Pauline telephoned Anne in terrible agitation. She had a sore throat and did Miss Shirley think it could possibly be the mumps? Anne ran down to reassure her, taking the gray poplin in a brown paper parcel. She hid it in the lilac bush and late that night Pauline, in a cold perspiration, managed to smuggle it upstairs to the little room where she kept her clothes and dressed, though she was never permitted to sleep there. Pauline was not quite easy about the dress. Perhaps her sore throat was a judgment on her for deception. But she couldn't go to Louisa's silver wedding in that dreadful old black taffeta...she simply couldn't.

Saturday morning Anne was at the Gibson house bright and early. Anne always looked her best on a sparkling summer morning such as this. She seemed to sparkle with it and she moved through the golden air like a slender figure on a Grecian urn. The dullest room sparkled, too...lived... when she came into it.

"Walking as if you owned the earth," commented Mrs. Gibson sarcastically.

"So I do," said Anne gayly.

"Ah, you're very young," said Mrs. Gibson maddeningly.

"'I withhold not my heart from any joy,'" quoted Anne. "That is Bible authority for you, Mrs. Gibson."

"'Man is born to trouble as the sparks fly upward.' That's in the Bible, too," retorted Mrs. Gibson. The fact that she had so neatly countered Miss Shirley, B.A., put her in comparatively good humor. "I never was one to flatter, Miss Shirley, but that chip hat of yours with the blue flower kind of sets you. Your hair don't look so red under it, seems to me. Don't you admire a fresh young girl like this, Pauline? Wouldn't you like to be a fresh young girl yourself, Pauline?"

Pauline was too happy and excited to want to be any one but herself just then. Anne went to the upstairs room with her to help her dress.

"It's so lovely to think of all the pleasant things that must happen today, Miss Shirley. My throat is quite well and Ma is in such a good humor. You mightn't think so, but I know she is because she is talking, even if she is sarcastic. If she was mad or riled she'd be sulking. I've peeled the potatoes and the steak is in the ice-box and Ma's blanc mange is down cellar. There's canned chicken for supper and a sponge cake in the pantry. I'm just on tenterhooks Ma'll change her mind yet. I couldn't bear it if she did. Oh, Miss Shirley, do you think I'd better wear that gray dress...really?"

"Put it on," said Anne in her best school-teacherish manner.

Pauline obeyed and emerged a transformed Pauline. The gray dress fitted her beautifully. It was collarless and had dainty lace ruffles in the elbow sleeves. When Anne had done her hair Pauline hardly knew herself.

"I hate to cover it up with that horrid old black taffeta, Miss Shirley."

But it had to be. The taffeta covered it very securely. The old hat went on...but it would be taken off, too, when she got to Louisa's...and Pauline had a new pair of shoes. Mrs. Gibson had actually allowed her to get a new pair of shoes, though she thought the heels "scandalous high." "I'll make quite a sensation going away on the train alone. I hope people won't think it's a death. I wouldn't want Louisa's silver wedding to be connected in any way with the thought of death. Oh, perfume, Miss Shirley! Apple-blossom! Isn't that lovely? Just a whiff... so lady-like, I always think. Ma won't let me buy any. Oh, Miss Shirley, you won't forget to feed my dog, will you? I've left his bones in the pantry in the covered dish. I do hope"...dropping her voice to a shamed whisper..."that he won't...misbehave...in the house while you're here."

Pauline had to pass her mother's inspection before leaving. Excitement over her outing and guilt in regard to the hidden poplin combined to give her a very unusual flush. Mrs. Gibson gazed at her discontentedly.

"Oh me, oh my! Going to London to look at the Queen, are we? You've got too much color. People will think you're painted. Are you sure you ain't?"

"Oh, no, Ma...no," in shocked tones.

"Mind your manners now and when you set down, cross your ankles decently. Mind you don't set in a draught or talk too much."

"I won't, Ma," promised Pauline earnestly, with a nervous glance at the clock.

"I'm sending Louisa a bottle of my sarsaparilla wine to drink the toasts in. I never cared for Louisa, but her mother was a Tackaberry. Mind you bring back the bottle and don't let her give you a kitten. Louisa's always giving people kittens."

"I won't, Ma."

"You're sure you didn't leave the soap in the water?"

"Quite sure, Ma," with another anguished glance at the clock.

"Are your shoe-laces tied?"

"Yes, Ma."

"You don't smell respectable...drenched with scent."

"Oh, no, Ma dear...just a little...the tiniest bit..."

"I said drenched and I mean drenched. There isn't, a rip under your arm, is there?"

"Oh, no, Ma."

"Let me see..." inexorably.

Pauline quaked. Suppose the skirt of the gray dress showed when she lifted her arms!

"Well, go, then." With a long sigh. "If I ain't here when you come back, remember that I want to be laid out in my lace shawl and my black satin slippers. And see that my hair is crimped."

"Do you feel any worse, Ma?" The poplin dress had made Pauline's conscience very sensitive. "If you do...I'll not go..."

"And waste the money for them shoes! 'Course you're going. And mind you don't slide down the banister."

But at this the worm turned.

"Ma! Do you think I would?"

"You did at Nancy Parker's wedding."

'Thirty-five years ago! Do you think I would do it now?"

"It's time you were off. What are you jabbering here for? Do you want to miss your train?"

Pauline hurried away and Anne sighed with relief. She had been afraid that old Mrs. Gibson had, at the last moment, been taken with a fiendish impulse to detain Pauline until the train was gone.

"Now for a little peace," said Mrs. Gibson. "This house is in an awful condition of untidiness, Miss Shirley. I hope you realize it ain't always so. Pauline hasn't known which end of her was up these last few days. Will you please set that vase an inch to the left? No, move it back again. That lamp shade is crooked. Well, that's a little straighter. But that blind is an inch lower than the other. I wish you'd fix it."

Anne unluckily gave the blind too energetic a twist; it escaped her fingers and went whizzing to the top.

"Ah, now you see," said Mrs. Gibson.

Anne didn't see but she adjusted the blind meticulously.

"And now wouldn't you like me to make you a nice cup of tea, Mrs. Gibson?"

"I do need something...I'm clean wore out with all this worry and fuss. My stomach seems to be dropping out of me," said Mrs. Gibson pathetically. "Kin you make a decent cup of tea? I'd as soon drink mud as the tea some folks make."

"Marilla Cuthbert taught me how to make tea. You'll see. But first I'm going to wheel you out to the porch so that you can enjoy the sunshine."

"I ain't been out on the porch for years," objected Mrs. Gibson.

"Oh, it's so lovely today, it can't hurt you. I want you to see the crab tree in bloom. You can't see it unless you go out. And the wind is south today, so you'll get the clover scent from Norman Johnson's field. I'll bring you your tea and we'll drink it together and then I'll get my embroidery and we'll sit there and criticize everybody who passes."

"I don't hold with criticizing people," said Mrs. Gibson virtuously. "It ain't Christian. Would you mind telling me if that is all your own hair?"

"Every bit," laughed Anne.

"Pity it's red. Though red hair seems to be gitting popular now. I sort of like your laugh. That nervous giggle of poor Pauline's always gits on my nerves. Well, if I've got to git out, I s'pose I've got to. I'll likely ketch my death of cold, but the responsibility is yours, Miss Shirley. Remember I'm eighty...every day of it, though I hear old Davy Ackham has been telling all around Summerside I'm only seventy-nine. His mother was a Watt. The Watts were always jealous."

Anne moved the wheel-chair deftly out, and proved that she had a knack of arranging pillows. Soon after she brought out the tea and Mrs. Gibson deigned approval.

"Yes, this is drinkable, Miss Shirley. Ah me, for one year

I had to live entirely on liquids. They never thought I'd pull through. I often think it might have been better if I hadn't. Is that the crab tree you was raving about?"

"Yes...isn't it lovely...so white against that deep blue sky?"

"It ain't poetical," was Mrs. Gibson's sole comment. But she became rather mellow after two cups of tea and the forenoon wore away until it was time to think of dinner.

"I'll go and get it ready and then I'll bring it out here on a little table."

"No, you won't, miss. No crazy monkey-shines like that for me! People would think it awful queer, us eating out here in public. I ain't denying it's kind of nice out here...though the smell of clover always makes me kind of squalmish...and the forenoon's passed awful quick to what it mostly does, but I ain't eating my dinner out-of-doors for any one. I ain't a gypsy. Mind you wash your hands clean before you cook the dinner. My, Mrs. Storey must be expecting more company. She's got all the spare-room bed-clothes airing on the line. It ain't real hospitality...just a desire for sensation. Her mother was a Carey."

The dinner Anne produced pleased even Mrs. Gibson.

"I didn't think any one who wrote for the papers could cook. But of course Marilla Cuthbert brought you up. Her mother was a Johnson. I s'pose Pauline will eat herself sick at that wedding. She don't know when she's had enough...just like her father. I've seen him gorge on strawberries when he knew he'd be doubled up with pain an hour afterwards. Did I ever show you his picture, Miss Shirley? Well, go to the spare-room and bring it down. You'll find it under the bed. Mind you don't go prying into the drawers while you're up there. But take a peep and see if there's any dust curls under the bureau. I don't trust Pauline...Ah, yes, that's him. His mother was a Walker. There's no men like that nowadays. This is a degenerate age, Miss Shirley."

"Homer said the same thing eight hundred years, B.C.," smiled Anne.

"Some of them Old Testament writers was always croaking," said Mrs. Gibson. "I daresay you're shocked to hear me say so, Miss Shirley, but my husband was very broad in his views. I hear you're engaged...to a medical student. Medical students mostly drink, I believe...have to, to stand the dissecting-room. Never marry a man who drinks, Miss Shirley. Nor one who ain't a good provider. Thistledown and moonshine ain't much to live on, I kin tell you. Mind you clean the sink and rinse the dish-towels. I can't abide greasy dish-towels. I s'pose you'll have to feed the dog. He's too fat now, but Pauline just stuffs him. Sometimes I think I'll have to get rid of him."

"Oh, I wouldn't do that, Mrs. Gibson. There are always burglaries, you know...and your house is lonely, off here by itself. You really do need protection."

"Oh, well, have it your own way. I'd ruther do anything than argue with people, 'specially when I've such a queer throbbing in the back of my neck. I s'pose it means I'm going to have a stroke."

"You need your nap. When you've had it you'll feel better. I'll tuck you up and lower your chair. Would you like to go out on the porch for your nap?"

"Sleeping in public! That'd be worse than eating. You do have the queerest ideas. You just fix me up right here in the sitting-room and draw the blinds down and shut the door to keep the flies out. I daresay you'd like a quiet spell yourself...your tongue's been going pretty steady."

Mrs. Gibson had a good long nap, but woke up in a bad humor. She would not let Anne wheel her out to the porch again.

"Want me to ketch my death in the night air, I s'pose," she grumbled, although it was only five o'clock. Nothing suited her. The drink Anne brought her was too cold...the next one wasn't cold enough...of course anything would do for her. Where was the dog? Misbehaving, no doubt. Her back ached...her knees ached...her head ached...her breastbone ached. Nobody sympathized with her...nobody knew what she went through. Her chair was too high...her chair was too low...She wanted a shawl for her shoulders and an afghan for her knees and a cushion for her feet. And would Miss Shirley see where that awful draught was coming from? She could do with a cup of tea, but she didn't want to be a trouble to any one and she would soon be at rest in her grave. Maybe they might appreciate her when she was gone.

"Be the day short or be the day long, at last it weareth to evening song." There were moments when Anne thought it never would, but it did. Sunset came and Mrs. Gibson began to wonder why Pauline wasn't coming. Twilight came...still no Pauline. Night and moonshine and no Pauline.

"I knew it," said Mrs. Gibson cryptically.

"You know she can't come till Mr. Gregor comes and he's generally the last dog hung," soothed Anne. "Won't you let me put you to bed, Mrs. Gibson? You're tired...I know it's a bit of a strain having a stranger round instead of some one you're accustomed to."

The little puckery lines about Mrs. Gibson's mouth deepened obstinately.

"I'm not going to bed till that girl comes home. But if you're so anxious to be gone, go. I can stay alone...or die alone."

At half past nine Mrs. Gibson decided that Jim Gregor was not coming home till Monday.

"Nobody could ever depend on Jim Gregor to stay in the

same mind twenty-four hours. And he thinks it's wrong to travel on Sunday even to come home. He's on your school board, ain't he? What do you really think of him and his opinions on eddication?"

Anne went wicked. After all, she had endured a good deal at Mrs. Gibson's hands that day.

"I think he's a psychological anachronism," she answered gravely.

Mrs. Gibson did not bat an eyelash.

"I agree with you," she said. But she pretended to go to sleep after that.

14

It was ten o'clock when Pauline came at last...a flushed, starry-eyed Pauline, looking ten years younger, in spite of the resumed taffeta and the old hat, and carrying a beautiful bouquet which she hurriedly presented to the grim lady in the wheelchair.

"The bride sent you her bouquet, Ma. Isn't it lovely? Twenty-five white roses."

"Cat's hindfoot! I don't s'pose any one thought of sending me a crumb of wedding-cake. People nowadays don't seem to have any family feeling. Ah, well, I've seen the day..."

"But they did. I've a great big piece here in my bag. And everybody asked about you and sent you their love, Ma."

"Did you have a nice time?" asked Anne.

Pauline sat down on a hard chair because she knew her mother would resent it if she sat on a soft one.

"Very nice," she said cautiously. "We had a lovely wedding-dinner and Mr. Freeman, the Gull Cove minister, married Louisa and Maurice over again..."

"I call that sacrilegious..."

"And then the photographer took all our pictures. The flowers were simply wonderful. The parlor was a bower..."

"Like a funeral I s'pose..."

"And, oh, Ma. Mary Luckley was there from the west...Mrs. Flemming, you know. You remember what friends she and I always were. We used to call each other Polly and Molly..."

"Very silly names..."

"And it was so nice to see her again and have a long talk over old times. Her sister Em was there, too, with such a delicious baby."

"You talk as if it was something to eat," grunted Mrs. Gibson. "Babies are common enough."

"Oh, no, babies are never common," said Anne, bringing a bowl of water for Mrs. Gibson's roses. "Every one is a miracle."

"Well, I had ten and I never saw much that was miraculous about any of them. Pauline, do sit still if you kin. You fidget me. I notice you ain't asking how I got along. But I s'pose I couldn't expect it."

"I can tell how you got along without asking, Ma...you look so bright and cheerful." Pauline was still so uplifted by the day that she could be a little arch even with her mother. "I'm sure you and Miss Shirley had a nice time together."

"We got on well enough. I just let her have her own way. I admit it's the first time in years I've heard some interesting conversation. I ain't so near the grave as some people would like to make out. Thank heaven I've never got deaf or childish. Well, I s'pose the next thing you'll be off to the moon. And I s'pose they didn't care for my sarsaparilla wine by any chance?"

"Oh, they did. They thought it delicious."

"You've taken your own time telling me that. Did you bring back the bottle...or would it be too much to expect you'd remember that?"

"The...the bottle got broke," faltered Pauline. "Some one knocked it over in the pantry. But Louisa gave me another just exactly the same, Ma, so you needn't worry."

"I've had that bottle ever since I started housekeeping. Louisa's can't be exactly the same. They don't make such bottles nowadays. I wish you'd bring me another shawl. I'm sneezing...I expect I've got a terrible cold. You can't either of you seem to remember not to let the night air git at me. Likely it'll bring my neuritis back."

An old neighbor up the street dropped in at this Juncture and Pauline snatched at the chance to go a little way with Anne.

"Good night, Miss Shirley," said Mrs. Gibson quite graciously. "I'm much obliged to you. If there was more people like you in this town, it would be the better for it." She grinned toothlessly and pulled Anne down to her. "I don't care what people say...I think you're real nice-looking," she whispered.

Pauline and Anne walked along the street, through the cool, green night, and Pauline let herself go, as she had not dared do before her mother.

"Oh, Miss Shirley, it was heavenly. How can I ever repay you? I've never spent such a wonderful day...I'll live on it for years. It was such fun being a bridesmaid again. And Captain Isaac Kent was groomsman. He...he used to be an old beau of mine...well, no, hardly a beau...I don't think he ever had any real intentions but we drove round together...and he paid me two compliments. He said, 'I remember how pretty you looked at Louisa's wedding in that wine-colored dress.' Wasn't it wonderful his remembering the dress? And he said, 'Your hair looks just as much like molasses taffy as it ever did.' There wasn't anything improper in his saying that, was there, Miss Shirley?"

"Nothing whatever."

"Lou and Molly and I had such a nice supper together after everybody had gone. I was so hungry...I don't think I've been so hungry for years. It was so nice to eat just what I wanted and nobody to warn me about things that wouldn't agree with my stomach. After supper Mary and I went over to her old home and wandered around the garden, talking over old times. We saw the lilac bushes we planted years ago. We had some beautiful summers together when we were girls. Then when it came sunset we went down to the dear old shore and sat there on a rock in silence. There was a bell ringing down at the harbor and it was lovely to feel the wind from the sea again and see the stars trembling in the water. I had forgotten night on the gulf could be so beautiful. When it got quite dark we went back and Mr. Gregor was ready to start...and so," concluded Pauline with a laugh, "The Old Woman Got Home That Night."

"I wish...I wish you didn't have such a hard time at home, Pauline..."

"Oh, dear Miss Shirley, I won't mind it now," said Pauline quickly. "After all, poor Ma needs me. And it's nice to be needed, my dear."

Yes, it was nice to be needed. Anne thought of this in her tower room, where Dusty Miller, having evaded both Rebecca Dew and the widows, was curled up on her bed. She thought of Pauline trotting back to her bondage but companied by "the immortal spirit of one happy day."

"I hope some one will always need me," said Anne to Dusty Miller. "And it's wonderful, Dusty Miller, to be able to give happiness to somebody. It has made me feel so rich, giving Pauline this day. But, oh, Dusty Miller, you don't think I'll ever be like Mrs. Adoniram Gibson, even if I live to be eighty? Do you, Dusty Miller?"

Dusty Miller, with rich, throaty purrs, assured her he didn't.

15

Anne went down to Bonnyview on the Friday night before the wedding. The Nelsons were giving a dinner for some family friends and wedding-guests arriving by the boat train. The big, rambling house which was Dr. Nelson's "summer home" was built among spruces on a long point with the bay on both sides and a stretch of golden-breasted dunes beyond that knew all there was to be known about winds.

Anne liked it the moment she saw it. An old stone house

always looks reposeful and dignified. It fears not what rain or wind or changing fashion can do. And on this June evening it was bubbling over with young life and excitement, the laughter of girls, the greetings of old friends, buggies coming and going, children running everywhere, gifts arriving, every one in the delightful turmoil of a wedding, while Dr. Nelson's two black cats, who rejoiced in the names of Barnabas and Saul, sat on the railing of the veranda and watched everything like two imperturbable sable sphinxes.

Sally detached herself from a mob and whisked Anne upstairs.

"We've saved the north gable room for you. Of course you'll have to share it with at least three others. There's a perfect riot here. Father's having a tent put up for the boys down among the spruces and later on we can have cots in the glassed-in porch at the back. And we can pack most of the children in the hay-loft of course. Oh, Anne, I'm so excited. It's really no end of fun getting married. My wedding-dress just came from Montreal today. It's a dream...cream corded silk with a lace bertha and pearl embroidery. The loveliest gifts have come. This is your bed. Mamie Gray and Dot Fraser and Sis Palmer have the others. Mother wanted to put Amy Stewart here but I wouldn't let her. Amy hates you because she wanted to be my bridesmaid. But I couldn't have any one so fat and dumpy, could I now? Besides, she looks like somebody seasick in Nile green. Oh, Anne, Aunt Mouser is here. She came just a few minutes ago and we're simply horror-stricken. Of course we had to invite her, but we never thought of her coming before tomorrow."

"Who in the world is Aunt Mouser?"

"Dad's aunt, Mrs. James Kennedy. Oh, of course she's really Aunt Grace, but Tommy nicknamed her Aunt Mouser because she's always mousing round pouncing on things we don't want her to find out. There's no escaping her. She even gets up early in the morning for fear of missing something and she's the last to go to bed at night. But that isn't the worst. If there's a wrong thing to say she's certain to say it and she's never learned that there are questions that mustn't be asked. Dad calls her speeches 'Aunt Mouser's felicities.' I know she'll spoil the dinner. Here she comes now."

The door opened and Aunt Mouser came in...a fat, brown, pop-eyed little woman, moving in an atmosphere of moth-balls and wearing a chronically worried expression. Except for the expression she really did look a good deal like a hunting pussy-cat.

"So you're the Miss Shirley I've always heard so much of. You ain't a bit like a Miss Shirley I once knew. She had such beautiful eyes. Well, Sally, so you're to be married at last. Poor

Nora is the only one left. Well, your mother is lucky to be rid of five of you. Eight years ago I said to her, 'Jane,' sez I, 'do you think you'll ever get all those girls married off?' Well, a man is nothing but trouble as I sees it and of all the uncertain things marriage is the uncertainest, but what else is there for a woman in this world? That's what I've just been saying to poor Nora. 'Mark my words, Nora,' I said to her, 'there isn't much fun in being an old maid. What's Jim Wilcox thinking of?' I said to her."

"Oh, Aunt Grace, I wish you hadn't! Jim and Nora had some sort of a quarrel last January and he's never been round since."

"I believe in saying what I think. Things is better said. I'd heard of that quarrel. That's why I asked her about him. 'It's only right,' I told her, 'that you should know they say he's driving Eleanor Pringle.' She got red and mad and flounced off. What's Vera Johnson doing here? She ain't any relation."

"Vera's always been a great friend of mine, Aunt Grace. She's going to play the wedding-march."

"Oh, she is, is she? Well, all I hope is she won't make a mistake and play the Dead March like Mrs. Tom Scott did at Dora Best's wedding. Such a bad omen. I don't know where you're going to put the mob you've got here for the night. Some of us will have to sleep on the clothes-line I reckon."

"Oh, we'll find a place for every one, Aunt Grace."

"Well, Sally, all I hope is you won't change your mind at the last moment like Helen Summers did. It clutters things up so. Your father is in terrible high spirits. I never was one to go looking for trouble but all I hope is it ain't the forerunner of a stroke. I've seen it happen that way."

"Oh, Dad's fine, Aunt Mouser. He's just a bit excited."

"Ah, you're too young, Sally, to know all that can happen. Your mother tells me the ceremony is at high noon tomorrow. The fashions in weddings are changing like everything else and not for the better. When I was married it was in the evening and my father laid in twenty gallons of liquor for the wedding. Ah, dear me, times ain't what they used to be. What's the matter with Mercy Daniels? I met her on the stairs and her complexion has got terrible muddy."

"'The quality of mercy is not strained,'" giggled Sally, wriggling into her dinner-dress.

"Don't quote the Bible flippantly," rebuked Aunt Mouser. "You must excuse her, Miss Shirley. She just ain't used to getting married. Well, all I hope is the groom won't have a hunted look like so many of them do. I s'pose they do feel that way, but they needn't show it so plain. And I hope he won't forget the ring. Upton Hardy did. Him and Flora had to be married with a ring off one of the curtain poles. Well, I'll be taking another look at the wedding-presents. You've got a lot of nice things, Sally. All I hope is it won't be as hard to keep the handles of them spoons polished as I think likely."

Dinner that night in the big, glassed-in porch was a gay affair. Chinese lanterns had been hung all about it, shedding mellow-tinted lights on the pretty dresses and glossy hair and white, unlined brows of girls. Barnabas and Saul sat like ebony statues on the broad arms of the Doctor's chair, where he fed them tidbits alternately.

"Just about as bad as Parker Pringle," said Aunt Mouser. "He has his dog sit at the table with a chair and napkin of his own. Well, sooner or later there'll be a judgment."

It was a large party, for all the married Nelson girls and their husbands were there, besides ushers and bridesmaids; and it was a merry one, in spite of Aunt Mouser's "felicities"...or perhaps because of them. Nobody took Aunt Mouser very seriously; she was evidently a joke among the young fry. When she said, on being introduced to Gordon Hill, "Well, well, you ain't a bit like I expected. I always thought Sally would pick out a tall handsome man," ripples of laughter ran through the porch. Gordon Hill, who was on the short side and called no more than "pleasant-faced" by his best friends, knew he would never hear the last of it. When she said to Dot Fraser, "Well, well, a new dress every time I see you! All I hope is your father's purse will be able to stand it for a few years yet," Dot could, of course, have boiled her in oil, but some of the other girls found it amusing. And when Aunt Mouser mournfully remarked, apropos of the preparations of the wedding-dinner, "All I hope is everybody will get her teaspoons afterwards. Five were missing after Gertie Paul's wedding. They never turned up," Mrs. Nelson, who had borrowed three dozen and the sisters-in-law she had borrowed them from all looked harried. But Dr. Nelson haw-hawed cheerfully.

"We'll make everyone turn out their pockets before they go, Aunt Grace."

"Ah, you may laugh, Samuel. It is no joking-matter to have anything like that happen in the family. Some one must have those teaspoons. I never go anywhere but I keep my eyes open for them. I'd know them wherever I saw them, though it was twenty-eight years ago. Poor Nora was just a baby then. You remember you had her there, Jane, in a little white embroidered dress? Twenty-eight years! Ah, Nora, you're getting on, though in this light you don't show your age so much."

Nora did not join in the laugh that followed. She looked as if she might flash lightning at any moment. In spite of her daffodil-hued dress and the pearls in her dark hair, she made Anne think of a black moth. In direct contrast with Sally, who was a cool, snowy blonde, Nora Nelson had magnificent black hair, dusky eyes, heavy black brows and velvety red cheeks. Her nose was beginning to look a trifle hawk-like and she had never been accounted pretty, but Anne felt an odd attraction to her in spite of her sulky, smoldering expression. She felt that she would prefer Nora as a friend to the popular Sally.

They had a dance after dinner and music and laughter came tumbling out of the broad low windows of the old stone house in a flood. At ten Nora had disappeared. Anne was a little tired of the noise and merriment. She slipped through the hall to a back door that opened almost on the bay, and flitted down a flight of rocky steps to the shore, past a little grove of pointed firs. How divine the cool salt air was after the sultry evening! How exquisite the silver patterns of moonlight on the bay! How dream-like that ship which had sailed at the rising of the moon and was now approaching the harbor bar! It was a night when you might expect to stray into a dance of mermaids.

Nora was hunched up in the grim black shadow of a rock by the water's edge, looking more like a thunderstorm than ever.

"May I sit with you for a while?" asked Anne. "I'm a little tired of dancing and it's a shame to miss this wonderful night. I envy you with the whole harbor for a back yard like this."

"What would you feel like at a time like this if you had no beau?" asked Nora abruptly and sullenly. "Or any likelihood of one," she added still more sullenly.

"I think it must be your own fault if you haven't," said Anne, sitting down beside her. Nora found herself telling Anne her troubles. There was always something about Anne that made people tell her their troubles.

"You're saying that to be polite of course. You needn't. You know as well as I do that I'm not a girl men are likely to fall in love with...I'm 'the plain Miss Nelson.' It isn't my fault that I haven't anybody. I couldn't stand it in there any longer. I had to come down here and just let myself be unhappy. I'm tired of smiling and being agreeable to every one and pretending not to care when they give me digs about not being married. I'm not going to pretend any longer. I do care...I care horribly. I'm the only one of the Nelson girls left. Five of us are married or will be tomorrow. You heard Aunt Mouser casting my age up to me at the dinnertable. And I heard her telling Mother before dinner that I had 'aged quite a bit' since last summer. Of course I have. I'm twenty-eight. In twelve more years I'll be forty. How will I endure life at forty, Anne, if I haven't got any roots of my own by that time?"

"I wouldn't mind what a foolish old woman said."

"Oh, wouldn't you? You haven't a nose like mine. I'll be as beaky as Father in ten more years. And I suppose you wouldn't care, either, if you'd waited years for a man to propose...and he just wouldn't?"

"Oh, yes, I think I would care about that."

"Well, that's my predicament exactly. Oh, I know you've heard of Jim Wilcox and me. It's such an old story. He's been hanging around me for years...but he's never said anything about getting married."

"Do you care for him?"

"Of course I care. I've always pretended I didn't but, as I've told you, I'm through with pretending. And he's never been near me since last January. We had a fight...but we've had hundreds of fights. He always came back before...but he hasn't come this time...and he never will. He doesn't want to. Look at his house across the bay, shining in the moonlight. I suppose he's there...and I'm here...and all the harbor between us. That's the way it always will be. It...it's terrible! And I can't do a thing."

"If you sent for him, wouldn't he come back?"

"Send for him! Do you think I'd do that? I'd die first. If he wants to come, there's nothing to prevent him coming. If he doesn't, I don't want him to. Yes, I do...I do! I love Jim...and I want to get married. I want to have a home of my own and be 'Mrs.' and shut Aunt Mouser's mouth. Oh, I wish I could be Barnabas or Saul for a few moments just to swear at her! If she calls me 'poor Nora' again I'll throw a scuttle at her. But after all, she only says what everybody thinks. Mother has despaired long ago of my ever marrying, so she leaves me alone, but the rest rag me. I hate Sally...of course I'm dreadful...but I hate her. She's getting a nice husband and a lovely home. It isn't fair she should have everything and I nothing. She isn't better or cleverer or much prettier than me...only luckier. I suppose you think I'm awful...not that I care what you think."

"I think you're very, very tired, after all these weeks of preparation and strain, and that things which were always hard have become too hard all at once."

"You understand...oh, yes, I always knew you would. I've wanted to be friends with you, Anne Shirley. I like the way you laugh. I've always wished I could laugh like that. I'm not as sulky as I look...it's these eyebrows. I really think they're what scare the men away. I never had a real girl friend in my life. But of course I always had Jim. We've been...friends...ever since we were kids. Why, I used to put a light up in that little window in the attic whenever I wanted him over particularly and he'd sail across at once. We went everywhere together. No other boy ever had a chance...not that any one wanted it, I suppose. And now it's all over. He was just tired of me and was glad of the excuse of a quarrel to get free. Oh, won't I hate you tomorrow because I've told you this!"

"Why?"

"We always hate people who surprise our secrets, I suppose," said Nora drearily. "But there's something gets into you at a wedding...and I just don't care...I don't care for anything. Oh, Anne Shirley, I'm so miserable! Just let me have a good cry on your shoulder. I've got to smile and look happy all day tomorrow. Sally thinks it's because I'm superstitious that I wouldn't be her bridesmaid...'Three times a bridesmaid, never a bride,' you know. 'Tisn't! I just couldn't endure to stand there and hear her saying, 'I will,' and know I'd never have a chance to say it for Jim. I'd have flung back my head and howled. I want to be a bride...and have a trousseau...and monogrammed linen...and lovely presents. Even Aunt Mouser's silver butter-dish. She always gives a butter-dish to every bride...awful things with tops like the dome of St. Peter's. We could have had it on the breakfast table just for Jim to make fun of. Anne, I think I'm going crazy."

The dance was over when the girls went back to the house, hand in hand. People were being stowed away for the night. Tommy Nelson was taking Barnabas and Saul to the barn. Aunt Mouser was still sitting on a sofa, thinking of all the dreadful things she hoped wouldn't happen on the morrow.

"I hope nobody will get up and give a reason why they shouldn't be joined together. That happened at Tillie Hatfield's wedding."

"No such good luck for Gordon as that," said the groomsman. Aunt Mouser fixed him with a stony brown eye.

"Young man, marriage isn't exactly a joke."

"You bet it isn't," said the unrepentant. "Hello, Nora, when are we going to have a chance to dance at your wedding?"

Nora did not answer in words. She went closer up to him and deliberately slapped him, first on one side of his face and then on the other. The slaps were not make-believe ones. Then she went upstairs without looking behind her.

"That girl," said Aunt Mouser, "is overwrought."

16

The forenoon of Saturday passed in a whirl of last-minute things. Anne, shrouded in one of Mrs. Nelson's aprons, spent it in the kitchen helping Nora with the salads. Nora was all prickles, evidently repenting, as she had foretold, her confidences of the night before.

"We'll be all tired out for a month," she snapped, "and Father can't really afford all this splurge. But Sally was set on having what she calls a 'pretty wedding' and Father gave in. He's always spoiled her."

"Spite and jealousy," said Aunt Mouser, suddenly popping her head out of the pantry, where she was driving Mrs. Nelson frantic with her hopings against hope.

"She's right," said Nora bitterly to Anne. "Quite right. I am spiteful and jealous...I hate the very look of happy people. But all the same I'm not sorry I slapped Jud Taylor's face last night. I'm only sorry I didn't tweak his nose into the bargain. Well, that finishes the salads. They do look pretty. I love fussing things up when I'm normal. Oh, after all, I hope everything will go off nicely for Sally's sake. I suppose I do love her underneath everything, though just now I feel as if I hated every one and Jim Wilcox worst of all."

"Well, all I hope is the groom won't be missing just before the ceremony," floated out from the pantry in Aunt Mouser's lugubrious tones. "Austin Creed was. He just forgot he was to be married that day. The Creeds were always forgetful, but I call that carrying things too far."

The two girls looked at each other and laughed. Nora's whole face changed when she laughed...lightened...glowed...rippled. And then some one came out to tell her that Barnabas had been sick on the stairs...too many chicken livers probably. Nora rushed off to repair the damage and Aunt Mouser came out of the pantry to hope that the wedding-cake wouldn't disappear as had happened at Alma Clark's wedding ten years before.

By noon everything was in immaculate readiness...the table laid, the beds beautifully dressed, baskets of flowers everywhere; and in the big north room upstairs Sally and her three bridesmaids were in quivering splendor. Anne, in her Nile green dress and hat, looked at herself in the mirror, and wished that Gilbert could see her.

"You're wonderful," said Nora half enviously.

"You're looking wonderful yourself, Nora. That smoke-blue chiffon and that picture hat bring out the gloss of your hair and the blue of your eyes."

"There's nobody to care how I look," said Nora bitterly. "Well, watch me grin, Anne. I mustn't be the death's head at the feast, I suppose. I have to play the wedding-march after all...Vera's got a terrible headache. I feel more like playing the Dead March, as Aunt Mouser foreboded."

Aunt Mouser, who had wandered round all the morning, getting in everybody's way, in a none too clean old kimono and a wilted "boudoir cap," now appeared resplendent in maroon grosgrain and told Sally one of her sleeves didn't fit and she hoped nobody's petticoat would show below her dress as had happened at Annie Crewson's wedding. Mrs. Nelson came in and cried because Sally looked so lovely in her wedding-dress.

"Now, now, don't be sentimental, Jane," soothed Aunt Mouser. "You've still got one daughter left...and likely to have her by all accounts. Tears ain't lucky at weddings. Well, all I hope is nobody'll drop dead like old Uncle Cromwell at Roberta Pringle's wedding, right in the middle of the ceremony. The bride spent two weeks in bed from shock."

With this inspiring send-off the bridal party went downstairs, to the strains of Nora's wedding-march somewhat stormily played, and Sally and Gordon were married without anybody dropping dead or forgetting the ring. It was a pretty wedding group and even Aunt Mouser gave up worrying about the universe for a few moments. "After all," she told Sally hopefully later on, "even if you ain't very happy married, it's likely you'd be more unhappy not." Nora alone continued to glower from the piano stool, but she went up to Sally and gave her a fierce hug, wedding-veil and all.

"So that's finished," said Nora drearily, when the dinner was over and the bridal party and most of the guests had gone. She glanced around at the room which looked as forlorn and disheveled as rooms always do in the aftermath...a faded, trampled corsage lying on the floor...chairs awry...a torn piece of lace...two dropped handkerchiefs...crumbs the children had scattered...a dark stain on the ceiling where the water from a jug Aunt Mouser had overturned in a guest-room had seeped through.

"I must clear up this mess," went on Nora savagely. "There's a lot of young fry waiting for the boat train and some staying over Sunday. They're going to wind up with a bonfire on the shore and a moonlit rock dance. You can imagine how much I feel like moonlight dancing. I want to go to bed and cry."

"A house after a wedding is over does seem a rather forsaken place," said Anne. "But I'll help you clear up and then we'll have a cup of tea."

"Anne Shirley, do you think a cup of tea is a panacea for everything? It's you who ought to be the old maid, not me. Never mind. I don't want to be horrid, but I suppose it's my native disposition. I hate the thought of this shore dance more than the wedding. Jim always used to be at our shore dances. Anne, I've made up my mind to go and train for a nurse. I know I'll hate it...and heaven help my future patients...but I'm not going to hang around Summerside and be teased about being on the shelf any longer. Well, let's tackle this pile of greasy plates and look as if we liked it."

"I do like it...I've always liked washing dishes. It's fun to make dirty things clean and shining again."

"Oh, you ought to be in a museum," snapped Nora.

By moonrise everything was ready for the shore dance. The boys had a huge bonfire of driftwood ablaze on the point, and the waters of the harbor were creaming and shimmering in the moonlight. Anne was expecting to enjoy herself hugely, but a glimpse of Nora's face, as the latter went down the steps carrying a basket of sandwiches, gave her pause.

"She's so unhappy. If there was anything I could do!"

An idea popped into Anne's head. She had always been a prey to impulse. Darting into the kitchen, she snatched up a little hand-lamp alight there, sped up the back stairs and up another flight to the attic. She set the light in the dormer-window that looked out across the harbor. The trees hid it from the dancers.

"He may see it and come. I suppose Nora will be furious with me, but that won't matter if he only comes. And now to wrap up a bit of wedding-cake for Rebecca Dew."

Jim Wilcox did not come. Anne gave up looking for him after a while and forgot him in the merriment of the evening. Nora had disappeared and Aunt Mouser had for a wonder gone to bed. It was eleven o'clock when the revelry ceased and the tired moonlighters yawned their way upstairs. Anne was so sleepy, she never thought of the light in the attic. But at two o'clock Aunt Mouser crept into the room and flashed a candle in the girls' faces.

"Goodness, what's the matter?" gasped Dot Fraser, sitting up in bed.

"S-s-s-sh," warned Aunt Mouser, her eyes nearly popping out of her head, "I think there's some one in the house...I know there is. What is that noise?"

"Sounds like a cat mewing or a dog barking," giggled Dot.

"Nothing of the sort," said Aunt Mouser severely. "I know

there's a dog barking in the barn, but that is not what wakened me. It was a bump...a loud, distinct bump."

"'From ghosties and ghoulies and long-legged beasties and things that go bump in the night, good Lord, deliver us,'" murmured Anne.

"Miss Shirley, this ain't any laughing-matter. There's burglars in this house. I'm going to call Samuel."

Aunt Mouser disappeared and the girls looked at each other.

"Do you suppose...all the wedding-presents are down in the library..." said Anne.

"I'm going to get up, anyhow," said Mamie. "Anne, did you ever see anything like Aunt Mouser's face when she held the candle low and the shadows fell upward...and all those wisps of hair hanging about it? Talk of the Witch of Endor!"

Four girls in kimonos slipped out into the hall. Aunt Mouser was coming along it, followed by Dr. Nelson in dressing-gown and slippers. Mrs. Nelson, who couldn't find her kimono, was sticking a terrified face out of her door.

"Oh, Samuel...don't take any risks...if it's burglars they may shoot..."

"Nonsense! I don't believe there's anything," said the Doctor.

"I tell you I heard a bump," quavered Aunt Mouser.

A couple of boys joined the party. They crept cautiously

down the stairs with the Doctor at the head and Aunt Mouser, candle in one hand and poker in the other, bringing up the rear.

There were undoubtedly noises in the library. The Doctor opened the door and walked in.

Barnabas, who had contrived to be overlooked in the library when Saul had been taken to the barn, was sitting on the back of the chesterfield, blinking amused eyes. Nora and a young man were standing in the middle of the room, which was dimly lighted by another flickering candle. The young man had his arms around Nora and was holding a large white handkerchief to her face.

"He's chloroforming her!" shrieked Aunt Mouser, letting the poker fall with a tremendous crash.

The young man turned, dropped the handkerchief and looked foolish. Yet he was a rather nice-looking young man, with crinkly russet eyes and crinkly red-brown hair, not to mention a chin that gave the world assurance of a chin.

Nora snatched the handkerchief up and applied it to her face.

"Jim Wilcox, what does this mean?" said the Doctor, with exceeding sternness.

"I don't know what it means," said Jim Wilcox rather sulkily. "All I know is Nora signaled for me. I didn't see the light till I got home at one from a Masonic banquet in Summerside. And I sailed right over."

"I didn't signal for you," stormed Nora. "For pity's sake don't look like that, Father. I wasn't asleep...I was sitting at my window...I hadn't undressed...and I saw a man coming up from the shore. When he got near the house I knew it was Jim, so I ran down. And I...I ran into the library door and made my nose bleed. He's just been trying to stop it."

"I jumped in at the window and knocked over that bench..."

"I told you I heard a bump," said Aunt Mouser.

"...and now Nora says she didn't signal for me, so I'll just relieve you of my unwelcome presence, with apologies to all concerned."

"It's really too bad to have disturbed your night's rest and brought you all the way over the bay on a wild-goose chase," said Nora as icily as possible, consistent with hunting for a bloodless spot on Jim's handkerchief.

"Wild-goose chase is right," said the Doctor.

"You'd better try a door-key down your back," said Aunt Mouser.

"It was I who put the light in the window," said Anne shamefacedly, "and then I forgot..."

"You dared!" cried Nora, "I'll never forgive you..."

"Have you all gone crazy?" said the Doctor irritably. "What's all this fuss about, anyhow? For heaven's sake put that window down, Jim...there's a wind blowing in fit to chill you to the bone. Nora, hang your head back and your nose will be all right."

Nora was shedding tears of rage and shame. Mingled with the blood on her face they made her a fearsome sight. Jim Wilcox looked as if he wished the floor would open and gently drop him in the cellar.

"Well," said Aunt Mouser belligerently, "all you can do now is marry her, Jim Wilcox. She'll never get a husband if it gets round that she was found here with you at two o'clock at night."

"Marry her!" cried Jim in exasperation. "What have I wanted all my life but to marry her...never wanted anything else!"

"Then why didn't you say so long ago?" demanded Nora, whirling about to face him.

"Say so? You've snubbed and frozen and jeered at me for years. You've gone out of your way times without number to show me how you despised me. I didn't think it was the least use to ask you. And last January you said..."

"You goaded me into saying it..."

"I goaded you! I like that! You picked a quarrel with me just to get rid of me..."

"I didn't...I..."

"And yet I was fool enough to tear over here in the dead of night because I thought you'd put our old signal in the window and wanted me! Ask you to marry me! Well, I'll ask you now and have done with it and you can have the fun of turning me down before all this gang. Nora Edith Nelson, will you marry me?"

"Oh, won't I...won't I!" cried Nora so shamelessly that even Barnabas blushed for her.

Jim gave her one incredulous look...then sprang at her. Perhaps her nose had stopped bleeding...perhaps it hadn't. It didn't matter.

"I think you've all forgotten that this is the Sabbath morn," said Aunt Mouser, who had just remembered it herself. "I could do with a cup of tea if any one would make it. I ain't used to demonstrations like this. All I hope is poor Nora has really landed him at last. At least, she has witnesses."

They went to the kitchen and Mrs. Nelson came down and made tea for them...all except Jim and Nora, who remained closeted in the library with Barnabas for chaperon. Anne did not see Nora until the morning...such a different Nora, ten years younger, flushed with happiness.

"I owe this to you, Anne. If you hadn't set the light...though just for two and a half minutes last night I could have chewed your ears off!"

"And to think I slept through it all," moaned Tommy Nelson heart-brokenly.

But the last word was with Aunt Mouser.

"Well, all I hope is it won't be a case of marrying in haste and repenting at leisure."

17

(Extract from letter to Gilbert.)

"School closed today. Two months of Green Gables and dew-wet, spicy ferns ankle-deep along the brook and lazy, dappling shadows in Lover's Lane and wild strawberries in Mr. Bell's pasture and the dark loveliness of firs in the Haunted Wood! My very soul has wings.

"Jen Pringle brought me a bouquet of lilies of the valley and wished me a happy vacation. She's coming down to spend a week-end with me some time. Talk of miracles!

"But little Elizabeth is heart-broken. I wanted her for a visit, too, but Mrs. Campbell did not 'deem it advisable.' Luckily, I hadn't said anything to Elizabeth about it, so she was spared that disappointment.

"'I believe I'll be Lizzie all the time you're away, Miss Shirley,' she told me. 'I'll feel like Lizzie anyway.'

"'But think of the fun we'll have when I come back,' I said. 'Of course you won't be Lizzie. There's no such person as Lizzie in you. And I'll write you every week, little Elizabeth.'

"'Oh, Miss Shirley, will you! I've never had a letter in my life. Won't it be fun! And I'll write you if they'll let me have a stamp. If they don't, you'll know I'm thinking of you just the same. I've called the chipmunk in the back yard after you...Shirley. You don't mind, do you? I thought at first of calling it Anne Shirley...but then I thought that mightn't be respectful...and, anyway, Anne doesn't sound chipmunky. Besides, it might be a gentleman chipmunk. Chipmunks are such darling things, aren't they? But the Woman says they eat the rosebush roots.'

"'She would!' I said.

"I asked Katherine Brooke where she was going to spend the summer and she briefly answered, 'Here. Where did you suppose?'

"I felt as if I ought to ask her to Green Gables, but I just couldn't. Of course I don't suppose she'd have come, anyway. And she's such a kill-joy. She'd spoil everything. But when I think of her alone in that cheap boarding-house all summer, my conscience gives me unpleasant jabs.

"Dusty Miller brought in a live snake the other day and dropped it on the floor of the kitchen. If Rebecca Dew could have turned pale she would have. 'This is really the last straw!' she said. But Rebecca Dew is just a little peevish these days because she has to spend all her spare time picking big gray-green beetles off the rose trees and dropping them in a can of kerosene. She thinks there are entirely too many insects in the world.

"'It's just going to be eaten up by them some day,' she predicts mournfully.

"Nora Nelson is to be married to Jim Wilcox in September. Very quietly...no fuss, no guests, no bridesmaids. Nora told me that was the only way to escape Aunt Mouser, and she will not have Aunt Mouser to see her married. I'm to be present, however, sort of unofficially. Nora says Jim would never have come back if I hadn't set that light in the window. He was going to sell his store and go west. Well, when I think of all the matches I'm supposed to have made...

"Sally says they'll fight most of their time but that they'll be happier fighting with each other than agreeing with anybody else. But I don't think they'll fight...much. I think it is just misunderstanding that makes most of the trouble in the world. You and I for so long, now...

"Good night, belovedest. Your sleep will be sweet if there is any influence in the wishes of

"YOUR OWN.

"P.S. The above sentence is quoted verbatim from a letter of Aunt Chatty's grandmother."

THE SECOND YEAR

1

"Windy Poplars,

"Spook's Lane,

"September 14th.

"I can hardly reconcile myself to the fact that our beautiful two months are over. They were beautiful, weren't they, dearest? And now it will be only two years before...

(Several paragraphs omitted.)

"But there has been a good deal of pleasure in coming back to Windy Poplars...to my own private tower and my own special chair and my own lofty bed...and even Dusty Miller basking on the kitchen window-sill.

"The widows were glad to see me and Rebecca Dew said frankly, 'It's good to have you back.' Little Elizabeth felt the same way. We had a rapturous meeting at the green gate.

"'I was a little afraid you might have got into Tomorrow before me,' said little Elizabeth.

"'Isn't this a lovely evening?' I said.

"'Where you are it's always a lovely evening, Miss Shirley,' said little Elizabeth.

"Talk of compliments!

"'How have you put in the summer, darling?' I asked.

"'Thinking,' said little Elizabeth softly, 'of all the lovely things that will happen in Tomorrow.'

"Then we went up to the tower room and read a story about elephants. Little Elizabeth is very much interested in elephants at present.

"'There is something bewitching about the very name of elephant, isn't there?' she said gravely, holding her chin in her small hands after a fashion she has. 'I expect to meet lots of elephants in Tomorrow.'

"We put an elephant park in our map of fairyland. It is no use looking superior and disdainful, my Gilbert, as I know you will be looking when you read this. Not a bit of use. The world always will have fairies. It can't get along without them. And somebody has to supply them.

"It's rather nice to be back in school, too. Katherine Brooke isn't any more companionable but my pupils seemed glad to see me and Jen Pringle wants me to help her make the tin halos for the angels' heads in a Sunday-school concert.

"I think the course of study this year will be much more interesting than last year. Canadian History has been added to the curriculum. I have to give a little 'lecturette' tomorrow on the War of 1812. It seems so strange to read over the stories of those old wars...things that can never happen again. I don't suppose any of us will ever have more than an academic interest in 'battles long ago.' It's impossible to think of Canada ever being at war again. I am so thankful that phase of history is over.

"We are going to reorganize the Dramatic Club at once and canvass every family connected with the school for a subscription. Lewis Allen and I are going to take the Dawlish Road as our territory and canvass it next Saturday afternoon. Lewis will try to kill two birds with one stone, as he is competing for a prize offered by Country Homes for the best photograph of an attractive farmhouse. The prize is twenty-five dollars and that will mean a badly needed new suit and overcoat for Lewis. He worked on a farm all summer and is doing housework and waiting on the table at his boarding-house again this year. He must hate it, but he never says a word about it. I do like Lewis...he is so plucky and ambitious, with a charming grin in place of a smile. And he really isn't over-strong. I was afraid last year he would break down. But his summer on the farm seems to have built him up a bit. This is his last year in High and then he hopes to achieve a year at Queen's. The widows are going to ask him to Sunday-night supper as often as possible this winter. Aunt Kate and I have had a conference on ways and means and I persuaded her to let me put up the extras. Of course we didn't try to persuade Rebecca Dew. I merely asked Aunt Kate in Rebecca's hearing if I could have Lewis Allen in on Sunday nights at least twice a month. Aunt Kate said coldly she was afraid they couldn't afford it, in addition to their usual lonely girl.

"Rebecca Dew uttered a cry of anguish.

"'This is the last straw. Getting so poor we can't afford a bite now and again to a poor, hard-working, sober boy who is trying to get an education! You pay more for liver for That Cat and him ready to burst. Well, take a dollar off my wages and have him.'

"The gospel according to Rebecca was accepted. Lewis Allen is coming and neither Dusty Miller's liver nor Rebecca Dew's wages will be less. Dear Rebecca Dew!

"Aunt Chatty crept into my room last night to tell me she wanted to get a beaded cape but that Aunt Kate thought she was too old for it and her feelings had been hurt.

"'Do you think I am, Miss Shirley? I don't want to be undignified...but I've always wanted a beaded cape so much. I always thought they were what you might call jaunty...and now they're in again."

"'Too old! Of course you're not too old, dearest,' I assured her. 'Nobody is ever too old to wear just what she wants to wear. You wouldn't want to wear it if you were too old.' 'I shall get it and defy Kate,' said Aunt Chatty, anything but defiantly. But I think she will...and I think I know how to reconcile Aunt Kate.

"I'm alone in my tower. Outside there is a still, still night and the silence is velvety. Not even the poplars are stirring. I have just leaned out of my window and blown a kiss in the direction of somebody not a hundred miles away from Kingsport."

2

The Dawlish Road was a meandering sort of road, and the afternoon was made for wanderers...or so Anne and Lewis thought as they prowled along it, now and then pausing to enjoy a sudden sapphire glimpse of the strait through the trees or to snap a particularly lovely bit of scenery or picturesque little house in a leafy hollow. It was not, perhaps, quite so pleasant to call at the houses themselves and ask for subscriptions for the benefit of the Dramatic Club, but Anne and Lewis took turns doing the talking...he taking on the women while Anne manipulated the men.

"Take the men if you're going in that dress and hat," Rebecca Dew had advised. "I've had a good bit of experience in canvassing in my day and it all went to show that the better-dressed and better-looking you are the more money...or promise of it...you'll get, if it's the men you have to tackle. But if it's the women, put on the oldest and ugliest things you have."

"Isn't a road an interesting thing, Lewis?" said Anne dreamily. "Not a straight road, but one with ends and kinks around which anything of beauty and surprise may be lurking. I've always loved bends in roads."

"Where does this Dawlish Road go to?" asked Lewis practically...though at the same moment he was reflecting that Miss Shirley's voice always made him think of spring.

"I might be horrid and school-teacherish, Lewis, and say that it doesn't go anywhere...it stays right here. But I won't. As to where it goes or where it leads to...who cares? To the end of the world and back, perhaps. Remember what Emerson says...'Oh, what have I to do with time?' That's our motto for today. I expect the universe will muddle on if we let it alone for a while. Look at those cloud shadows...and that tranquillity of green valleys...and that house with an apple tree at each of its corners. Imagine it in spring. This is one of the days people feel alive and every wind of the world is a sister. I'm glad there are so many clumps of spice ferns along this road...spice ferns with gossamer webs on them. It brings back the days when I pretended...or believed...I think I really did believe...that gossamer webs were fairies' tablecloths."

They found a wayside spring in a golden hollow and sat down on a moss that seemed made of tiny ferns, to drink from a cup that Lewis twisted out of birch bark.

"You never know the real joy of drinking till you're dry with thirst and find water," he said. "That summer I worked out west on the railroad they were building, I got lost on the prairie one hot day and wandered for hours. I thought I'd die of thirst and then I came to a settler's shack, and he had a little spring like this in a clump of willows. How I drank! I've understood the Bible and its love of good water better ever since."

"We're going to get some water from another quarter," said Anne rather anxiously. "There's a shower coming up and...Lewis, I love showers, but I've got on my best hat and my second-best dress. And there isn't a house within half a mile."

"There's an old deserted blacksmith's forge over there," said Lewis, "but we'll have to run for it."

Run they did and from its shelter enjoyed the shower as they had enjoyed everything else on that carefree, gypsying afternoon. A veiled hush had fallen over the world. All the young breezes that had been whispering and rustling so importantly along the Dawlish Road had folded their wings and become motionless and soundless. Not a leaf stirred, not a shadow flickered. The maple leaves at the bend of the road turned wrong side out until the trees looked as if they were turning pale from fear. A huge cool shadow seemed to engulf them like a green wave...the cloud had reached them. Then the rain, with a rush and sweep of wind. The shower pattered sharply down on the leaves, danced along the smoking red road and pelted the roof of the old forge right merrily.

"If this lasts..." said Lewis.

But it didn't. As suddenly as it had come up, it was over and the sun was shining on the wet, glistening trees. Dazzling glimpses of blue sky appeared between the torn white clouds. Far away they could see a hill still dim with rain, but below them the cup of the valley seemed to brim over with peach-tinted mists. The woods around were pranked out with a sparkle and glitter as of springtime, and a bird began to sing in the big maple over the forge as if he were cheated into believing it really was springtime, so amazingly fresh and sweet did the world seem all at once.

"Let's explore this," said Anne, when they resumed their tramp, looking along a little side road running between old rail fences smothered in goldenrod.

"I don't think there's anybody living along that road," said Lewis doubtfully. "I think it's only a road running down to the harbor."

"Never mind...let's go along it. I've always had a weakness for side roads...something off the beaten track, lost and green and lonely. Smell the wet grass, Lewis. Besides, I feel in my bones that there is a house on it...a certain kind of house...a very snappable house."

Anne's bones did not deceive her. Soon there was a house...and a snappable house to boot. It was a quaint, old-fashioned one, low in the eaves, with square, small-paned windows. Big willows stretched patriarchal arms over it and an apparent wilderness of perennials and shrubs crowded all about it. It was weather-gray and shabby, but the big barns beyond it were snug and prosperous-looking, up-to-date in every respect. "I've always heard, Miss Shirley, that when a man's barns are better than his house, it's a sign that his income exceeds his expenditure," said Lewis, as they sauntered up the deep-rutted grassy lane.

"I should think it was a sign that he thought more of his horses than of his family," laughed Anne. "I'm not expecting a subscription to our club here, but that's the most likely house for a prize contest we've encountered yet. It's grayness won't matter in a photograph."

"This lane doesn't look as if it were much traveled," said Lewis with a shrug. "Evidently the folks who live here aren't strongly sociable. I'm afraid we'll find they don't even know what a dramatic club is. Anyhow, I'm going to secure my picture before we rouse any of them from their lair."

The house seemed deserted, but after the picture was taken they opened a little white gate, crossed the yard and knocked on a faded blue kitchen door, the front door evidently being like that of Windy Poplars, more for show than for use...if a door literally hidden in Virginia creeper could be said to be for show.

They expected at least the civility which they had hitherto met in their calls, whether backed up with generosity or not. Consequently they were decidedly taken aback when the door was jerked open and on the threshold appeared, not the smiling farmer's wife or daughter they had expected to see, but a tall, broad-shouldered man of fifty, with grizzled hair and bushy eyebrows, who demanded unceremoniously,

"What do you want?"

"We have called, hoping to interest you in our High School Dramatic Club," began Anne, rather lamely. But she was spared further effort.

"Never heard of it. Don't want to hear about it. Nothing to do with it," was the uncompromising interruption, and the door was promptly shut in their faces.

"I believe we've been snubbed," said Anne as they walked away.

"Nice amiable gentleman, that," grinned Lewis. "I'm sorry for his wife, if he has one."

"I don't think he can have, or she would civilize him a trifle," said Anne, trying to recover her shattered poise. "I wish Rebecca Dew had the handling of him. But we've got his house, at least, and I've a premonition that it's going to win the prize. Bother! I've just got a pebble in my shoe and I'm going to sit down on my gentleman's stone dyke, with or without his permission, and remove it."

"Luckily it's out of sight of the house," said Lewis.

Anne had just retied her shoe-lace when they heard something pushing softly through the jungle of shrubbery on their right. Then a small boy about eight years of age came into view and stood surveying them bashfully, with a big apple turnover clasped tightly in his chubby hands. He was a pretty child, with glossy brown curls, big trustful brown eyes and delicately modeled features. There was an air of refinement about him, in spite of the fact that he was bare-headed and bare-legged, with only a faded blue cotton shirt and a pair of threadbare velvet knickerbockers between head and legs. But he looked like a small prince in disguise.

Just behind him was a big black Newfoundland dog whose head was almost on a level with the lad's shoulder.

Anne looked at him with a smile that always won children's hearts.

"Hello, sonny," said Lewis. "Who belongs to you?"

The boy came forward with an answering smile, holding out his turnover.

"This is for you to eat," he said shyly. "Dad made it for me, but I'd rather give it to you. I've lots to eat."

Lewis, rather tactlessly, was on the point of refusing to take the little chap's snack, but Anne gave him a quick nudge. Taking the hint, he accepted it gravely and handed it to Anne, who, quite as gravely, broke it in two and gave half of it back to him. They knew they must eat it and they had painful doubts as to "Dad's" ability in the cooking line, but the first mouthful reassured them. "Dad" might not be strong on courtesy but he could certainly make turnovers.

"This is delicious," said Anne. "What is your name, dear?"

"Teddy Armstrong," said the small benefactor. "But Dad always calls me Little Fellow. I'm all he has, you know. Dad is awful fond of me and I'm awful fond of Dad. I'm afraid you think my dad is impolite 'cause he shut that door so quick, but he doesn't mean to be. I heard you asking for something to eat." ("We didn't but it doesn't matter," thought Anne.)

"I was in the garden behind the hollyhocks, so I just thought I'd bring you my turnover 'cause I'm always so sorry for poor people who haven't plenty to eat. I have, always. My dad is a splendid cook. You ought to see the rice puddings he can make."

"Does he put raisins in them?" asked Lewis with a twinkle.

"Lots and lots. There's nothing mean about my dad."

"Haven't you any mother, darling?" asked Anne.

"No. My mother is dead. Mrs. Merrill told me once she'd gone to heaven, but my dad says there's no such place and I guess he ought to know. My dad is an awful wise man. He's read thousands of books. I mean to be just 'zackly like him when I grow up...only I'll always give people things to eat when they want them. My dad isn't very fond of people, you know, but he's awful good to me."

"Do you go to school?" asked Lewis.

"No. My dad teaches me at home. The trustees told him I'd have to go next year, though. I think I'd like to go to school and have some other boys to play with. 'Course I've got Carlo and Dad himself is splendid to play with when he has time. My dad is pretty busy, you know. He has to run the farm and keep the house clean, too. That's why he can't be bothered having people around, you see. When I get bigger I'll be able to help him lots and then he'll have more time to be polite to folks."

"That turnover was just about right, Little Fellow," said Lewis, swallowing the last crumb.

The Little Fellow's eyes beamed.

"I'm so glad you liked it," he said.

"Would you like to have your picture taken?" said Anne, feeling that it would never do to offer this generous small soul money. "If you would, Lewis will take it."

"Oh, wouldn't I!" said the Little Fellow eagerly. "Carlo, too?"

"Certainly Carlo, too."

Anne posed the two prettily before a background of shrubs, the little lad standing with his arm about his big, curly playmate's neck, both dog and boy seeming equally well pleased, and Lewis took the picture with his last remaining plate.

"If it comes out well I'll send you one by mail," he promised. "How shall I address it?"

"Teddy Armstrong, care of Mr. James Armstrong, Glencove Road," said the Little Fellow. "Oh, won't it be fun to have something coming to me mineself through the post-office! I tell you I'll feel awful proud. I won't say a word to Dad about it so that it'll be a splendid surprise for him."

"Well, look out for your parcel in two or three weeks," said Lewis, as they bade him good-by. But Anne suddenly stooped and kissed the little sunburned face. There was something about it that tugged at her heart. He was so sweet...so gallant... so motherless!

They looked back at him before a curve in the lane and saw him standing on the dyke, with his dog, waving his hand to them.

Of course Rebecca Dew knew all about the Armstrongs.

"James Armstrong has never got over his wife's death five years ago," she said. "He wasn't so bad before that...agreeable enough, though a bit of a hermit. Kind of built that way. He was just wrapped up in his bit of a wife...she was twenty years younger than he was. Her death was an awful shock to him I've heard...just seemed to change his nature completely. He got sour and cranky. Wouldn't even get a housekeeper...looked after his house and child himself. He kept bachelor's hall for years before he was married, so he ain't a bad hand at it."

"But it's no life for the child," said Aunt Chatty. "His father never takes him to church or anywhere he'd see people."

"He worships the boy, I've heard," said Aunt Kate.

"'Thou shalt have no other gods before me,'" quoted Rebecca Dew suddenly.

3

It was almost three weeks before Lewis found time to develop his pictures. He brought them up to Windy Poplars the first Sunday night he came to supper. Both the house and the Little Fellow came out splendidly. The Little Fellow smiled up from the picture "as real as life," said Rebecca Dew.

"Why, he looks like you, Lewis!" exclaimed Anne.

"He does that," agreed Rebecca Dew, squinting at it judicially. "The minute I saw it, his face reminded me of somebody but I couldn't think who."

"Why, the eyes...the forehead...the whole expression...are yours, Lewis," said Anne.

"It's hard to believe I was ever such a good-looking little chap," shrugged Lewis. "I've got a picture of myself somewhere, taken when I was eight. I must hunt it out and compare it. You'd laugh to see it, Miss Shirley. I'm the most sober-eyed kid, with long curls and a lace collar, looking stiff as a ramrod. I suppose I had my head clamped in one of those three-clawed contraptions they used to use. If this picture really resembles me, it must be only a coincidence. The Little Fellow can't be any relation of mine. I haven't an relative on the Island...now."

"Where were you born?" asked Aunt Kate.

"N. B. Father and Mother died when I was ten and I came over here to live with a cousin of mother's...I called her Aunt Ida. She died too, you know...three years ago."

"Jim Armstrong came from New Brunswick," said Rebecca Dew. "He ain't a real islander...wouldn't be such a crank if he was. We have our peculiarities but we're civilized."

"I'm not sure that I want to discover a relation in the amiable Mr. Armstrong," grinned Lewis, attacking Aunt Chatty's cinnamon toast. "However, I think when I get the photograph finished and mounted I'll take it out to Glencove Road myself and investigate a little. He may be a distant cousin or something. I really know nothing about my mother's people, if she had any living. I've always been under the impression that she hadn't. Father hadn't, I know."

"If you take the picture out in person, won't the Little Fellow be a bit disappointed over losing his thrill of getting something through the post-office?" said Anne.

"I'll make it up to him...I'll send him something else by mail."

The next Saturday afternoon Lewis came driving along Spook's Lane in an antiquated buggy behind a still more antiquated mare.

"I'm going out to Glencove to take little Teddy Armstrong his picture, Miss Shirley. If my dashing turn-out doesn't give you heart-failure I'd like to have you come, too. I don't think any of the wheels will fall off."

"Where on earth did you pick up that relic, Lewis?" demanded Rebecca Dew.

"Don't poke fun at my gallant steed, Miss Dew. Have some respect for age. Mr. Bender lent me both mare and buggy on condition I'd do an errand for him along the Dawlish Road. I hadn't time to walk out to Glencove today and back."

"Time!" said Rebecca Dew. "I could walk there and back myself faster than that animal."

"And carry a bag of potatoes back for Mr. Bender? You wonderful woman!"

Rebecca Dew's red cheeks grew even redder.

"It ain't nice to make fun of your elders," she said rebukingly. Then, by way of coals of fire..."Could you do with a few doughnuts afore you start out?"

The white mare, however, developed surprising powers of locomotion when they were once more out in the open. Anne giggled to herself as they jogged along the road. What would Mrs. Gardiner or even Aunt Jamesina say if they could see her now? Well, she didn't care. It was a wonderful day for a drive through a land that was keeping its old lovely ritual of autumn, and Lewis was a good companion. Lewis would attain his ambitions. Nobody else of her acquaintance, she reflected, would dream of asking her to go driving in the Bender buggy behind the Bender mare. But it never occurred to Lewis that there was anything odd about it. What difference how you traveled as long as you got there? The calm rims of the upland hills were as blue, the roads as red, the maples as gorgeous, no matter what vehicle you rode in. Lewis was a philosopher and cared as little what people might say as he did when some of the High School pupils called him "Sissy" because he did housework for his board. Let them call! Some day the laugh would be on the other side. His pockets might be empty but his head wasn't. Meanwhile the afternoon was an idyl and they were going to see the Little Fellow again. They told Mr. Bender's brother-in-law about their errand when he put the bag of potatoes in the back of the buggy.

"Do you mean to say you've got a photo of little Teddy Armstrong?" exclaimed Mr. Merrill.

"That I have and a good one." Lewis unwrapped it and held it proudly out. "I don't believe a professional photographer could have taken a better."

Mr. Merrill slapped his leg resoundingly.

"Well, if that don't beat all! Why, little Teddy Armstrong is dead..."

"Dead!" exclaimed Anne in horror. "Oh, Mr. Merrill...no...don't tell me...that dear little boy..."

"Sorry, miss, but it's a fact. And his father is just about wild and all the worse that he hasn't got any kind of a picture of him at all. And now you've got a good one. Well, well!"

"It...it seems impossible," said Anne, her eyes full of tears. She was seeing the slender little figure waving his farewell from the dyke.

"Sorry to say it's only too true. He died nearly three weeks ago. Pneumonia. Suffered awful but he was just as brave and patient as any one could be, they say. I dunno what'll become of Jim Armstrong now. They say he's like a crazy man—just moping and muttering to himself all the time. 'If I only had a picture of my Little Fellow,' he keeps saying."

"I'm sorry for that man," said Mrs. Merrill suddenly. She had not hitherto spoken, standing by her husband, a gaunt, square-built gray woman in wind-whipped calico and check apron. "He's well-to-do and I've always felt he looked down on us because we were poor. But we have our boy...and it don't never matter how poor you are as long as you've got something to love."

Anne looked at Mrs. Merrill with a new respect. Mrs. Merrill was not beautiful, but as her sunken gray eyes met Anne's, something of spirit kinship was acknowledged between them. Anne had never seen Mrs. Merrill before and never saw her again, but she always remembered her as a woman who had attained to the ultimate secret of life. You were never poor as long as you had something to love.

The golden day was spoiled for Anne. Somehow, the Little Fellow had won her heart in their brief meeting. She and Lewis drove in silence down the Glencove Road and up the grassy lane. Carlo was lying on the stone before the blue door. He got up and came down over to them, as they descended from the buggy, licking Anne's hand and looking up at her with big wistful eyes as if asking for news of his little playmate. The door was open and in the dim room beyond they saw a man with his head bowed on the table.

At Anne's knock he started up and came to the door. She was shocked at the change in him. He was hollow-cheeked, haggard and unshaven, and his deep-set eyes flashed with a fitful fire.

She expected a repulse at first, but he seemed to recognize her, for he said listlessly,

"So you're back? The Little Fellow said you talked to him and kissed him. He liked you. I was sorry I'd been so churlish to you. What is it you want?"

"We want to show you something," said Anne gently.

"Will you come in and sit down?" he said drearily.

Without a word Lewis took the Little Fellow's picture from its wrappings and held it out to him. He snatched it up, gave it one amazed, hungry look, then dropped on his chair and burst into tears and sobs. Anne had never seen a man weep so before. She and Lewis stood in mute sympathy until he had regained his self-control.

"Oh, you don't know what this means to me," he said brokenly at last. "I hadn't any picture of him. And I'm not like other folks...I can't recall a face...I can't see faces as most folks can in their mind. It's been awful since the Little Fellow died... I couldn't even remember what he looked like. And now you've brought me this...after I was so rude to you. Sit down...sit down. I wish I could express my thanks in some way. I guess you've saved my reason...maybe my life. Oh, miss, isn't it like him? You'd think he was going to speak. My dear Little Fellow! How am I going to live without him? I've nothing to live for now. First his mother...now him."

"He was a dear little lad," said Anne tenderly.

"That he was. Little Teddy...Theodore, his mother named him...her 'gift of Gods' she said he was. And he was so patient and never complained. Once he smiled up in my face and said, 'Dad, I think you've been mistaken in one thing...just one. I guess there is a heaven, isn't there? Isn't there, Dad?' I said to him, yes, there was...God forgive me for ever trying to teach him anything else. He smiled again, contented like, and said, 'Well, Dad, I'm going there and Mother and God are there, so

I'll be pretty well off. But I'm worried about you, Dad. You'll be so awful lonesome without me. But just do the best you can and be polite to folks and come to us by and by.' He made me promise I'd try, but when he was gone I couldn't stand the blankness of it. I'd have gone mad if you hadn't brought me this. It won't be so hard now."

He talked about his Little Fellow for some time, as if he found relief and pleasure in it. His reserve and gruffness seemed to have fallen from him like a garment. Finally Lewis produced the small faded photograph of himself and showed it to him.

"Have you ever seen anybody who looked like that, Mr. Armstrong?" asked Anne.

Mr. Armstrong peered at it in perplexity.

"It's awful like the Little Fellow," he said at last. "Whose might it be?"

"Mine," said Lewis, "when I was seven years old. It was because of the strange resemblance to Teddy that Miss Shirley made me bring it to show you. I thought it possible that you and I or the Little Fellow might be some distant relation. My name is Lewis Allen and my father was George Allen. I was born in New Brunswick."

James Armstrong shook his head. Then he said,

"What was your mother's name?"

"Mary Gardiner."

James Armstrong looked at him for a moment in silence.

"She was my half-sister," he said at last. "I hardly knew her...never saw her but once. I was brought up in an uncle's family after my father's death. My mother married again and moved away. She came to see me once and brought her little daughter. She died soon after and I never saw my half-sister again. When I came over to the Island to live, I lost all trace of her. You are my nephew and the Little Fellow's cousin."

This was surprising news to a lad who had fancied himself alone in the world. Lewis and Anne spent the whole evening with Mr. Armstrong and found him to be a well-read and intelligent man. Somehow, they both took a liking to him. His former inhospitable reception was quite forgotten and they saw only the real worth of the character and temperament below the unpromising shell that had hitherto concealed them.

"Of course the Little Fellow couldn't have loved his father so much if it hadn't been so," said Anne, as she and Lewis drove back to Windy Poplars through the sunset.

When Lewis Allen went the next week-end to see his uncle, the latter said to him,

"Lad, come and live with me. You are my nephew and I can do well for you...what I'd have done for my Little Fellow if he'd lived. You're alone in the world and so am I. I need you.

I'll grow hard and bitter again if I live here alone. I want you to help me keep my promise to the Little Fellow. His place is empty. Come you and fill it."

"Thank you, Uncle; I'll try," said Lewis, holding out his hand.

"And bring that teacher of yours here once in a while. I like that girl. The Little Fellow liked her. 'Dad,' he said to me, 'I didn't think I'd ever like anybody but you to kiss me, but I liked it when she did. There was something in her eyes, Dad.'"

4

"The old porch thermometer says it's zero and the new side-door one says it's ten above," remarked Anne, one frosty December night. "So I don't know whether to take my muff or not."

"Better go by the old thermometer," said Rebecca Dew cautiously. "It's probably more used to our climate. Where are you going this cold night, anyway?"

"I'm going round to Temple Street to ask Katherine Brooke to spend the Christmas holidays with me at Green Gables."

"You'll spoil your holidays, then," said Rebecca Dew solemnly. "She'd go about snubbing the angels, that one...that is, if she ever condescended to enter heaven. And the worst of it is, she's proud of her bad manners...thinks it shows her strength of mind no doubt!"

"My brain agrees with every word you say but my heart simply won't," said Anne. "I feel, in spite of everything, that Katherine Brooke is only a shy, unhappy girl under her disagreeable rind. I can never make any headway with her in Summerside, but if I can get her to Green Gables I believe it will thaw her out."

"You won't get her. She won't go," predicted Rebecca Dew. "Probably she'll take it as an insult to be asked...think you're offering her charity. We asked her here once to Christmas dinner...the year afore you came...you remember, Mrs. MacComber, the year we had two turkeys give us and didn't know how we was to get 'em et...and all she said was, 'No, thank you. If there's anything I hate, it's the word Christmas!'"

"But that is so dreadful...hating Christmas! Something has to be done, Rebecca Dew. I'm going to ask her and I've a queer feeling in my thumbs that tells me she will come."

"Somehow," said Rebecca Dew reluctantly, "when you say a thing is going to happen, a body believes it will. You haven't got a second sight, have you? Captain MacComber's mother had it. Useter give me the creeps."

"I don't think I have anything that need give you creeps.

It's only just...I've had a feeling for some time that Katherine Brooke is almost crazy with loneliness under her bitter outside and that my invitation will come pat to the psychological moment, Rebecca Dew."

"I am not a B.A.," said Rebecca with awful humility, "and I do not deny your right to use words I cannot always understand. Neither do I deny that you can wind people round your little finger. Look how you managed the Pringles. But I do say I pity you if you take that iceberg and nutmeg grater combined home with you for Christmas."

Anne was by no means as confident as she pretended to be during her walk to Temple Street. Katherine Brooke had really been unbearable of late. Again and again Anne, rebuffed, had said, as grimly as Poe's raven, "Nevermore." Only yesterday Katherine had been positively insulting at a staff meeting. But in an unguarded moment Anne had seen something looking out of the older girl's eyes...a passionate, half-frantic something like a caged creature mad with discontent. Anne spent the first half of the night trying to decide whether to invite Katherine Brooke to Green Gables or not. Finally she fell asleep with her mind irrevocably made up.

Katherine's landlady showed Anne into the parlor and shrugged a fat shoulder when she asked for Miss Brooke.

"I'll tell her you're here but I dunno if she'll come down.

She's sulking. I told her at dinner tonight that Mrs. Rawlins says its scandalous the way she dresses, for a teacher in Summerside High, and she took it high and mighty as usual."

"I don't think you should have told Miss Brooke that," said Anne reproachfully.

"But I thought she ought to know," said Mrs. Dennis somewhat waspishly.

"Did you also think she ought to know that the Inspector said she was one of the best teachers in the Maritimes?" asked Anne. "Or didn't you know it?"

"Oh, I heard it. But she's stuck-up enough now without making her any worse. Proud's no name for it...though what she's got to be proud of, I dunno. Of course she was mad anyhow tonight because I'd said she couldn't have a dog. She's took a notion into her head she'd like to have a dog. Said she'd pay for his rations and see he was no bother. But what'd I do with him when she was in school? I put my foot down. 'I'm boarding no dogs,' sez I."

"Oh, Mrs. Dennis, won't you let her have a dog? He wouldn't bother you...much. You could keep him in the basement while she was in school. And a dog really is such a protection at night. I wish you would...please."

There was always something about Anne Shirley's eyes when she said "please" that people found hard to resist. Mrs.

Dennis, in spite of fat shoulders and a meddlesome tongue, was not unkind at heart. Katherine Brooke simply got under her skin at times with her ungracious ways.

"I dunno why you should worry as to her having a dog or not. I didn't know you were such friends. She hasn't any friends. I never had such an unsociable boarder."

"I think that is why she wants a dog, Mrs. Dennis. None of us can live without some kind of companionship."

"Well, it's the first human thing I've noticed about her," said Mrs. Dennis. "I dunno's I have any awful objection to a dog, but she sort of vexed me with her sarcastic way of asking...'I s'pose you wouldn't consent if I asked you if I might have a dog, Mrs. Dennis,' she sez, haughty like. Set her up with it! 'You're s'posing right,' sez I, as haughty as herself. I don't like eating my words any more than most people, but you can tell her she can have a dog if she'll guarantee he won't misbehave in the parlor."

Anne did not think the parlor could be much worse if the dog did misbehave. She eyed the dingy lace curtains and the hideous purple roses on the carpet with a shiver.

"I'm sorry for any one who has to spend Christmas in a boarding-house like this," she thought. "I don't wonder Katherine hates the word. I'd like to give this place a good airing...it smells of a thousand meals. Why does Katherine go on boarding here when she has a good salary?"

"She says you can come up," was the message Mrs. Dennis brought back, rather dubiously, for Miss Brooke had run true to form.

The narrow, steep stair was repellent. It didn't want you. Nobody would go up who didn't have to. The linoleum in the hall was worn to shreds. The little back hall-bedroom where Anne presently found herself was even more cheerless than the parlor. It was lighted by one glaring unshaded gas jet. There was an iron bed with a valley in the middle of it and a narrow, sparsely draped window looking out on a backyard garden where a large crop of tin cans flourished. But beyond it was a marvelous sky and a row of lombardies standing out against long, purple, distant hills.

"Oh, Miss Brooke, look at that sunset," said Anne rapturously from the squeaky, cushionless rocker to which Katherine had ungraciously pointed her.

"I've seen a good many sunsets," said the latter coldly, without moving. ("Condescending to me with your sunsets!" she thought bitterly.)

"You haven't seen this one. No two sunsets are alike. Just sit down here and let us let it sink into our souls," said Anne. Thought Anne, "Do you ever say anything pleasant?"

"Don't be ridiculous, please."

The most insulting words in the world! With an added edge of insult in Katherine's contemptuous tones. Anne turned from her sunset and looked at Katherine, much more than half inclined to get up and walk out. But Katherine's eyes looked a trifle strange. Had she been crying? Surely not...you couldn't imagine Katherine Brooke crying.

"You don't make me feel very welcome," Anne said slowly.

"I can't pretend things. I haven't your notable gift for doing the queen act...saying exactly the right thing to every one. You're not welcome. What sort of room is this to welcome any one to?"

Katherine made a scornful gesture at the faded walls, the shabby bare chairs and the wobbly dressing-table with its petticoat of limp muslin.

"It isn't a nice room, but why do you stay here if you don't like it?"

"Oh...why...Why? You wouldn't understand. It doesn't matter. I don't care what anybody thinks. What brought you here tonight? I don't suppose you came just to soak in the sunset."

"I came to ask if you would spend the Christmas holidays with me at Green Gables."

("Now," thought Anne, "for another broadside of sarcasm! I do wish she'd sit down at least. She just stands there as if waiting for me to go.")

But there was silence for a moment. Then Katherine said slowly,

"Why do you ask me? It isn't because you like me...even you couldn't pretend that."

"It's because I can't bear to think of any human being spending Christmas in a place like this," said Anne candidly.

The sarcasm came then.

"Oh, I see. A seasonable outburst of charity. I'm hardly a candidate for that yet, Miss Shirley."

Anne got up. She was out of patience with this strange, aloof creature. She walked across the room and looked Katherine squarely in the eye. "Katherine Brooke, whether you know it or not, what you want is a good spanking."

They gazed at each other for a moment.

"It must have relieved you to say that," said Katherine. But somehow the insulting tone had gone out of her voice. There was even a faint twitch at the corner of her mouth.

"It has," said Anne. "I've been wanting to tell you just that for some time. I didn't ask you to Green Gables out of charity...you know that perfectly well. I told you my true reason. Nobody ought to spend Christmas here...the very idea is indecent."

"You asked me to Green Gables just because you are sorry for me."

"I am sorry for you. Because you've shut out life...and now life is shutting you out. Stop, it, Katherine. Open your doors to life...and life will come in."

"The Anne Shirley version of the old bromide, 'If you bring a smiling visage to the glass you meet a smile,'" said Katherine with a shrug.

"Like all bromides, that's absolutely true. Now, are you coming to Green Gables or are you not?"

"What would you say if I accepted...to yourself, not to me?"

"I'd say you were showing the first faint glimmer of common sense I'd ever detected in you," retorted Anne.

Katherine laughed...surprisingly. She walked across to the window, scowled at the fiery streak which was all that was left of the scorned sunset and then turned.

"Very well...I'll go. Now you can go through the motions of telling me you're delighted and that we'll have a jolly time."

"I am delighted. But I don't know if you'll have a jolly time or not. That will depend a good deal on yourself, Miss Brooke."

"Oh, I'll behave myself decently. You'll be surprised. You won't find me a very exhilarating guest, I suppose, but I promise you I won't eat with my knife or insult people when they tell me it's a fine day. I tell you frankly that the only reason I'm going is because even I can't stick the thought of spending the holidays here alone. Mrs. Dennis is going to spend Christmas week with her daughter in Charlottetown. It's a bore to think of getting my own meals. I'm a rotten cook. So much for the triumph of matter over mind. But will you give me your word of honor that you won't wish me a merry Christmas? I just don't want to be merry at Christmas."

"I won't. But I can't answer for the twins."

"I'm not going to ask you to sit down here...you'd freeze...but I see that there's a very fine moon in place of your sunset and I'll walk home with you and help you to admire it if you like."

"I do like," said Anne, "but I want to impress on your mind that we have much finer moons in Avonlea."

"So she's going?" said Rebecca Dew as she filled Anne's hot-water bottle. "Well, Miss Shirley, I hope you'll never try to induce me to turn Mohammedan...because you'd likely succeed. Where is That Cat? Out frisking round Summerside and the weather at zero."

"Not by the new thermometer. And Dusty Miller is curled up on the rocking-chair by my stove in the tower, snoring with happiness."

"Ah well," said Rebecca Dew with a little shiver as she shut the kitchen door, "I wish every one in the world was as warm and sheltered as we are tonight."

5

Anne did not know that a wistful little Elizabeth was watching out of one of the mansard windows of The Evergreens as she drove away from Windy Poplars...an Elizabeth with tears in her eyes who felt as if everything that made life worth living had gone out of her life for the time being and that she was the very Lizziest of Lizzies. But when the livery sleigh vanished from her sight around the corner of Spook's Lane Elizabeth went and knelt down by her bed.

"Dear God," she whispered, "I know it isn't any use to ask You for a merry Christmas for me because Grandmother and The Woman couldn't be merry, but please let my dear Miss Shirley have a merry, merry Christmas and bring her back safe to me when it's over.

"Now," said Elizabeth, getting up from her knees, "I've done all that I can."

Anne was already tasting Christmas happiness. She fairly sparkled as the train left the station. The ugly streets slipped past her...she was going home...home to Green Gables. Out in the open country the world was all golden-white and pale violet, woven here and there with the dark magic of spruces and the leafless delicacy of birches. The low sun behind the bare woods seemed rushing through the trees like a splendid god, as the train sped on. Katherine was silent but did not seem ungracious.

"Don't expect me to talk," she had warned Anne curtly.

"I won't. I hope you don't think I'm one of those terrible people who make you feel that you have to talk to them all the time. We'll just talk when we feel like it. I admit I'm likely to feel like it a good part of the time, but you're under no obligation to take any notice of what I'm saying."

Davy met them at Bright River with a big two-seated sleigh full of furry robes...and a bear hug for Anne. The two girls snuggled down in the back seat. The drive from the station to Green Gables had always been a very pleasant part of Anne's week-ends home. She always recalled her first drive home from Bright River with Matthew. That had been in spring and this was December, but everything along the road kept saying to her, "Do you remember?" The snow crisped under the runners; the music of the bells tinkled through the ranks of tall pointed firs, snow-laden. The White Way of Delight had little festoons of stars tangled in the trees. And on the last hill but one they saw the great gulf, white and mystical under the moon but not yet ice-bound.

"There's just one spot on this road where I always feel suddenly...'I'm home,'" said Anne. "It's the top of the next hill, where we'll see the lights of Green Gables. I'm just thinking of the supper Marilla will have ready for us. I believe I can smell it here. Oh, it's good...good...good to be home again!"

At Green Gables every tree in the yard seemed to welcome her back...every lighted window was beckoning. And how good Marilla's kitchen smelled as they opened the door. There were hugs and exclamations and laughter. Even Katherine seemed somehow no outsider, but one of them. Mrs. Rachel Lynde had set her cherished parlor lamp on the supper-table and lighted it. It was really a hideous thing with a hideous red globe, but what a warm rosy becoming light it cast over everything! How warm and friendly were the shadows! How pretty Dora was growing! And Davy really seemed almost a man.

There was news to tell. Diana had a small daughter...Josie Pye actually had a young man...and Charlie Sloane was said to be engaged. It was all just as exciting as news of empire could have been. Mrs. Lynde's new patchwork quilt, just completed, containing five thousand pieces, was on display and received its meed of praise.

"When you come home, Anne," said Davy, "everything seems to come alive."

"Ah, this is how life should be," purred Dora's kitten.

"I've always found it hard to resist the lure of a moonlight night," said Anne after supper. "How about a snow-shoe tramp,

Miss Brooke? I think that I've heard that you snowshoe."

"Yes...it's the only thing I can do...but I haven't done it for six years," said Katherine with a shrug.

Anne rooted out her snow-shoes from the garret and Davy shot over to Orchard Slope to borrow an old pair of Diana's for Katherine. They went through Lover's Lane, full of lovely tree shadows, and across fields where little fir trees fringed the fences and through woods which were full of secrets they seemed always on the point of whispering to you but never did...and through open glades that were like pools of silver.

They did not talk or want to talk. It was as if they were afraid to talk for fear of spoiling something beautiful. But Anne had never felt so near Katherine Brooke before. By some magic of its own the winter night had brought them together...almost together but not quite.

When they came out to the main road and a sleigh flashed by, bells ringing, laughter tinkling, both girls gave an involuntary sigh. It seemed to both that they were leaving behind a world that had nothing in common with the one to which they were returning...a world where time was not...which was young with immortal youth...where souls communed with each other in some medium that needed nothing so crude as words.

"It's been wonderful," said Katherine so obviously to herself that Anne made no response.

They went down the road and up the long Green Gables lane but just before they reached the yard gate, they both paused as by a common impulse and stood in silence, leaning against the old mossy fence and looked at the brooding, motherly old house seen dimly through its veil of trees. How beautiful Green Gables was on a winter night!

Below it the Lake of Shining Waters was locked in ice, patterned around its edges with tree shadows. Silence was everywhere, save for the staccato clip of a horse trotting over the bridge. Anne smiled to recall how often she had heard that sound as she lay in her gable room and pretended to herself that it was the gallop of fairy horses passing in the night.

Suddenly another sound broke the stillness.

"Katherine...you're...why, you're not crying!"

Somehow, it seemed impossible to think of Katherine crying. But she was. And her tears suddenly humanized her. Anne no longer felt afraid of her.

"Katherine...dear Katherine...what is the matter? Can I help?"

"Oh...you can't understand!" gasped Katherine. "Things have always been made easy for you. You...you seem to live in a little enchanted circle of beauty and romance. 'I wonder what delightful discovery I'll make today'...that seems to be your attitude to life, Anne. As for me, I've forgotten how to live...no,

I never knew how. I'm...I'm like a creature caught in a trap. I can never get out...and it seems to me that somebody is always poking sticks at me through the bars. And you...you have more happiness than you know what to do with...friends everywhere, a lover! Not that I want a lover...I hate men...but if I died tonight, not one living soul would miss me. How would you like to be absolutely friendless in the world?"

Katherine's voice broke in another sob.

"Katherine, you say you like frankness. I'm going to be frank. If you are as friendless as you say, it is your own fault. I've wanted to be friends with you. But you've been all prickles and stings."

"Oh, I know...I know. How I hated you when you came first! Flaunting your circlet of pearls..."

"Katherine, I didn't 'flaunt' it!"

"Oh, I suppose not. That's just my natural hatefulness. But it seemed to flaunt itself...not that I envied you your beau...I've never wanted to be married...I saw enough of that with father and mother...but I hated your being over me when you were younger than I...I was glad when the Pringles made trouble for you. You seemed to have everything I hadn't...charm...friendship...youth. Youth! I never had anything but starved youth. You know nothing about it. You don't know...you haven't the least idea what it is like not to be wanted by any one...any one!"

"Oh, haven't I?" cried Anne.

In a few poignant sentences she sketched her childhood before coming to Green Gables.

"I wish I'd known that," said Katherine. "It would have made a difference. To me you seemed one of the favorites of fortune. I've been eating my heart out with envy of you. You got the position I wanted...oh, I know you're better qualified than I am, but there it was. You're pretty...at least you make people believe you're pretty. My earliest recollection is of some one saying, 'What an ugly child!' You come into a room delightfully...oh, I remember how you came into school that first morning. But I think the real reason I've hated you so is that you always seemed to have some secret delight...as if every day of life was an adventure. In spite of my hatred there were times when I acknowledged to myself that you might just have come from some far-off star."

"Really, Katherine, you take my breath with all these compliments. But you don't hate me any longer, do you? We can be friends now."

"I don't know...I've never had a friend of any kind, much less one of anything like my own age. I don't belong anywhere...never have belonged. I don't think I know how to be a friend. No, I don't hate you any longer...I don't know how I feel about you...oh, I suppose it's your noted charm beginning to work on me. I only know that I feel I'd like to tell you what my life has been like. I could never have told you if you hadn't told me about your life before you came to Green Gables. I want you to understand what has made me as I am. I don't know why I should want you to understand...but I do."

"Tell me, Katherine dear. I do want to understand you."

"You do know what it is like not to be wanted, I admit...but not what it is like to know that your father and mother don't want you. Mine didn't. They hated me from the moment I was born...and before...and they hated each other. Yes, they did. They quarreled continually...just mean, nagging, petty quarrels. My childhood was a nightmare. They died when I was seven and I went to live with Uncle Henry's family. They didn't want me either. They all looked down on me because I was 'living on their charity.' I remember all the snubs I got...every one. I can't remember a single kind word. I had to wear my cousins' castoff clothes. I remember one hat in particular...it made me look like a mushroom. And they made fun of me whenever I put it on. One day I tore it off and threw it on the fire. I had to wear the most awful old tam to church all the rest of the winter. I never even had a dog...and I wanted one so. I had some brains...I longed so for a B.A. course...but naturally I might just as well have yearned for the moon. However, Uncle Henry agreed to put me through Queen's if I would pay him back when I got a school. He paid my board in a miserable third-rate boarding-house where I had a room over the kitchen that was ice cold in winter and boiling hot in summer, and full of stale cooking smells in all seasons. And the clothes I had to wear to Queen's! But I got my license and I got the second room in Summerside High...the only bit of luck I've ever had. Even since then I've been pinching and scrimping to pay Uncle Henry...not only what he spent putting me through Queen's, but what my board through all the years I lived there cost him. I was determined I would not owe him one cent. That is why I've boarded with Mrs. Dennis and dressed shabbily. And I've just finished paying him. For the first time in my life I feel free. But meanwhile I've developed the wrong way. I know I'm unsocial...I know I can never think of the right thing to say. I know it's my own fault that I'm always neglected and overlooked at social functions. I know I've made being disagreeable into a fine art. I know I'm sarcastic. I know I'm regarded as a tyrant by my pupils. I know they hate me. Do you think it doesn't hurt me to know it? They always look afraid of me...I hate people who look as if they were afraid of me. Oh, Anne...hate's got to be a disease with me. I do want to be like other people...and I never can now. That is what makes me so bitter."

"Oh, but you can!" Anne put her arm about Katherine. "You

can put hate out of your mind...cure yourself of it. Life is only beginning for you now...since at last you're quite free and independent. And you never know what may be around the next bend in the road."

"I've heard you say that before...I've laughed at your 'bend in the road.' But the trouble is there aren't any bends in my road. I can see it stretching straight out before me to the sky-line...endless monotony. Oh, does life ever frighten you, Anne, with its blankness... its swarms of cold, uninteresting people? No, of course it doesn't. You don't have to go on teaching all the rest of your life. And you seem to find everybody interesting, even that little round red being you call Rebecca Dew. The truth is, I hate teaching...and there's nothing else I can do. A school-teacher is simply a slave of time. Oh, I know you like it...I don't see how you can. Anne, I want to travel. It's the one thing I've always longed for. I remember the one and only picture that hung on the wall of my attic room at Uncle Henry's...a faded old print that had been discarded from the other rooms with scorn. It was a picture of palms around a spring in the desert, with a string of camels marching away in the distance. It literally fascinated me. I've always wanted to go and find it...I want to see the Southern Cross and the Taj Mahal and the pillars of Karnak. I want to know... not just believe... that the world is round. And I can never do it on a teacher's salary. I'll just have to go on forever, prating of King Henry the Eighth's wives and the inexhaustible resources of the Dominion."

Anne laughed. It was safe to laugh now, for the bitterness had gone out of Katherine's voice. It sounded merely rueful and impatient.

"Anyhow, we're going to be friends...and we're going to have a jolly ten days here to begin our friendship. I've always wanted to be friends with you, Katherine...spelled with a K! I've always felt that underneath all your prickles was something that would make you worth while as a friend."

"So that is what you've really thought of me? I've often wondered. Well, the leopard will have a go at changing its spots if it's at all possible. Perhaps it is. I can believe almost anything at this Green Gables of yours. It's the first place I've ever been in that felt like a home. I should like to be more like other people...if it isn't too late. I'll even practice a sunny smile for that Gilbert of yours when he arrives tomorrow night. Of course I've forgotten how to talk to young men...if I ever knew. He'll just think me an old-maid gooseberry. I wonder if, when I go to bed tonight, I'll feel furious with myself for pulling off my mask and letting you see into my shivering soul like this."

"No, you won't. You'll think, 'I'm glad she's found out I'm human.' We're going to snuggle down among the warm fluffy blankets, probably with two hot-water bottles, for likely Marilla and Mrs. Lynde will each put one in for us for fear the other has forgotten it. And you'll feel deliciously sleepy after this walk in the frosty moonshine...and first thing you'll know, it will be morning and you'll feel as if you were the first person to discover that the sky is blue. And you'll grow learned in lore of plum puddings because you're going to help me make one for Tuesday...a great big plummy one."

Anne was amazed at Katherine's good looks when they went in. Her complexion was radiant after her long walk in the keen air and color made all the difference in the world to her.

"Why, Katherine would be handsome if she wore the right kind of hats and dresses," reflected Anne, trying to imagine Katherine with a certain dark, richly red velvet hat she had seen in a Summerside shop, on her black hair and pulled over her amber eyes. "I've simply got to see what can be done about it."

6

Saturday and Monday were full of gay doings at Green Gables. The plum pudding was concocted and the Christmas tree brought home. Katherine and Anne and Davy and Dora went to the woods for it...a beautiful little fir to whose cutting down Anne was only reconciled by the fact that it was in a little clearing of Mr. Harrison's which was going to be stumped and plowed in the spring anyhow.

They wandered about, gathering creeping spruce and ground pine for wreaths...even some ferns that kept green in a certain deep hollow of the woods all winter...until day smiled back at night over white-bosomed hills and they came back to Green Gables in triumph...to meet a tall young man with hazel eyes and the beginnings of a mustache which made him look so much older and maturer that Anne had one awful moment of wondering if it were really Gilbert or a stranger.

Katherine, with a little smile that tried to be sarcastic but couldn't quite succeed, left them in the parlor and played games with the twins in the kitchen all the evening. To her amazement she found she was enjoying it. And what fun it was to go down cellar with Davy and find that there were really such things as sweet apples still left in the world.

Katherine had never been in a country cellar before and had no idea what a delightful, spooky, shadowy place it could be by candle-light. Life already seemed warmer. For the first time it came home to Katherine that life might be beautiful, even for her.

Davy made enough noise to wake the Seven Sleepers, at an

unearthly hour Christmas morning, ringing an old cowbell up and down the stairs. Marilla was horrified at his doing such a thing when there was a guest in the house, but Katherine came down laughing. Somehow, an odd camaraderie had sprung up between her and Davy. She told Anne candidly that she had no use for the impeccable Dora but that Davy was somehow tarred with her own brush.

They opened the parlor and distributed the gifts before breakfast because the twins, even Dora, couldn't have eaten anything if they hadn't. Katherine, who had not expected anything except, perhaps, a duty gift from Anne, found herself getting presents from every one. A gay, crocheted afghan from Mrs. Lynde...a sachet of orris root from Dora...a paper-knife from Davy...a basketful of tiny jars of jam and jelly from Marilla...even a little bronze chessy cat for a paper-weight from Gilbert.

And, tied under the tree, curled up on a bit of warm and woolly blanket, a dear little brown-eyed puppy, with alert, silken ears and an ingratiating tail. A card tied to his neck bore the legend, "From Anne, who dares, after all, to wish you a Merry Christmas."

Katherine gathered his wriggling little body up in her arms and spoke shakily.

"Anne...he's a darling! But Mrs. Dennis won't let me keep

him. I asked her if I might get a dog and she refused."

"I've arranged it all with Mrs. Dennis. You'll find she won't object. And, anyway, Katherine, you're not going to be there long. You must find a decent place to live, now that you've paid off what you thought were your obligations. Look at the lovely box of stationery Diana sent me. Isn't it fascinating to look at the blank pages and wonder what will be written on them?"

Mrs. Lynde was thankful it was a white Christmas...there would be no fat graveyards when Christmas was white...but to Katherine it seemed a purple and crimson and golden Christmas. And the week that followed was just as beautiful. Katherine had often wondered bitterly just what it would be like to be happy and now she found out. She bloomed out in the most astonishing way. Anne found herself enjoying their companionship.

"To think I was afraid she would spoil my Christmas holiday!" she reflected in amazement.

"To think," said Katherine to herself, "that I was on the verge of refusing to come here when Anne invited me!"

They went for long walks...through Lover's Lane and the Haunted Wood, where the very silence seemed friendly...over hills where the light snow whirled in a winter dance of goblins...through old orchards full of violet shadows...through the glory of sunset woods. There were no birds to chirp or sing, no brooks to gurgle, no squirrels to gossip. But the wind made occasional music that had in quality what it lacked in quantity.

"One can always find something lovely to look at or listen to," said Anne.

They talked of "cabbages and kings," and hitched their wagons to stars, and came home with appetites that taxed even the Green Gables pantry. One day it stormed and they couldn't go out. The east wind was beating around the eaves and the gray gulf was roaring. But even a storm at Green Gables had charms of its own. It was cozy to sit by the stove and dreamily watch the firelight flickering over the ceiling while you munched apples and candy. How jolly supper was with the storm wailing outside!

One night Gilbert took them to see Diana and her new baby daughter.

"I never held a baby in my life before," said Katherine as they drove home. "For one thing, I didn't want to, and for another I'd have been afraid of it going to pieces in my grasp. You can't imagine how I felt...so big and clumsy with that tiny, exquisite thing in my arms. I know Mrs. Wright thought I was going to drop it every minute. I could see her striving heroically to conceal her terror. But it did something to me...the baby I mean...I haven't decided just what."

"Babies are such fascinating creatures," said Anne dreamily.

"They are what I heard somebody at Redmond call 'terrific bundles of potentialities.' Think of it, Katherine...Homer must have been a baby once...a baby with dimples and great eyes full of light...he couldn't have been blind then, of course."

"What a pity his mother didn't know he was to be Homer," said Katherine.

"But I think I'm glad Judas' mother didn't know he was to be Judas," said Anne softly. "I hope she never did know."

There was a concert in the hall one night, with a party at Abner Sloane's after it, and Anne persuaded Katherine to go to both.

"I want you to give us a reading for our program, Katherine. I've heard you read beautifully."

"I used to recite...I think I rather liked doing it. But the summer before last I recited at a shore concert which a party of summer resorters got up...and I heard them laughing at me afterwards."

"How do you know they were laughing at you?"

"They must have been. There wasn't anything else to laugh at."

Anne hid a smile and persisted in asking for the reading.

"Give Genevra for an encore. I'm told you do that splendidly. Mrs. Stephen Pringle told me she never slept a wink the night after she heard you give it."

"No; I've never liked Genevra. It's in the reading, so I try occasionally to show the class how to read it. I really have no patience with Genevra. Why didn't she scream when she found herself locked in? When they were hunting everywhere for her, surely somebody would have heard her."

Katherine finally promised the reading but was dubious about the party. "I'll go, of course. But nobody will ask me to dance and I'll feel sarcastic and prejudiced and ashamed. I'm always miserable at parties...the few I've ever gone to. Nobody seems to think I can dance...and you know I can fairly well, Anne. I picked it up at Uncle Henry's, because a poor bit of a maid they had wanted to learn, too, and she and I used to dance together in the kitchen at night to the music that went on in the parlor. I think I'd like it...with the right kind of partner."

"You won't be miserable at this party, Katherine. You won't be outside looking in. There's all the difference in the world, you know, between being inside looking out and outside looking in. You have such lovely hair, Katherine. Do you mind if I try a new way of doing it?"

Katherine shrugged.

"Oh, go ahead. I suppose my hair does look dreadful...but I've no time to be always primping. I haven't a party dress. Will my green taffeta do?"

"It will have to do...though green is the one color above all others that you should never wear, my Katherine. But you're going to wear a red, pin-tucked chiffon collar I've made for you. Yes, you are. You ought to have a red dress, Katherine."

"I've always hated red. When I went to live with Uncle Henry, Aunt Gertrude always made me wear aprons of bright Turkey-red. The other children in school used to call out 'Fire,' when I came in with one of those aprons on. Anyway, I can't be bothered with clothes."

"Heaven grant me patience! Clothes are very important," said Anne severely, as she braided and coiled. Then she looked at her work and saw that it was good. She put her arm about Katherine's shoulders and turned her to the mirror.

"Don't you truly think we are a pair of quite good-looking girls?" she laughed. "And isn't it really nice to think people will find some pleasure in looking at us? There are so many homely people who would actually look quite attractive if they took a little pains with themselves. Three Sundays ago in church...you remember the day poor old Mr. Milvain preached and had such a terrible cold in his head that nobody could make out what he was saying?...well, I passed the time making the people around me beautiful. I gave Mrs. Brent a new nose, I waved Mary Addison's hair and gave Jane Marden's a lemon rinse...I dressed Emma Dill in blue instead of brown...I dressed Charlotte Blair in stripes instead of checks...I removed several moles...and I shaved off Thomas Anderson's long, sandy Piccadilly weepers. You couldn't have known them when I got through with them. And, except perhaps for Mrs. Brent's nose, they could have done everything I did, themselves. Why, Katherine, your eyes are just the color of tea...amber tea. Now, live up to your name this evening...a brook should be sparkling...limpid...merry."

"Everything I'm not."

"Everything you've been this past week. So you can be it."

"That's only the magic of Green Gables. When I go back to Summerside, twelve o'clock will have struck for Cinderella."

"You'll take the magic back with you. Look at yourself... looking for once as you ought to look all the time."

Katherine gazed at her reflection in the mirror as if rather doubting her identity.

"I do look years younger," she admitted. "You were right... clothes do do things to you. Oh, I know I've been looking older than my age. I didn't care. Why should I? Nobody else cared. And I'm not like you, Anne. Apparently you were born knowing how to live. And I don't know anything about it...not even the A B C. I wonder if it's too late to learn. I've been sarcastic so long, I don't know if I can be anything else. Sarcasm seemed to me to be the only way I could make any impression on people. And it seems to me, too, that I've always been afraid when I was in the company of other people...afraid of saying something stupid...afraid of being laughed at."

"Katherine Brooke, look at yourself in that mirror; carry that picture of yourself with you...magnificent hair framing your face instead of trying to pull it backward...eyes sparkling like dark stars...a little flush of excitement on your cheeks...and you won't feel afraid. Come, now. We're going to be late, but fortunately all the performers have what I heard Dora referring to as 'preserved' seats."

Gilbert drove them to the hall. How like old times it was...only Katherine was with her in place of Diana. Anne sighed. Diana had so many other interests now. No more running round to concerts and parties for her.

But what an evening it was! What silvery satin roads with a pale green sky in the west after a light snowfall! Orion was treading his stately march across the heavens, and hills and fields and woods lay around them in a pearly silence.

Katherine's reading captured her audience from the first line, and at the party she could not find dances for all her would-be partners. She suddenly found herself laughing without bitterness. Then home to Green Gables, warming their toes at the sitting-room fire by the light of two friendly candles on the mantel; and Mrs. Lynde tiptoeing into their room, late as it was, to ask them if they'd like another blanket and assure Katherine that her little dog was snug and warm in a basket behind the kitchen stove.

"I've got a new outlook on life," thought Katherine as she drifted off to slumber. "I didn't know there were people like this."

"Come again," said Marilla when she left.

Marilla never said that to any one unless she meant it.

"Of course she's coming again," said Anne. "For week-ends...and for weeks in the summer. We'll build bonfires and hoe in the garden...and pick apples and go for the cows...and row on the pond and get lost in the woods. I want to show you Little Hester Gray's garden, Katherine, and Echo Lodge and Violet Vale when it's full of violets."

7

"Windy Poplars,

"January 5th,

"The street where ghosts (should) walk.

"MY ESTEEMED FRIEND:

"That isn't anything Aunt Chatty's grandmother wrote. It's only something she would have written if she'd thought of it.

"I've made a New Year resolution to write sensible love-letters. Do you suppose such a thing is possible?

"I have left dear Green Gables but I have returned to dear Windy Poplars. Rebecca Dew had a fire lighted in the tower room for me and a hot-water bottle in the bed.

"I'm so glad I like Windy Poplars. It would be dreadful to live in a place I didn't like...that didn't seem friendly to me...that didn't say, 'I'm glad you're back.' Windy Poplars does. It's a bit old-fashioned and a bit prim, but it likes me.

"And I was glad to see Aunt Kate and Aunt Chatty and Rebecca Dew again. I can't help seeing their funny sides but I love them well for all that.

"Rebecca Dew said such a nice thing to me yesterday.

"'Spook's Lane has been a different place since you came here, Miss Shirley.'

"I'm glad you liked Katherine, Gilbert. She was surprisingly nice to you. It's amazing to find how nice she can be when she tries. And I think she is just as much amazed at it herself as any one else. She had no idea it would be so easy.

"It's going to make so much difference in school, having a Vice you can really work with. She is going to change her boarding-house, and I have already persuaded her to get that velvet hat and have not yet given up hope of persuading her to sing in the choir.

"Mr. Hamilton's dog came down yesterday and chivied

Dusty Miller. 'This is the last straw,' said Rebecca Dew. And with her red cheeks redder still, her chubby back shaking with anger, and in such a hurry that she put her hat on hindside before and never knew it, she toddled up the road and gave Mr. Hamilton quite a large piece of her mind. I can just see his foolish, amiable face while he was listening to her.

"'I do not like That Cat,' she told me, 'but he is OURS and no Hamilton dog is going to come here and give him impudence in his own back yard. "He only chased your cat in fun," said Jabez Hamilton. "The Hamilton ideas of fun are different from the MacComber ideas of fun or the MacLean ideas of fun or, if it comes to that, the Dew ideas of fun," I told him. "Tut, tut, you must have had cabbage for dinner, Miss Dew," said he. "No," I said, "but I could have had. Mrs. Captain MacComber didn't sell all her cabbages last fall and leave her family without any because the price was so good. There are some people," sez I, "that can't hear anything because of the jingle in their pocket." And I left that to sink in. But what could you expect from a Hamilton? Low scum!'

"There is a crimson star hanging low over the white Storm King. I wish you were here to watch it with me. If you were, I really think it would be more than a moment of esteem and friendship."

"January 12th.

"Little Elizabeth came over two nights ago to find out if I could tell her what peculiar kind of terrible animals Papal bulls were, and to tell me tearfully that her teacher had asked her to sing at a concert the public school is getting up but that Mrs. Campbell put her foot down and said 'no' most decidedly. When Elizabeth attempted to plead, Mrs. Campbell said,

"'Have the goodness not to talk back to me, Elizabeth, if you please.'

"Little Elizabeth wept a few bitter tears in the tower room that night and said she felt it would make her Lizzie forever. She could never be any of her other names again.

"'Last week I loved God, this week I don't,' she said defiantly.

"All her class were taking part in the program and she felt 'like a leopard.' I think the sweet thing meant she felt like a leper and that was sufficiently dreadful. Darling Elizabeth must not feel like a leper.

"So I manufactured an errand to The Evergreens next evening. The Woman...who might really have lived before the flood, she looks so ancient...gazed at me coldly out of great gray, expressionless eyes, showed me grimly into the drawing-room and went to tell Mrs. Campbell that I had asked for her.

"I don't think there has been any sunshine in that drawing-room since the house was built. There was a piano, but I'm sure it could never have been played on. Stiff chairs, covered with silk brocade, stood against the wall...All the furniture stood against the wall except a central marble-topped table, and none of it seemed to be acquainted with the rest.

"Mrs. Campbell came in. I had never seen her before. She has a fine, sculptured old face that might have been a man's, with black eyes and black bushy brows under frosty hair. She has not quite eschewed all vain adornment of the body, for she wore large black onyx earrings that reached to her shoulders. She was painfully polite to me and I was painlessly polite to her. We sat and exchanged civilities about the weather for a few moments...both, as Tacitus remarked a few thousand years ago, 'with countenances adjusted to the occasion.' I told her, truthfully, that I had come to see if she would lend me the Rev. James Wallace Campbell's Memoirs for a short time, because I understood there was a good deal about the early history of Prince County in them which I wished to make use of in school.

"Mrs. Campbell thawed quite markedly and summoning Elizabeth, told her to go up to her room and bring down the Memoirs. Elizabeth's face showed signs of tears and Mrs. Campbell condescended to explain that it was because little Elizabeth's teacher had sent another note begging that she be allowed to sing at the concert, and that she, Mrs. Campbell, had written a very stinging reply which little Elizabeth would have to carry to her teacher the next morning.

"'I do not approve of children of Elizabeth's age singing in public,' said Mrs. Campbell. 'It tends to make them bold and forward.'

"As if anything could make little Elizabeth bold and forward!

"'I think perhaps you are wise, Mrs. Campbell,' I remarked in my most patronizing tone. 'In any event Mabel Phillips is going to sing, and I am told that her voice is really so wonderful that she will make all the others seem as nothing. No doubt it is much better that Elizabeth should not appear in competition with her.'

"Mrs. Campbell's face was a study. She may be Campbell outside but she is Pringle at the core. She said nothing, however, and I knew the psychological moment for stopping. I thanked her for the Memoirs and came away.

"The next evening when little Elizabeth came to the garden gate for her milk, her pale, flower-like face was literally a-star. She told me that Mrs. Campbell had told her she might sing after all, if she were careful not to let herself get puffed up about it.

"You see, Rebecca Dew had told me that the Phillips and the

Campbell clans have always been rivals in the matter of good voices!

"I gave Elizabeth a bit of a picture for Christmas to hang above her bed...just a light-dappled woodland path leading up a hill to a quaint little house among some trees. Little Elizabeth says she is not so frightened now to go to sleep in the dark, because as soon as she gets into bed she pretends that she is walking up the path to the house and that she goes inside and it is all lighted and her father is there.

"Poor darling! I can't help detesting that father of hers!"

"January 19th.

"There was a dance at Carry Pringle's last night. Katherine was there in a dark red silk with the new side flounces and her hair had been done by a hairdresser. Would you believe it, people who had known her ever since she came to teach in Summerside actually asked one another who she was when she came into the room. But I think it was less the dress and hair that made the difference than some indefinable change in herself.

"Always before, when she was out with people, her attitude seemed to be, 'These people bore me. I expect I bore them and I hope I do.' But last night it was as if she had set lighted candles in all the windows of her house of life.

"I've had a hard time winning Katherine's friendship. But

nothing worth while is ever easy come by and I have always felt that her friendship would be worth while.

"Aunt Chatty has been in bed for two days with a feverish cold and thinks she may have the doctor tomorrow, in case she is taking pneumonia. So Rebecca Dew, her head tied up in a towel, has been cleaning the house madly all day to get it in perfect order before the doctor's possible visit. Now she is in the kitchen ironing Aunt Chatty's white cotton nighty with the crochet yoke, so that it will be ready for her to slip over her flannel one. It was spotlessly clean before, but Rebecca Dew thought it was not quite a good color from lying in the bureau drawer."

"January 28th.

"January so far has been a month of cold gray days, with an occasional storm whirling across the harbor and filling Spook's Lane with drifts. But last night we had a silver thaw and today the sun shone. My maple grove was a place of unimaginable splendors. Even the commonplaces had been made lovely. Every bit of wire fencing was a wonder of crystal lace.

"Rebecca Dew has been poring this evening over one of my magazines containing an article on 'Types of Fair Women,' illustrated by photographs.

"'Wouldn't it be lovely, Miss Shirley, if some one could just wave a wand and make everybody beautiful?' she said wistfully. 'Just fancy my feelings, Miss Shirley, if I suddenly found myself beautiful! But then'...with a sigh...'if we were all beauties who would do the work?'"

8

"I'm so tired," sighed Cousin Ernestine Bugle, dropping into her chair at the Windy Poplars supper-table. "I'm afraid sometimes to sit down for fear I'll never be able to git up again."

Cousin Ernestine, a cousin three times removed of the late Captain MacComber, but still, as Aunt Kate used to reflect, much too close, had walked in from Lowvale that afternoon for a visit to Windy Poplars. It cannot be said that either of the widows had welcomed her very heartily, in spite of the sacred ties of family. Cousin Ernestine was not an exhilarating person, being one of those unfortunates who are constantly worrying not only about their own affairs but everybody else's as well and will not give themselves or others any rest at all. The very look of her, Rebecca Dew declared, made you feel that life was a vale of tears.

Certainly Cousin Ernestine was not beautiful and it was extremely doubtful if she ever had been. She had a dry, pinched little face, faded, pale blue eyes, several badly placed moles and a whining voice. She wore a rusty black dress and a decrepit neck-piece of Hudson seal which she would not remove even at the table, because she was afraid of draughts.

Rebecca Dew might have sat at the table with them had she wished, for the widows did not regard Cousin Ernestine as any particular "company." But Rebecca always declared she couldn't "savor her victuals" in that old kill-joy's society. She preferred to "eat her morsel" in the kitchen, but that did not prevent her from saying her say as she waited on the table.

"Likely it's the spring getting into your bones," she remarked unsympathetically.

"Ah, I hope it's only that, Miss Dew. But I'm afraid I'm like poor Mrs. Oliver Gage. She et mushrooms last summer but there must-a been a toadstool among them, for she's never felt the same since.

"But you can't have been eating mushrooms as early as this," said Aunt Chatty.

"No, but I'm afraid I've et something else. Don't try to cheer me up, Charlotte. You mean well, but it ain't no use. I've been through too much. Are you sure there ain't a spider in that cream jug, Kate? I'm afraid I saw one when you poured my cup."

"We never have spiders in our cream jugs," said Rebecca Dew ominously, and slammed the kitchen door.

"Mebbe it was only a shadder," said Cousin Ernestine meekly. "My eyes ain't what they were. I'm afraid I'll soon be blind. That reminds me...I dropped in to see Martha MacKay this afternoon and she was feeling feverish and all out in some kind of a rash. 'Looks to me as though you had the measles,' I told her. 'Likely they'll leave you almost blind. Your family all have weak eyes.' I thought she ought to be prepared. Her mother isn't well either. The doctor says it's indigestion, but I'm afraid it's a growth. 'And if you have to have an operation and take chloroform,' I told her, 'I'm afraid you'll never come out of it. Remember you're a Hillis and the Hillises all had weak hearts. Your father died of heart-failure, you know.'"

"At eighty-seven!" said Rebecca Dew, whisking away a plate.

"And you know three score and ten is the Bible limit," said Aunt Chatty cheerfully.

Cousin Ernestine helped herself to a third teaspoonful of sugar and stirred her tea sadly.

"So King David said, Charlotte, but I'm afraid David wasn't a very nice man in some respects."

Anne caught Aunt Chatty's eye and laughed before she could help herself.

Cousin Ernestine looked at her disapprovingly.

"I've heerd you was a great girl to laugh. Well, I hope it'll last, but I'm afraid it won't. I'm afraid you'll find out all too soon that life's a melancholy business. Ah well, I was young myself once."

"Was you really?" inquired Rebecca Dew sarcastically, bringing in the muffins. "Seems to me you must always have been afraid to be young. It takes courage, I can tell you that, Miss Bugle."

"Rebecca Dew has such an odd way of putting things," complained Cousin Ernestine. "Not that I mind her of course. And it's well to laugh when you can, Miss Shirley, but I'm afraid you're tempting Providence by being so happy. You're awful like our last minister's wife's aunt...she was always laughing and she died of a parralattic stroke. The third one kills you. I'm afraid our new minister out at Lowvale is inclined to be frivolous. The minute I saw him I sez to Louisy, 'I'm afraid a man with legs like that must be addicted to dancing.' I s'pose he's give it up since he turned minister, but I'm afraid the strain will come out in his family. He's got a young wife and they say she's scandalously in love with him. I can't seem to git over the thought of any one marrying a minister for love. I'm afraid it's awful irreverent. He preaches pretty fair sermons, but I'm afraid from what he said of Elijah the Tidbit last Sunday that he's far too liberal in his views of the Bible."

"I see by the papers that Peter Ellis and Fanny Bugle were

married last week," said Aunt Chatty.

"Ah, yes. I'm afraid that'll be a case of marrying in haste and repenting at leisure. They've only known each other three years. I'm afraid Peter'll find out that fine feathers don't always make fine birds. I'm afraid Fanny's very shiftless. She irons her table napkins on the right side first and only. Not much like her sainted mother. Ah, she was a thorough woman if ever there was one. When she was in mourning she always wore black nightgowns. Said she felt as bad in the night as in the day. I was down at Andy Bugle's, helping them with the cooking, and when I come downstairs on the wedding morning if there wasn't Fanny eating an egg for her breakfast...and her gitting married that day. I don't s'pose you'll believe that...I wouldn't if I hadn't a-seen it with my own eyes. My poor dead sister never et a thing for three days afore she was married. And after her husband died we was all afraid she was never going to eat again. There are times when I feel I can't understand the Bugles any longer. There was a time when you knew where you was with your own connection, but it ain't that way now."

"Is it true that Jean Young is going to be married again?" asked Aunt Kate.

"I'm afraid it is. Of course Fred Young is supposed to be dead, but I'm dreadful afraid he'll turn up yet. You could never trust that man. She's going to marry Ira Roberts. I'm afraid he's only marrying her to make her happy. His Uncle Philip once wanted to marry me, but I sez to him, sez I, 'Bugle I was born and Bugle I will die. Marriage is a leap in the dark,' sez I, 'and I ain't going to be drug into it.' There's been an awful lot of weddings in Lowvale this winter. I'm afraid there'll be funerals all summer to make up for it. Annie Edwards and Chris Hunter were married last month. I'm afraid they won't be as fond of each other in a few years' time as they are now. I'm afraid she was just swept off her feet by his dashing ways. His Uncle Hiram was crazy...he belieft he was a dog for years."

"If he did his own barking nobody need have grudged him the fun of it," said Rebecca Dew, bringing in the pear preserves and the layer cake.

"I never heerd that he barked," said Cousin Ernestine. "He just gnawed bones and buried them when nobody was looking. His wife felt it."

"Where is Mrs. Lily Hunter this winter?" asked Aunt Chatty.

"She's been spending it with her son in San Francisco and I'm awful afraid there'll be another earthquake afore she gits out of it. If she does, she'll likely try to smuggle and have trouble at the border. If it ain't one thing, it's another when you're traveling. But folks seem to be crazy for it. My cousin Jim Bugle spent the winter in Florida. I'm afraid he's gitting rich and worldly. I said to him afore he went, sez I...I remember it was the night afore the Colemans' dog died...or was it?...yes, it was...'Pride goeth afore destruction and a haughty spirit afore a fall,' sez I. His daughter is teaching over in the Bugle Road school and she can't make up her mind which of her beaus to take. 'There's one thing I can assure you of, Mary Annetta,' sez I, 'and that is you'll never git the one you love best. So you'd better take the one as loves you...if you kin be sure he does.' I hope she'll make a better choice than Jessie Chipman did. I'm afraid she's just going to marry Oscar Green because he was always round. 'Is that what you've picked out?' I sez to her. His brother died of galloping consumption. 'And don't be married in May,' sez I, 'for May's awful unlucky for a wedding.'"

"How encouraging you always are!" said Rebecca Dew, bringing in a plate of macaroons.

"Can you tell me," said Cousin Ernestine, ignoring Rebecca Dew and taking a second helping of pears, "if a calceolaria is a flower or a disease?"

"A flower," said Aunt Chatty.

Cousin Ernestine looked a little disappointed.

"Well, whatever it is, Sandy Bugle's widow's got it. I heerd her telling her sister in church last Sunday that she had a calceolaria at last. Your geraniums are dreadful scraggy, Charlotte. I'm afraid you don't fertilize them properly. Mrs. Sandy's gone out of mourning and poor Sandy only dead four years. Ah well, the dead are soon forgot nowadays. My sister wore crape for her husband twenty-five years."

"Did you know your placket was open?" said Rebecca, setting a coconut pie before Aunt Kate.

"I haven't time to be always staring at my face in the glass," said Cousin Ernestine acidly. "What if my placket is open? I've got three petticoats on, haven't I? They tell me the girls nowadays only wear one. I'm afraid the world is gitting dreadful gay and giddy. I wonder if they ever think of the judgment day."

"Do you s'pose they'll ask us at the judgment day how many petticoats we've got on?" asked Rebecca Dew, escaping to the kitchen before any one could register horror. Even Aunt Chatty thought Rebecca Dew really had gone a little too far.

"I s'pose you saw old Alec Crowdy's death last week in the paper," sighed Cousin Ernestine. "His wife died two years ago, lit'rally harried into her grave, poor creetur. They say he's been awful lonely since she died, but I'm afraid that's too good to be true. And I'm afraid they're not through with their troubles with him yet, even if he is buried. I hear he wouldn't make a will and I'm afraid there'll be awful ructions over the estate. They say Annabel Crowdy is going to marry a jack-of-all-trades. Her mother's first husband was one, so mebbe it's heredit'ry. Annabel's had a hard life of it, but I'm afraid she'll find it's out of the frying-pan into the fire, even if it don't turn out he's got a wife already."

"What is Jane Goldwin doing with herself this winter?" asked Aunt Kate. "She hasn't been in to town for a long time."

"Ah, poor Jane! She's just pining away mysteriously. They don't know what's the matter with her, but I'm afraid it'll turn out to be an alibi. What is Rebecca Dew laughing like a hyenus out in the kitchen for? I'm afraid you'll have her on your hands yet. There's an awful lot of weak minds among the Dews."

"I see Thyra Cooper has a baby," said Aunt Chatty.

"Ah, yes, poor little soul. Only one, thank mercy. I was afraid it would be twins. Twins run so in the Coopers."

"Thyra and Ned are such a nice young couple," said Aunt Kate, as if determined to salvage something from the wreck of the universe.

But Cousin Ernestine would not admit that there was any balm in Gilead much less in Lowvale.

"Ah, she was real thankful to git him at last. There was a time she was afraid he wouldn't come back from the west. I warned her. 'You may be sure he'll disappoint you,' I told her. 'He's always disappointed people. Every one expected him to die afore he was a year old, but you see he's alive yet.' When he bought the Holly place I warned her again. 'I'm afraid that well is full of typhoid,' I told her. 'The Holly hired man died of typhoid there five years ago.' They can't blame me if anything happens. Joseph Holly has some misery in his back. He calls it lumbago, but I'm afraid it's the beginning of spinal meningitis."

"Old Uncle Joseph Holly is one of the best men in the world," said Rebecca Dew, bringing in a replenished teapot.

"Ah, he's good," said Cousin Ernestine lugubriously. "Too good! I'm afraid his sons will all go to the bad. You see it like that so often. Seems as if an average has to be struck. No, thank you, Kate, I won't have any more tea...well, mebbe a macaroon. They don't lie heavy on the stomach, but I'm afraid I've et far too much. I must be taking French leave, for I'm afraid it'll be dark afore I git home. I don't want to git my feet wet; I'm so afraid of ammonia. I've had something traveling from my arm to my lower limbs all winter. Night after night I've laid awake with it. Ah, nobody knows what I've gone through, but I ain't one of the complaining sort. I was determined I'd git up to see you once more, for I may not be here another spring. But you've both failed terrible, so you may go afore me yet. Ah well, it's best to go while there's some one of your own left to lay you out. Dear me, how the wind is gitting up! I'm afraid our barn roof will blow off if it comes to a gale. We've had so much wind this spring I'm afraid the climate is changing. Thank you, Miss Shirley..." as Anne helped her into her coat..."Be careful of yourself. You look awful washed out.

I'm afraid people with red hair never have real strong constitutions."

"I think my constitution is all right," smiled Anne, handing Cousin Ernestine an indescribable bit of millinery with a stringy ostrich feather dripping from its back. "I have a touch of sore throat tonight, Miss Bugle, that's all."

"Ah!" Another of Cousin Ernestine's dark forebodings came to her. "You want to watch a sore throat. The symptoms of diptheria and tonsillitis are exactly the same till the third day. But there's one consolation...you'll be spared an awful lot of trouble if you die young."

9

"Tower Room,

"Windy Poplars,

"April 20th.

"POOR DEAR GILBERT:

"'I said of laughter, it is mad, and of mirth, what doeth it?' I'm afraid I'll turn gray young...I'm afraid I'll end up in the poorhouse...I'm afraid none of my pupils will pass their finals...Mr. Hamilton's dog barked at me Saturday night and I'm afraid I'll have hydrophobia...I'm afraid my umbrella will turn inside out when I keep a tryst with Katherine tonight...I'm afraid Katherine likes me so much now that she can't always like me as much...I'm afraid my hair isn't auburn after all...I'm afraid I'll have a mole on the end of my nose when I'm fifty...I'm afraid my school is a fire-trap...I'm afraid I'll find a mouse in my bed tonight...I'm afraid you got engaged to me just because I was always around...I'm afraid I'll soon be picking at the counterpane.

"No, dearest, I'm not crazy...not yet. It's only that Cousin Ernestine Bugle is catching.

"I know now why Rebecca Dew has always called her 'Miss Much-afraid.' The poor soul has borrowed so much trouble, she must be hopelessly in debt to fate.

"There are so many Bugles in the world...not many quite so far gone in Buglism as Cousin Ernestine, perhaps, but so many kill-joys, afraid to enjoy today because of what tomorrow will bring.

"Gilbert darling, don't let's ever be afraid of things. It's such dreadful slavery. Let's be daring and adventurous and expectant. Let's dance to meet life and all it can bring to us, even if it brings scads of trouble and typhoid and twins!

"Today has been a day dropped out of June into April. The snow is all gone and the fawn meadows and golden hills just sing of spring. I know I heard Pan piping in the little green hollow in my maple bush and my Storm King was bannered with the airiest of purple hazes. We've had a great deal of rain lately and I've loved sitting in my tower in the still, wet hours of the spring twilights. But tonight is a gusty, hurrying night...even the clouds racing over the sky are in a hurry and the moonlight that gushes out between them is in a hurry to flood the world.

"Suppose, Gilbert, we were walking hand in hand down one of the long roads in Avonlea tonight!

"Gilbert, I'm afraid I'm scandalously in love with you. You don't think it's irreverent, do you? But then, you're not a minister."

10

"I'm so different," sighed Hazel.

It was really dreadful to be so different from other people...and yet rather wonderful, too, as if you were a being strayed from another star. Hazel would not have been one of the common herd for anything...no matter what she suffered by reason of her differentness.

"Everybody is different," said Anne amusedly.

"You are smiling." Hazel clasped a pair of very white, very dimpled hands and gazed adoringly at Anne. She emphasized at least one syllable in every word she uttered. "You have such a fascinating smile...such a haunting smile. I knew the moment I first saw you that you would understand everything. We are on the same plane. Sometimes I think I must be psychic, Miss Shirley. I always know so instinctively the moment I meet any one whether I'm going to like them or not. I felt at once that you were sympathetic...that you would understand. It's so sweet to be understood. Nobody understands me, Miss Shirley...nobody. But when I saw you, some inner voice whispered to me, 'She will understand...with her you can be your real self.' Oh, Miss Shirley, let's be real... let's always be real. Oh, Miss Shirley, do you love me the leastest, tiniest bit?"

"I think you're a dear," said Anne, laughing a little and ruffling Hazel's golden curls with her slender fingers. It was quite easy to be fond of Hazel.

Hazel had been pouring out her soul to Anne in the tower room, from which they could see a young moon hanging over the harbor and the twilight of a late May evening filling the crimson cups of the tulips below the windows.

"Don't let's have any light yet," Hazel had begged, and Anne had responded,

"No...it's lovely here when the dark is your friend, isn't it? When you turn on the light, it makes the dark your enemy...and it glowers in at you resentfully."

"I can think things like that but I can never express them so beautifully," moaned Hazel in an anguish of rapture. "You talk in the language of the violets, Miss Shirley."

Hazel couldn't have explained in the least what she meant by that, but it didn't matter. It sounded so poetic.

The tower room was the only peaceful room in the house. Rebecca Dew had said that morning, with a hunted look, "We must get the parlor and spare-room papered before the Ladies' Aid meets here," and had forthwith removed all the furniture from both to make way for a paper-hanger who then refused to come until the next day. Windy Poplars was a wilderness of confusion, with one sole oasis in the tower room.

Hazel Marr had a notorious "crush" on Anne. The Marrs were new-comers in Summerside, having moved there from Charlottetown during the winter. Hazel was an "October blonde," as she liked to describe herself, with hair of golden bronze and brown eyes, and, so Rebecca Dew declared, had never been much good in the world since she found out she was pretty. But Hazel was popular, especially among the boys, who found her eyes and curls a quite irresistible combination.

Anne liked her. Earlier in the evening she had been tired and a trifle pessimistic, with the fag that comes with late afternoon in a schoolroom, but she felt rested now; whether as a result of the May breeze, sweet with apple blossom, blowing in at the window, or of Hazel's chatter, she could not have told. Perhaps both. Somehow, to Anne, Hazel recalled her own early youth, with all its raptures and ideals and romantic visions.

Hazel caught Anne's hand and pressed her lips to it reverently.

"I hate all the people you have loved before me, Miss Shirley. I hate all the other people you love now. I want to possess you exclusively."

"Aren't you a bit unreasonable, honey? You love other people besides me. How about Terry, for example?"

"Oh, Miss Shirley! It's that I want to talk to you about. I can't endure it in silence any longer...I cannot. I must talk to some one about it...some one who understands. I went out the night before last and walked round and round the pond all night...well, nearly...till twelve, anyhow. I've suffered everything...everything."

Hazel looked as tragic as a round, pink-and-white face, long-lashed eyes and a halo of curls would let her.

"Why, Hazel dear, I thought you and Terry were so happy...that everything was settled."

Anne could not be blamed for thinking so. During the preceding three weeks, Hazel had raved to her about Terry Garland, for Hazel's attitude was, what was the use of having a beau if you couldn't talk to some one about him?

"Everybody thinks that," retorted Hazel with great bitterness. "Oh, Miss Shirley, life seems so full of perplexing problems. I feel sometimes as if I wanted to lie down somewhere...anywhere... and fold my hands and never think again."

"My dear girl, what has gone wrong?"

"Nothing...and everything. Oh, Miss Shirley, can I tell you all about it...can I pour out my whole soul to you?"

"Of course, dear."

"I have really no place to pour out my soul," said Hazel pathetically. "Except in my journal, of course. Will you let me show you my journal some day, Miss Shirley? It is a self-revelation. And yet I cannot write out what burns in my soul. It...it stifles me!" Hazel clutched dramatically at her throat.

"Of course I'd like to see it if you want me to. But what is this trouble between you and Terry?"

"Oh, Terry!! Miss Shirley, will you believe me when I tell you that Terry seems like a stranger to me? A stranger! Some one I'd never seen before," added Hazel, so that there might be no mistake.

"But, Hazel...I thought you loved him...you said..."

"Oh, I know. I thought I loved him, too. But now I know it was all a terrible mistake. Oh, Miss Shirley, you can't dream how difficult my life is...how impossible."

"I know something about it," said Anne sympathetically, remembering Roy Gardiner.

"Oh, Miss Shirley, I'm sure I don't love him enough to marry him. I realize that now...now that it is too late. I was just moonlighted into thinking I loved him. If it hadn't been for the moon I'm sure I would have asked for time to think it over. But I was swept off my feet...I can see that now. Oh, I'll run away...I'll do something desperate!"

"But, Hazel dear, if you feel you've made a mistake, why not just tell him..."

"Oh, Miss Shirley, I couldn't! It would kill him. He simply adores me. There isn't any way out of it really. And Terry's beginning to talk of getting married. Think of it...a child like me...I'm only eighteen. All the friends I've told about my engagement as a secret are congratulating me...and it's such a farce. They think Terry is a great catch because he comes into ten thousand dollars when he is twenty-five. His grandmother left it to him. As if I cared about such a sordid thing as money! Oh, Miss Shirley, why is it such a mercenary world...why?"

"I suppose it is mercenary in some respects, but not in all, Hazel. And if you feel like this about Terry...we all make mistakes...it's very hard to know our own minds sometimes..."

"Oh, isn't it? I knew you'd understand. I did think I cared for him, Miss Shirley. The first time I saw him I just sat and gazed at him the whole evening. Waves went over me when I met his eyes. He was so handsome...though I thought even then that his hair was too curly and his eyelashes too white. That should have warned me. But I always put my soul into everything, you know...I'm so intense. I felt little shivers of ecstasy whenever he came near me. And now I feel nothing...nothing! Oh, I've grown old these past few weeks, Miss Shirley...old! I've hardly eaten anything since I got engaged. Mother could tell you. I'm sure I don't love him enough to marry him. Whatever else I may be in doubt about, I know that."

"Then you shouldn't..."

"Even that moonlight night he proposed to me, I was thinking of what dress I'd wear to Joan Pringle's fancy dress party. I thought it would be lovely to go as Queen of the May in pale green, with a sash of darker green and a cluster of pale pink roses in my hair. And a May-pole decked with tiny roses and hung with pink and green ribbons. Wouldn't it have been fetching? And then Joan's uncle had to go and die and Joan couldn't have the party after all, so it all went for nothing. But the point is...I really couldn't have loved him when my thoughts were wandering like that, could I?"

"I don't know...our thoughts play us curious tricks some times."

"I really don't think I ever want to get married at all, Miss Shirley. Do you happen to have an orangewood stick handy?

Thanks. My half-moons are getting ragged. I might as well do them while I'm talking. Isn't it just lovely to be exchanging confidences like this? It's so seldom one gets the opportunity...the world intrudes itself so. Well, what was I talking of...oh, yes, Terry. What am I to do, Miss Shirley? I want your advice. Oh, I feel like a trapped creature!"

"But, Hazel, it's so very simple..."

"Oh, it isn't simple at all, Miss Shirley! It's dreadfully complicated. Mamma is so outrageously pleased, but Aunt Jean isn't. She doesn't like Terry, and everybody says she has such good judgment. I don't want to marry anybody. I'm ambitious...I want a career. Sometimes I think I'd like to be a nun. Wouldn't it be wonderful to be the bride of heaven? I think the Catholic church is so picturesque, don't you? But of course I'm not a Catholic...and anyway, I suppose you could hardly call it a career. I've always felt I'd love to be a nurse. It's such a romantic profession, don't you think? Smoothing fevered brows and all that...and some handsome millionaire patient falling in love with you and carrying you off to spend a honeymoon in a villa on the Riviera, facing the morning sun and the blue Mediterranean. I've seen myself in it. Foolish dreams, perhaps, but, oh, so sweet. I can't give them up for the prosaic reality of marrying Terry Garland and settling down in Summerside!"

Hazel shivered at the very idea and scrutinized a half-moon

critically.

"I suppose..." began Anne.

"We haven't anything in common, you know, Miss Shirley. He doesn't care for poetry and romance, and they're my very life. Sometimes I think I must be a reincarnation of Cleopatra...or would it be Helen of Troy?...one of those languorous, seductive creatures, anyhow. I have such wonderful thoughts and feelings...I don't know where I get them if that isn't the explanation. And Terry is so terribly matter-of-fact...he can't be a reincarnation of anybody. What he said when I told him about Vera Fry's quill pen proves that, doesn't it?"

"But I never heard of Vera Fry's quill pen," said Anne patiently.

"Oh, haven't you? I thought I'd told you. I've told you so much. Vera's fiance gave her a quill pen he'd made out of a feather he'd picked up that had fallen from a crow's wing. He said to her, 'Let your spirit soar to heaven with it whenever you use it, like the bird who once bore it.' Wasn't that just wonderful? But Terry said the pen would wear out very soon, especially if Vera wrote as much as she talked, and anyway he didn't think crows ever soared to heaven. He just missed the meaning of the whole thing completely...it's very essence."

"What was its meaning?"

"Oh...why...why...soaring, you know...getting away from the

clods of earth. Did you notice Vera's ring? A sapphire. I think sapphires are too dark for engagement rings. I'd rather have your dear, romantic little hoop of pearls. Terry wanted to give me my ring right away...but I said not yet a while...it would seem like a fetter...so irrevocable, you know. I wouldn't have felt like that if I'd really loved him, would I?"

"No, I'm afraid not..."

"It's been so wonderful to tell somebody what I really feel like. Oh, Miss Shirley, if I could only find myself free again... free to seek the deeper meaning of life! Terry wouldn't understand what I meant if I said that to him. And I know he has a temper...all the Garlands have. Oh, Miss Shirley...if you would just talk to him...tell him what I feel like...he thinks you're wonderful...he'd be guided by what you say."

"Hazel, my dear little girl, how could I do that?"

"I don't see why not." Hazel finished the last new moon and laid the orangewood stick down tragically. "If you can't, there isn't any help anywhere. But I can never, never, NEVER marry Terry Garland."

"If you don't love Terry, you ought to go to him and tell him so...no matter how badly it will make him feel. Some day you'll meet some one you can really love, Hazel dear...you won't have any doubts then...you'll know."

"I shall never love anybody again," said Hazel, stonily

calm. "Love brings only sorrow. Young as I am I have learned that. This would make a wonderful plot for one of your stories, wouldn't it, Miss Shirley? I must be going...I'd no idea it was so late. I feel so much better since I've confided in you...'touched your soul in shadowland,' as Shakespeare says."

"I think it was Pauline Johnson," said Anne gently.

"Well, I knew it was somebody...somebody who had lived. I think I shall sleep tonight, Miss Shirley. I've hardly slept since I found myself engaged to Terry, without the least notion how it had all come about."

Hazel fluffed out her hair and put on her hat, a hat with a rosy lining to its brim and rosy blossoms around it. She looked so distractingly pretty in it that Anne kissed her impulsively. "You're the prettiest thing, darling," she said admiringly.

Hazel stood very still.

Then she lifted her eyes and stared clear through the ceiling of the tower room, clear through the attic above it, and sought the stars.

"I shall never, never forget this wonderful moment, Miss Shirley," she murmured rapturously. "I feel that my beauty...if I have any...has been consecrated. Oh, Miss Shirley, you don't know how really terrible it is to have a reputation for beauty and to be always afraid that when people meet you they will not think you as pretty as you were reported to be. It's torture.

Sometimes I just die of mortification because I fancy I can see they're disappointed. Perhaps it's only my imagination...I'm so imaginative...too much so for my own good, I fear. I imagined I was in love with Terry, you see. Oh, Miss Shirley, can you smell the apple-blossom fragrance?"

Having a nose, Anne could.

"Isn't it just divine? I hope heaven will be all flowers. One could be good if one lived in a lily, couldn't one?"

"I'm afraid it might be a little confining," said Anne perversely.

"Oh, Miss Shirley, don't...don't be sarcastic with your little adorer. Sarcasm just shrivels me up like a leaf."

"I see she hasn't talked you quite to death," said Rebecca Dew, when Anne had come back after seeing Hazel to the end of Spook's Lane. "I don't see how you put up with her."

"I like her, Rebecca, I really do. I was a dreadful little chatterbox when I was a child. I wonder if I sounded as silly to the people who had to listen to me as Hazel does sometimes."

"I didn't know you when you was a child but I'm sure you didn't," said Rebecca. "Because you would mean what you said no matter how you expressed it and Hazel Marr doesn't. She's nothing but skim milk pretending to be cream."

"Oh, of course she dramatizes herself a bit as most girls do, but I think she means some of the things she says," said Anne, thinking of Terry. Perhaps it was because she had a rather poor opinion of the said Terry that she believed Hazel was quite in earnest in all she said about him. Anne thought Hazel was throwing herself away on Terry in spite of the ten thousand he was "coming into." Anne considered Terry a good-looking, rather weak youth who would fall in love with the first pretty girl who made eyes at him and would, with equal facility, fall in love with the next one if Number One turned him down or left him alone too long.

Anne had seen a good deal of Terry that spring, for Hazel had insisted on her playing gooseberry frequently; and she was destined to see more of him, for Hazel went to visit friends in Kingsport and during her absence Terry rather attached himself to Anne, taking her out for rides and "seeing her home" from places. They called each other "Anne" and "Terry," for they were about the same age, although Anne felt quite motherly towards him. Terry felt immensely flattered that "the clever Miss Shirley" seemed to like his companionship and he became so sentimental the night of May Connelly's party, in a moonlit garden, where the shadows of the acacias blew crazily about, that Anne amusedly reminded him of the absent Hazel.

"Oh, Hazel!" said Terry. "That child!"

"You're engaged to 'that child,' aren't you?" said Anne severely.

"Not really engaged...nothing but some boy-and-girl nonsense. I...I guess I was just swept off my feet by the moonlight."

Anne did a bit of rapid thinking. If Terry really cared so little for Hazel as this, the child was far better freed from him. Perhaps this was a heaven-sent opportunity to extricate them both from the silly tangle they had got themselves into and from which neither of them, taking things with all the deadly seriousness of youth, knew how to escape.

"Of course," went on Terry, misinterpreting her silence. "I'm in a bit of a predicament, I'll own. I'm afraid Hazel has taken me a little bit too seriously, and I don't just know the best way to open her eyes to her mistake."

Impulsive Anne assumed her most maternal look.

"Terry, you are a couple of children playing at being grown up. Hazel doesn't really care anything more for you than you do for her. Apparently the moonlight affected both of you. She wants to be free but is afraid to tell you so for fear of hurting your feelings. She's just a bewildered, romantic girl and you're a boy in love with love, and some day you'll both have a good laugh at yourselves."

("I think I've put that very nicely," thought Anne complacently.)

Terry drew a long breath.

"You've taken a weight off my mind, Anne. Hazel's a sweet little thing, of course, I hated to think of hurting her, but I've realized my...our...mistake for some weeks. When one meets a woman...the woman...you're not going in yet, Anne? Is all this good moonlight to be wasted? You look like a white rose in the moonlight...Anne..."

But Anne had flown.

11

Anne, correcting examination papers in the tower room one mid-June evening, paused to wipe her nose. She had wiped it so often that evening that it was rosy-red and rather painful. The truth was that Anne was the victim of a very severe and very unromantic cold in the head. It would not allow her to enjoy the soft green sky behind the hemlocks of The Evergreens, the silver-white moon hanging over the Storm King, the haunting perfume of the lilacs below her window or the frosty, blue-penciled irises in the vase on her table. It darkened all her past and overshadowed all her future.

"A cold in the head in June is an immoral thing," she told Dusty Miller, who was meditating on the window-sill. "But in two weeks from today I'll be in dear Green Gables instead of stewing here over examination papers full of howlers and wiping a worn-out nose. Think of it, Dusty Miller."

Apparently Dusty Miller thought of it. He may also have thought that the young lady who was hurrying along Spook's Lane and down the road and along the perennial path looked angry and disturbed and un-June-like. It was Hazel Marr, only a day back from Kingsport, and evidently a much disturbed Hazel Marr, who, a few minutes later, burst stormily into the tower room without waiting for a reply to her sharp knock.

"Why, Hazel dear..." (Kershoo!)... "are you back from Kingsport already? I didn't expect you till next week."

"No, I suppose you didn't," said Hazel sarcastically. "Yes, Miss Shirley, I am back. And what do I find? That you have been doing your best to lure Terry away from me...and all but succeeding."

"Hazel!" (Kershoo!)

"Oh, I know it all! You told Terry I didn't love him...that I wanted to break our engagement...our sacred engagement!"

"Hazel...child!" (Kershoo!)

"Oh, yes, sneer at me...sneer at everything. But don't try to deny it. You did it...and you did it deliberately."

"Of course, I did. You asked me to."

"I...asked...you...to!"

"Here, in this very room. You told me you didn't love him

and could never marry him."

"Oh, just a mood, I suppose. I never dreamed you'd take me seriously. I thought you would understand the artistic temperament. You're ages older than I am, of course, but even you can't have forgotten the crazy ways girls talk...feel. You who pretended to be my friend!"

"This must be a nightmare," thought poor Anne, wiping her nose. "Sit down, Hazel...do."

"Sit down!" Hazel flew wildly up and down the room. "How can I sit down...how can anybody sit down when her life is in ruins all about her? Oh, if that is what being old does to you... jealous of younger people's happiness and determined to wreck it...I shall pray never to grow old."

Anne's hand suddenly tingled to box Hazel's ears with a strange horrible primitive tingle of desire. She slew it so instantly that she would never believe afterwards that she had really felt it. But she did think a little gentle chastisement was indicated.

"If you can't sit down and talk sensibly, Hazel, I wish you would go away." (A very violent kershoo.) "I have work to do." (Sniff...sniff...snuffle!)

"I am not going away till I have told you just what I think of you. Oh, I know I've only myself to blame...I should have known...I did know. I felt instinctively the first time I saw you that you were dangerous. That red hair and those green eyes! But I never dreamed you'd go so far as to make trouble between me and Terry. I thought you were a Christian at least. I never heard of any one doing such a thing. Well, you've broken my heart, if that is any satisfaction to you."

"You little goose..."

"I won't talk to you! Oh, Terry and I were so happy before you spoiled everything. I was so happy...the first girl of my set to be engaged. I even had my wedding all planned out...four bridesmaids in lovely pale blue silk dresses with black velvet ribbon on the flounces. So chic! Oh, I don't know if I hate you the most or pity you the most! Oh, how could you treat me like this...after I've loved you so...trusted you so...believed in you so!"

Hazel's voice broke...her eyes filled with tears...she collapsed on a rocking-chair.

"You can't have many exclamation points left," thought Anne, "but no doubt the supply of italics is inexhaustible."

"This will just about kill poor Momma," sobbed Hazel. "She was so pleased...everybody was so pleased...they all thought it an ideal match. Oh, can anything ever again be like it used to be?"

"Wait till the next moonlight night and try," said Anne gently.

"Oh, yes, laugh, Miss Shirley...laugh at my suffering. I have not the least doubt that you find it all very amusing...very amusing indeed! You don't know what suffering is! It is terrible...terrible!"

Anne looked at the clock and sneezed.

"Then don't suffer," she said unpityingly.

"I will suffer. My feelings are very deep. Of course a shallow soul wouldn't suffer. But I am thankful I am not shallow whatever else I am. Have you any idea what it means to be in love, Miss Shirley? Really, terribly deeply, wonderfully in love? And then to trust and be deceived? I went to Kingsport so happy...loving all the world! I told Terry to be good to you while I was away...not to let you be lonesome. I came home last night so happy. And he told me he didn't love me any longer...that it was all a mistake...a mistake!...and that you had told him I didn't care for him any longer, and wanted to be free!"

"My intentions were honorable," said Anne, laughing. Her impish sense of humor had come to her rescue and she was laughing as much at herself as at Hazel.

"Oh, how did I live through the night?" said Hazel wildly. "I just walked the floor. And you don't know...you can't even imagine what I've gone through today. I've had to sit and listen...actually listen... to people talking about Terry's infatuation for you. Oh, people have been watching you! They know what you've been doing. And why...why! That is what I cannot understand. You had your own lover...why couldn't you have left me mine? What had you against me? What had I ever done to you?"

"I think," said Anne, thoroughly exasperated, "that you and Terry both need a good spanking. If you weren't too angry to listen to reason..."

"Oh, I'm not angry, Miss Shirley...only hurt...terribly hurt," said Hazel in a voice positively foggy with tears. "I feel that I have been betrayed in everything... in friendship as well as in love. Well, they say after your heart is broken you never suffer any more. I hope it's true, but I fear it isn't."

"What has become of your ambition, Hazel? And what about the millionaire patient and the honeymoon villa on the blue Mediterranean?"

"I'm sure I don't know what you're talking about, Miss Shirley. I'm not a bit ambitious...I'm not one of those dreadful new women. My highest ambition was to be a happy wife and make a happy home for my husband. Was...was! To think it should be in the past tense! Well, it doesn't do to trust any one. I've learned that. A bitter, bitter lesson!"

Hazel wiped her eyes and Anne wiped her nose, and Dusty Miller glared at the evening star with the expression of a misanthrope.

"You'd better go, I think, Hazel. I'm really very busy and I can't see that there is anything to be gained by prolonging this interview."

Hazel walked to the door with the air of Mary Queen of Scots advancing to the scaffold, and turned there dramatically.

"Farewell, Miss Shirley. I leave you to your conscience."

Anne, left alone with her conscience, laid down her pen, sneezed three times and gave herself a plain talking-to.

"You may be a B.A., Anne Shirley, but you have a few things to learn yet...things that even Rebecca Dew could have told you...did tell you. Be honest with yourself, my dear girl, and take your medicine like a gallant lady. Admit that you were carried off your feet by flattery. Admit that you really liked Hazel's professed adoration for you. Admit you found it pleasant to be worshiped. Admit that you liked the idea of being a sort of dea ex machina... saving people from their own folly when they didn't in the least want to be saved from it. And having admitted all this and feeling wiser and sadder and a few thousand years older, pick up your pen and proceed with your examination papers, pausing to note in passing that Myra Pringle thinks a seraph is 'an animal that abounds in Africa.'"

12

A week later a letter came for Anne, written on pale blue paper edged with silver.

"DEAR MISS SHIRLEY:

"I am writing this to tell you that all misunderstanding is cleared away between Terry and me and we are so deeply, intensely, wonderfully happy that we have decided we can forgive you. Terry says he was just moonlighted into making love to you but that his heart never really swerved in its allegiance to me. He says he really likes sweet, simple girls...that all men do...and has no use for intriguing, designing ones. We don't understand why you behaved to us as you did...we never will understand. Perhaps you just wanted material for a story and thought you could find it in tampering with the first sweet, tremulous love of a girl. But we thank you for revealing us to ourselves. Terry says he never realized the deeper meaning of life before. So really it was all for the best. We are so sympathetic...we can feel each other's thoughts. Nobody understands him but me and I want to be a source of inspiration to him forever. I am not clever like you but I feel I can be that, for we are soul-mates and have vowed eternal truth and constancy to each other, no matter how many jealous people and false friends may try to make trouble between us.

"We are going to be married as soon as I have my trousseau ready. I am going up to Boston to get it. There really isn't anything in Summerside. My dress is to be white moire and my traveling-suit will be dove gray with hat, gloves and blouse of delphinium blue. Of course I'm very young, but I want to be married when I am young, before the bloom goes off life.

"Terry is all that my wildest dreams could picture and every thought of my heart is for him alone. I know we are going to be rapturously happy. Once I believed all my friends would rejoice with me in my happiness, but I have learned a bitter lesson in worldly wisdom since then.

"Yours truly,

"HAZEL MARR.

"P.S. 1. You told me Terry had such a temper. Why, he's a perfect lamb, his sister says.

"H.M.

"P.S. 2. I've heard that lemon juice will bleach freckles. You might try it on your nose.

"H.M."

"To quote Rebecca Dew," remarked Anne to Dusty Miller, "postscript Number Two is the last straw."

13

Anne went home for her second Summerside vacation with mixed feelings. Gilbert was not to be in Avonlea that summer. He had gone west to work on a new railroad that was being built. But Green Gables was still Green Gables and Avonlea was still Avonlea. The Lake of Shining Waters shone and sparkled as of old. The ferns still grew as thickly over the Dryad's Bubble, and the log-bridge, though it was a little crumblier and mossier every year, still led up to the shadows and silences and wind-songs of the Haunted Wood.

And Anne had prevailed on Mrs. Campbell to let little Elizabeth go home with her for a fortnight...no more. But Elizabeth, looking forward to two whole weeks with Miss Shirley, asked no more of life.

"I feel like Miss Elizabeth today," she told Anne with a sigh of delightful excitement, as they drove away from Windy Poplars. "Will you please call me 'Miss Elizabeth' when you introduce me to your friends at Green Gables? It would make me feel so grown up."

"I will," promised Anne gravely, remembering a small, red-headed damsel who had once begged to be called Cordelia.

Elizabeth's drive from Blight River to Green Gables, over

a road which only Prince Edward Island in June can show, was almost as ecstatic a thing for her as it had been for Anne that memorable spring evening so many years ago. The world was beautiful, with wind-rippled meadows on every hand and surprises lurking around every corner. She was with her beloved Miss Shirley; she would be free from the Woman for two whole weeks; she had a new pink gingham dress and a pair of lovely new brown boots. It was almost as if Tomorrow were already there...with fourteen Tomorrows to follow. Elizabeth's eyes were shining with dreams when they turned into the Green Gables lane where the pink wild roses grew.

Things seemed to change magically for Elizabeth the moment she got to Green Gables. For two weeks she lived in a world of romance. You couldn't step outside the door without stepping into something romantic. Things were just bound to happen in Avonlea...if not today, then tomorrow. Elizabeth knew she hadn't quite got into Tomorrow yet, but she knew she was on the very fringes of it.

Everything in and about Green Gables seemed to be acquainted with her. Even Marilla's pink rosebud tea-set was like an old friend. The rooms looked at her as if she had always known and loved them; the very grass was greener than grass anywhere else; and the people who lived at Green Gables were the kind of people who lived in Tomorrow. She loved them and was beloved by them. Davy and Dora adored her and spoiled her; Marilla and Mrs. Lynde approved of her. She was neat, she was lady-like, she was polite to her elders. They knew Anne did not like Mrs. Campbell's methods, but it was plain to be seen that she had trained her great-granddaughter properly.

"Oh, I don't want to sleep, Miss Shirley," Elizabeth whispered when they were in bed in the little porch gable, after a rapturous evening. "I don't want to sleep away a single minute of these wonderful two weeks. I wish I could get along without any sleep while I'm here."

For a while she didn't sleep. It was heavenly to lie there and listen to the splendid low thunder Miss Shirley had told her was the sound of the sea. Elizabeth loved it and the sigh of the wind around the eaves as well. Elizabeth had always been "afraid of the night." Who knew what queer thing might jump at you out of it? But now she was afraid no longer. For the first time in her life the night seemed like a friend to her.

They would go to the shore tomorrow, Miss Shirley had promised, and have a dip in those silver-tipped waves they had seen breaking beyond the green dunes of Avonlea when they drove over the last hill. Elizabeth could see them coming in, one after the other. One of them was a great dark wave of sleep...it rolled right over her...Elizabeth drowned in it with a delicious sigh of surrender.

"It's...so...easy...to...love...God...here," was her last conscious thought.

But she lay awake for a while every night of her stay at Green Gables, long after Miss Shirley had gone to sleep, thinking over things. Why couldn't life at The Evergreens be like life at Green Gables?

Elizabeth had never lived where she could make a noise if she wanted to. Everybody at The Evergreens had to move softly...speak softly...even, so Elizabeth felt, think softly. There were times when Elizabeth desired perversely to yell loud and long.

"You may make all the noise you want to here," Anne had told her. But it was strange...she no longer wanted to yell, now that there was nothing to prevent her. She liked to go quietly, stepping gently among all the lovely things around her. But Elizabeth learned to laugh during that sojourn at Green Gables. And when she went back to Summerside she carried delightful memories with her and left equally delightful ones behind her. To the Green Gables folks Green Gables seemed for months full of memories of little Elizabeth. For "little Elizabeth" she was to them in spite of the fact that Anne had solemnly introduced her as "Miss Elizabeth." She was so tiny, so golden, so elf-like, that they couldn't think of her as anything but little Elizabeth...little Elizabeth dancing in a twilight garden among the white June lilies...coiled up on a bough of the big Duchess apple tree reading fairy tales, unlet and unhindered...little Elizabeth half drowned in a field of buttercups where her golden head seemed just a larger buttercup...chasing silver-green moths or trying to count the fireflies in Lover's Lane...listening to the bumblebees zooming in the canterbury-bells...being fed strawberries and cream by Dora in the pantry or eating red currants with her in the yard..."Red currants are such beautiful things, aren't they, Dora? It's just like eating jewels, isn't it?"...little Elizabeth singing to herself in the haunted dusk of the firs...with fingers sweet from gathering the big, fat, pink "cabbage roses"...gazing at the great moon hanging over the brook valley..."I think the moon has worried eyes, don't you, Mrs. Lynde?"...crying bitterly because a chapter in the serial story in Davy's magazine left the hero in a sad predicament..."Oh, Miss Shirley, I'm sure he can never live through it!"...little Elizabeth curled up, all flushed and sweet like a wild rose, for an afternoon nap on the kitchen sofa with Dora's kittens cuddled about her...shrieking with laughter to see the wind blowing the dignified old hens' tails over their backs...could it be little Elizabeth laughing like that?...helping Anne frost cupcakes, Mrs. Lynde cut the patches for a new "double Irish chain" quilt, and Dora rub the old brass candlesticks till they could see their faces in them...cutting out tiny biscuits with a thimble under Marilla's tutelage. Why, the Green Gables folks could hardly look at a place or thing without being reminded of little Elizabeth.

"I wonder if I'll ever have such a happy fortnight again," thought little Elizabeth, as she drove away from Green Gables. The road to the station was just as beautiful as it had been two weeks before, but half the time little Elizabeth couldn't see it for tears.

"I couldn't have believed I'd miss a child so much," said Mrs. Lynde.

When little Elizabeth went, Katherine Brooke and her dog came for the rest of the summer. Katherine had resigned from the staff of the High School at the close of the year and meant to go to Redmond in the fall to take a secretarial course at Redmond University. Anne had advised this.

"I know you'd like it and you've never liked teaching," said the latter, as they sat one evening in a ferny corner of a clover field and watched the glories of a sunset sky.

"Life owes me something more than it has paid me and I'm going out to collect it," said Katherine decidedly. "I feel so much younger than I did this time last year," she added with a laugh.

"I'm sure it's the best thing for you to do, but I hate to think of Summerside and the High without you. What will the tower room be like next year without our evenings of confab and argument, and our hours of foolishness, when we turned everybody and everything into a joke?"

The Third Year

1

"Windy Poplars,

"Spook's Lane,

"September 8th.

"Dearest:

"The summer is over...the summer in which I have seen you only that week-end in May. And I am back at Windy Poplars for my third and last year in Summerside High. Katherine and I had a delightful time together at Green Gables and I'm going to miss her dreadfully this year. The new Junior teacher is a jolly little personage, chubby and rosy and friendly as a puppy...but somehow, there's nothing more to her than that. She has sparkling shallow blue eyes with no thought behind them. I like her...I'll always like her...neither more nor less...there's nothing to discover in her. There was so much to discover in Katherine, when you once got past her guard.

"There is no change at Windy Poplars...yes there is. The old red cow has gone to her long home, so Rebecca Dew sadly informed me when I came down to supper Monday night. The widows have decided not to bother with another one but to get milk and cream from Mr. Cherry. This means that little Elizabeth will come no more to the garden gate for her new milk. But Mrs. Campbell seems to have grown reconciled to her coming over here when she wants to, so that does not make so much difference now.

"And another change is brewing. Aunt Kate told me, much to my sorrow, that they have decided to give Dusty Miller away as soon as they can find a suitable home for him. When I protested, she said they were really driven to it for peace' sake. Rebecca Dew has been constantly complaining about him all summer and there seems to be no other way of satisfying her. Poor Dusty Miller...and he is such a nice, prowly, purry darling!

"Tomorrow, being Saturday, I'm going to look after Mrs. Raymond's twins while she goes to Charlottetown to the funeral of some relative. Mrs. Raymond is a widow who came to our town last winter. Rebecca Dew and the Windy Poplars widows...really, Summerside is a great place for widows...think her a 'little too grand' for Summerside, but she was really a wonderful help to Katherine and me in our Dramatic Club activities. One good turn deserves another.

"Gerald and Geraldine are eight and are a pair of angelic-looking youngsters, but Rebecca Dew 'pulled a mouth,' to use one of her own expressions, when I told her what I was going to do.

"'But I love children, Rebecca.'

"'Children, yes, but them's holy terrors, Miss Shirley. Mrs. Raymond doesn't believe in punishing children no matter what they do. She says she's determined they'll have a "natural" life. They take people in by that saintly look of theirs, but I've heard what her neighbors have to say of them. The minister's wife called one afternoon...well, Mrs. Raymond was sweet as sugar pie to her, but when she was leaving a shower of Spanish onions came flying down the stairs and one of them knocked her hat off. "Children always behave so abominably when you 'specially want them to be good," was all Mrs. Raymond said... kinder as if she was rather proud of them being so unmanageable. They're from the States, you know'...as if that explained everything. Rebecca has about as much use for 'Yankees' as Mrs. Lynde has."

2

Saturday forenoon Anne betook herself to the pretty,

old-fashioned cottage on a street that straggled out into the country, where Mrs. Raymond and her famous twins lived. Mrs. Raymond was all ready to depart...rather gayly dressed for a funeral, perhaps...especially with regard to the beflowered hat perched on top of the smooth brown waves of hair that flowed around her head...but looking very beautiful. The eight-year-old twins, who had inherited her beauty, were sitting on the stairs, their delicate faces wreathed with a quite cherubic expression. They had complexions of pink and white, large China-blue eyes and aureoles of fine, fluffy, pale yellow hair.

They smiled with engaging sweetness when their mother introduced them to Anne and told them that dear Miss Shirley had been so kind as to come and take care of them while Mother was away at dear Aunty Ella's funeral, and of course they would be good and not give her one teeny-weeny bit of trouble, wouldn't they, darlings?

The darlings nodded gravely and contrived, though it hadn't seemed possible, to look more angelic than ever.

Mrs. Raymond took Anne down the walk to the gate with her.

"They're all I've got...now," she said pathetically. "Perhaps I may have spoiled them a little...I know people say I have...people always know so much better how you ought to bring up your children than you know yourself, haven't you noticed,

Miss Shirley? But I think loving is better than spanking any day, don't you, Miss Shirley? I'm sure you will have no trouble with them. Children always know whom they can play on and whom they can't, don't you think? That poor old Miss Prouty up the street...I had her to stay with them one day, but the poor darlings couldn't bear her. So of course they teased her a good bit...you know what children are. She has revenged herself by telling the most ridiculous tales about them all over town. But they'll just love you and I know they'll be angels. Of course, they have high spirits...but children should have, don't you think? It's so pitiful to see children with a cowed appearance, isn't it? I like them to be natural, don't you? Too good children don't seem natural, do they? Don't let them sail their boats in the bathtub or go wading in the pond, will you? I'm so afraid of them catching cold...their father died of pneumonia."

Mrs. Raymond's large blue eyes looked as if they were going to overflow, but she gallantly blinked the tears away.

"Don't worry if they quarrel a little—children always do quarrel, don't you think? But if any outsider attacks them...my dear!! They really just worship each other, you know. I could have taken one of them to the funeral, but they simply wouldn't hear of it. They've never been separated a day in their lives. And I couldn't look after twins at a funeral, could I now?"

"Don't worry, Mrs. Raymond," said Anne kindly. "I'm sure

Gerald and Geraldine and I will have a beautiful day together. I love children."

"I know it. I felt sure the minute I saw you that you loved children. One can always tell, don't you think? There's something about a person who loves children. Poor old Miss Prouty detests them. She looks for the worst in children and so of course she finds it. You can't conceive what a comfort it is to me to reflect that my darlings are under the care of one who loves and understands children. I'm sure I'll quite enjoy the day."

"You might take us to the funeral," shrieked Gerald, suddenly sticking his head out of an upstairs window. "We never have any fun like that."

"Oh, they're in the bathroom!" exclaimed Mrs. Raymond tragically. "Dear Miss Shirley, please go and take them out. Gerald darling, you know mother couldn't take you both to the funeral. Oh, Miss Shirley, he's got that coyote skin from the parlor floor tied round his neck by the paws again. He'll ruin it. Please make him take it off at once. I must hurry or I'll miss the train."

Mrs. Raymond sailed elegantly away and Anne ran upstairs to find that the angelic Geraldine had grasped her brother by the legs and was apparently trying to hurl him bodily out of the window.

"Miss Shirley, make Gerald stop putting out his tongue at me," she demanded fiercely.

"Does it hurt you?" asked Anne smilingly.

"Well, he's not going to put out his tongue at me," retorted Geraldine, darting a baleful look at Gerald, who returned it with interest.

"My tongue's my own and you can't stop me from putting it out when I like...can she, Miss Shirley?"

Anne ignored the question.

"Twins dear, it's just an hour till lunch-time. Shall we go and sit in the garden and play games and tell stories? And, Gerald, won't you put that coyote skin back on the floor?"

"But I want to play wolf," said Gerald.

"He wants to play wolf," cried Geraldine, suddenly aligning herself on her brother's side.

"We want to play wolf," they both cried together.

A peal from the door-bell cut the knot of Anne's dilemma.

"Come on and see who it is," cried Geraldine. They flew to the stairs and by reason of sliding down the banisters, got to the front door much quicker than Anne, the coyote skin coming unloosed and drifting away in the process.

"We never buy anything from peddlers," Gerald told the lady standing on the door-stone.

"Can I see your mother?" asked the caller.

"No, you can't. Mother's gone to Aunt Ella's funeral. Miss Shirley's looking after us. That's her coming down the stairs. She'll make you scat."

Anne did feel rather like making the caller "scat" when she saw who it was. Miss Pamela Drake was not a popular caller in Summerside. She was always "canvassing" for something and it was generally quite impossible to get rid of her unless you bought it, since she was utterly impervious to snubs and hints and had apparently all the time in the world at her command.

This time she was "taking orders" for an encyclopedia...something no school-teacher could afford to be without. Vainly Anne protested that she did not need an encyclopedia...the High School already possessed a very good one.

"Ten years out of date," said Miss Pamela firmly. "We'll just sit down here on this rustic bench, Miss Shirley, and I'll show you my prospectus."

"I'm afraid I haven't time, Miss Drake. I have the children to look after."

"It won't take but a few minutes. I've been meaning to call on you, Miss Shirley, and I call it real fortunate to find you here. Run away and play, children, while Miss Shirley and I skim over this beautiful prospectus."

"Mother's hired Miss Shirley to look after us," said Geraldine, with a toss of her aerial curls. But Gerald had tugged her backward and they slammed the door shut.

"You see, Miss Shirley, what this encyclopedia means. Look at the beautiful paper...feel it...the splendid engravings...no other encyclopedia on the market has half the number of engravings...the wonderful print—a blind man could read it—and all for eighty dollars...eight dollars down and eight dollars a month till it's all paid. You'll never have such another chance...we're just doing this to introduce it...next year it will be a hundred and twenty."

"But I don't want an encyclopedia, Miss Drake," said Anne desperately.

"Of course you want an encyclopedia...every one wants an encyclopedia...a National encyclopedia. I don't know how I lived before I became acquainted with the National encyclopedia. Live! I didn't live...I merely existed. Look at that engraving of the cassowary, Miss Shirley. Did you ever really see a cassowary before?"

"But, Miss Drake, I..."

"If you think the terms a little too onerous I feel sure I can make a special arrangement for you, being a school-teacher...six a month instead of eight. You simply can't refuse an offer like that, Miss Shirley."

Anne almost felt she couldn't. Wouldn't it be worth six dollars a month to get rid of this terrible woman who had so evidently made up her mind not to go until she had got an order? Besides, what were the twins doing? They were alarmingly quiet. Suppose they were sailing their boats in the bathtub. Or had sneaked out of the back door and gone wading in the pond.

She made one more pitiful effort to escape.

"I'll think this over, Miss Drake, and let you know..."

"There's no time like the present," said Miss Drake, briskly getting out her fountain-pen. "You know you're going to take the National, so you might just as well sign for it now as any other time. Nothing is ever gained by putting things off. The price may go up any moment and then you'd have to pay a hundred and twenty. Sign here, Miss Shirley."

Anne felt the fountain-pen being forced into her hand...another moment...and then there was such a blood-curdling shriek from Miss Drake that Anne dropped the fountain-pen under the clump of golden glow that flanked the rustic seat, and gazed in amazed horror at her companion.

Was that Miss Drake...that indescribable object, hatless, spectacleless, almost hairless? Hat, spectacles, false front were floating in the air above her head half-way up to the bathroom window, out of which two golden heads were hanging. Gerald was grasping a fishing-rod to which were tied two cords ending in fish-hooks. By what magic he had contrived to make a triple catch, only he could have told. Probably it was sheer luck.

Anne flew into the house and upstairs. By the time she reached the bathroom the twins had fled. Gerald had dropped the fishing-rod and a peep from the window revealed a furious Miss Drake retrieving her belongings, including the fountain-pen, and marching to the gate. For once in her life Miss Pamela Drake had failed to land her order.

Anne discovered the twins seraphically eating apples on the back porch. It was hard to know what to do. Certainly, such behavior could not be allowed to pass without a rebuke...but Gerald had undoubtedly rescued her from a difficult position and Miss Drake was an odious creature who needed a lesson. Still...

"You've et a great big worm!" shrieked Gerald. "I saw it disappear down your throat."

Geraldine laid down her apple and promptly turned sick...very sick. Anne had her hands full for some time. And when Geraldine was better, it was lunch-hour and Anne suddenly decided to let Gerald off with a very mild reproof. After all, no lasting harm had been done Miss Drake, who would probably hold her tongue religiously about the incident for her own sake.

"Do you think, Gerald," she said gently, "that what you did was a gentlemanly action?"

"Nope," said Gerald, "but it was good fun. Gee, I'm some

fisherman, ain't I?"

The lunch was excellent. Mrs. Raymond had prepared it before she left and whatever her shortcomings as a disciplinarian might be, she was a good cook. Gerald and Geraldine, being occupied with gorging, did not quarrel or display worse table manners than the general run of children. After lunch Anne washed the dishes, getting Geraldine to help dry them and Gerald to put them carefully away in the cupboard. They were both quite knacky at it and Anne reflected complacently that all they needed was wise training and a little firmness.

3

At two o'clock Mr. James Grand called. Mr. Grand was the chairman of the High School board of trustees and had matters of importance to talk of, which he wished to discuss fully before he left on Monday to attend an educational conference in Kingsport. Could he come to Windy Poplars in the evening? asked Anne. Unfortunately he couldn't.

Mr. Grand was a good sort of man in his own fashion, but Anne had long ago found out that he must be handled with gloves. Moreover, Anne was very anxious to get him on her side in a battle royal over new equipment that was looming up.

She went out to the twins.

"Darlings, will you play nicely out in the back yard while I have a little talk with Mr. Grand? I won't be very long...and then we'll have an afternoon-tea picnic on the banks of the pond...and I'll teach you to blow soap-bubbles with red dye in them...the loveliest things!"

"Will you give us a quarter apiece if we behave?" demanded Gerald.

"No, Gerald dear," said Anne firmly, "I'm not going to bribe you. I know you are going to be good, just because I ask you, as a gentleman should."

"We'll be good, Miss Shirley," promised Gerald solemnly.

"Awful good," echoed Geraldine, with equal solemnity.

It is possible they would have kept their promise if Ivy Trent had not arrived almost as soon as Anne was closeted with Mr. Grand in the parlor. But Ivy Trent did arrive and the Raymond twins hated Ivy Trent...the impeccable Ivy Trent who never did anything wrong and always looked as if she had just stepped out of a band-box.

On this particular afternoon there was no doubt that Ivy Trent had come over to show off her beautiful new brown boots and her sash and shoulder bows and hair bows of scarlet ribbon. Mrs. Raymond, whatever she lacked in some respects, had fairly sensible ideas about dressing children. Her charitable neighbors said she put so much money on herself that she had none to spend on the twins...and Geraldine never had a chance to parade the street in the style of Ivy Trent, who had a dress for every afternoon in the week. Mrs. Trent always arrayed her in "spotless white." At least. Ivy was always spotless when she left home. If she were not quite so spotless when she returned that, of course, was the fault of the "jealous" children with whom the neighborhood abounded.

Geraldine was jealous. She longed for scarlet sash and shoulder bows and white embroidered dresses. What would she not have given for buttoned brown boots like those?

"How do you like my new sash and shoulder bows?" asked Ivy proudly.

"How do you like my new sash and shoulder bows?" mimicked Geraldine tauntingly.

"But you haven't got shoulder bows," said Ivy grandly.

"But you haven't got shoulder bows," squeaked Geraldine.

Ivy looked puzzled.

"I have so. Can't you see them?"

"I have so. Can't you see them?" mocked Geraldine, very happy in this brilliant idea of repeating everything Ivy said scornfully.

"They ain't paid for," said Gerald.

Ivy Trent had a temper. It showed itself in her face, which

grew as red as her shoulder bows.

"They are, too. My mother always pays her bills."

"My mother always pays her bills," chanted Geraldine.

Ivy was uncomfortable. She didn't know exactly how to cope with this. So she turned to Gerald, who was undoubtedly the handsomest boy on the street. Ivy had made up her mind about him.

"I came over to tell you I'm going to have you for my beau," she said, looking eloquently at him out of a pair of brown eyes that, even at seven, Ivy had learned had a devastating effect on most of the small boys of her acquaintance.

Gerald turned crimson.

"I won't be your beau," he said.

"But you've got to be," said Ivy serenely.

"But you've got to be," said Geraldine, wagging her head at him.

"I won't be," shouted Gerald furiously. "And don't you give me any more of your lip, Ivy Trent."

"You have to be," said Ivy stubbornly.

"You have to be," said Geraldine.

Ivy glared at her.

"You just shut up, Geraldine Raymond!"

"I guess I can talk in my own yard," said Geraldine.

"'Course she can," said Gerald. "And if you don't shut up,

Ivy Trent, I'll just go over to your place and dig the eyes out of your doll."

"My mother would spank you if you did," cried Ivy.

"Oh, she would, would she? Well, do you know what my mother would do to her if she did? She'd just sock her on the nose."

"Well, anyway, you've got to be my beau," said Ivy, returning calmly to the vital subject.

"I'll...I'll duck your head in the rain-barrel," yelled the maddened Gerald..."I'll rub your face in an ant's nest...I'll...I'll tear them bows and sash off you..." triumphantly, for this at least was feasible.

"Let's do it," squealed Geraldine.

They pounced like furies on the unfortunate Ivy, who kicked and shrieked and tried to bite but was no match for the two of them. Together they hauled her across the yard and into the woodshed, where her howls could not be heard.

"Hurry," gasped Geraldine, "'fore Miss Shirley comes out."

No time was to be lost. Gerald held Ivy's legs while Geraldine held her wrists with one hand and tore off her hair bow and shoulder bows and sash with the other.

"Let's paint her legs," shouted Gerald, his eyes falling on a couple of cans of paint left there by some workmen the previous week. "I'll hold her and you paint her."

Ivy shrieked vainly in despair. Her stockings were pulled down and in a few moments her legs were adorned with wide stripes of red and green paint. In the process a good deal of the paint got spattered over her embroidered dress and new boots. As a finishing touch they filled her curls with burrs.

She was a pitiful sight when they finally released her. The twins howled mirthfully as they looked at her. Long weeks of airs and condescensions from Ivy had been avenged.

"Now you go home," said Gerald. "This'll teach you to go 'round telling people they have to be your beaus."

"I'll tell my mother," wept Ivy. "I'll go straight home and tell my mother on you, you horrid, horrid, hateful, ugly boy!"

"Don't you call my brother ugly, you stuck-up thing," cried Geraldine. "You and your shoulder bows! Here, take them with you. We don't want them cluttering up our woodshed."

Ivy, pursued by the bows, which Geraldine pelted after her, ran sobbing out of the yard and down the street.

"Quick...let's sneak up the back stairs to the bathroom and clean up 'fore Miss Shirley sees us," gasped Geraldine.

4

Mr. Grand had talked himself out and bowed himself away.

Anne stood for a moment on the door-stone, wondering uneasily where her charges were. Up the street and in at the gate came a wrathful lady, leading a forlorn and still sobbing atom of humanity by the hand.

"Miss Shirley, where is Mrs. Raymond?" demanded Mrs. Trent.

"Mrs. Raymond is..."

"I insist on seeing Mrs. Raymond. She shall see with her own eyes what her children have done to poor, helpless, innocent Ivy. Look at her, Miss Shirley...just look at her!"

"Oh, Mrs. Trent...I'm so sorry! It is all my fault. Mrs. Raymond is away...and I promised to look after them...but Mr. Grand came..."

"No, it isn't your fault, Miss Shirley. I don't blame you. No one can cope with those diabolical children. The whole street knows them. If Mrs. Raymond isn't here, there is no point in my remaining. I shall take my poor child home. But Mrs. Raymond shall hear of this...indeed she shall. Listen to that, Miss Shirley. Are they tearing each other limb from limb?"

"That" was a chorus of shrieks, howls and yells that came echoing down the stairs. Anne ran upwards. On the hall floor was a twisting, writhing, biting, tearing, scratching mass. Anne separated the furious twins with difficulty and, holding each firmly by a squirming shoulder, demanded the meaning of such behavior.

"She says I've got to be Ivy Trent's beau," snarled Gerald.

"So he has got to be," screamed Geraldine.

"I won't be!"

"You've got to be!"

"Children!" said Anne. Something in her tone quelled them. They looked at her and saw a Miss Shirley they had not seen before. For the first time in their young lives they felt the force of authority.

"You, Geraldine," said Anne quietly, "will go to bed for two hours. You, Gerald, will spend the same length of time in the hall closet. Not a word. You have behaved abominably and you must take your punishment. Your mother left you in my charge and you will obey me."

"Then punish us together," said Geraldine, beginning to cry.

"Yes...you've no right to sep'rate us...we've never been sep'rated," muttered Gerald.

"You will be now." Anne was still very quiet. Meekly Geraldine took off her clothes and got into one of the cots in their room. Meekly Gerald entered the hall closet. It was a large airy closet with a window and a chair and nobody could have called the punishment an unduly severe one. Anne locked the door and sat down with a book by the hall window. At least, for two hours she would know a little peace of mind.

A peep at Geraldine a few minutes later showed her to be sound asleep, looking so lovely in her sleep that Anne almost repented her sternness. Well, a nap would be good for her, anyway. When she wakened she should be permitted to get up, even if the two hours had not expired.

At the end of an hour Geraldine was still sleeping. Gerald had been so quiet that Anne decided that he had taken his punishment like a man and might be forgiven. After all, Ivy Trent was a vain little monkey and had probably been very irritating.

Anne unlocked the closet door and opened it.

There was no Gerald in the closet. The window was open and the roof of the side porch was just beneath it. Anne's lips tightened. She went downstairs and out into the yard. No sign of Gerald. She explored the woodshed and looked up and down the street. Still no sign.

She ran through the garden and through the gate into the lane that led through a patch of scrub woodland to the little pond in Mr. Robert Creedmore's field. Gerald was happily poling himself about on it in the small flat Mr. Creedmore kept there. Just as Anne broke through the trees Gerald's pole, which he had stuck rather deep in the mud, came away with unexpected ease at his third tug and Gerald promptly shot heels over head backward into the water.

Anne gave an involuntary shriek of dismay, but there was no

real cause for alarm. The pond at its deepest would not come up to Gerald's shoulders and where he had gone over, it was little deeper than his waist. He had somehow got on his feet and was standing there rather foolishly, with his aureole plastered drippingly down on his head, when Anne's shriek was re-echoed behind her, and Geraldine, in her nightgown, tore through the trees and out to the edge of the little wooden platform to which the flat was commonly moored.

With a despairing shriek of "Gerald!" she took a flying leap that landed her with a tremendous splash by Gerald's side and almost gave him another ducking.

"Gerald, are you drowned?" cried Geraldine. "Are you drowned, darling?"

"No...no...darling," Gerald assured her through his chattering teeth.

They embraced and kissed passionately.

"Children, come in here this minute," said Anne.

They waded to the shore. The September day, warm in the morning, had turned cold and windy in the late afternoon. They shivered terribly...their faces were blue. Anne, without a word of censure, hurried them home, got off their wet clothes and got them into Mrs. Raymond's bed, with hot-water bottles at their feet. They still continued to shiver. Had they got a chill? Were they headed for pneumonia?

"You should have taken better care of us, Miss Shirley," said Gerald, still chattering.

"'Course you should," said Geraldine.

A distracted Anne flew downstairs and telephoned for the doctor. By the time he came the twins had got warm, and he assured Anne that they were in no danger. If they stayed in bed till tomorrow they would be all right.

He met Mrs. Raymond coming up from the station on the way back, and it was a pale, almost hysterical lady who presently rushed in.

"Oh, Miss Shirley, how could you have let my little treasures get into such danger!"

"That's just what we told her, Mother," chorused the twins.

"I trusted you...I told you..."

"I hardly see how I was to blame, Mrs. Raymond," said Anne, with eyes as cold as gray mist. "You will realize this, I think, when you are calmer. The children are quite all right...I simply sent for the doctor as a precautionary measure. If Gerald and Geraldine had obeyed me, this would not have happened."

"I thought a teacher would have a little authority over children," said Mrs. Raymond bitterly.

"Over children perhaps...but not young demons," thought Anne. She said only,

"Since you are here, Mrs. Raymond, I think I will go home. I don't think I can be of any further service and I have some school work to do this evening."

As one child the twins hurled themselves out of bed and flung their arms around her.

"I hope there'll be a funeral every week," cried Gerald. "'Cause I like you, Miss Shirley, and I hope you'll come and look after us every time Mother goes away."

"So do I," said Geraldine.

"I like you ever so much better than Miss Prouty."

"Oh, ever so much," said Geraldine.

"Will you put us in a story?" demanded Gerald.

"Oh, do," said Geraldine.

"I'm sure you meant well," said Mrs. Raymond tremulously.

"Thank you," said Anne icily, trying to detach the twins' clinging arms.

"Oh, don't let's quarrel about it," begged Mrs. Raymond, her enormous eyes filling with tears. "I can't endure quarreling with anybody."

"Certainly not." Anne was at her stateliest and Anne could be very stately. "I don't think there is the slightest necessity for quarreling. I think Gerald and Geraldine have quite enjoyed the day, though I don't suppose poor little Ivy Trent did."

Anne went home feeling years older.

"To think I ever thought Davy was mischievous," she reflected.

She found Rebecca in the twilight garden gathering late pansies.

"Rebecca Dew, I used to think the adage, 'Children should be seen and not heard,' entirely too harsh. But I see its points now."

"My poor darling. I'll get you a nice supper," said Rebecca Dew. And did not say, "I told you so."

5

(Extract from letter to Gilbert.)

"Mrs. Raymond came down last night and, with tears in her eyes, begged me to forgive her for her 'hasty behavior.' 'If you knew a mother's heart, Miss Shirley, you would not find it hard to forgive.'

"I didn't find it hard to forgive as it was...there is really something about Mrs. Raymond I can't help liking and she was a duck about the Dramatic Club. Just the same I did not say, 'Any Saturday you want to be away, I'll look after your offspring.' One learns by experience...even a person so incorrigibly optimistic and trustful as myself.

"I find that a certain section of Summerside society is at present very much exercised over the loves of Jarvis Morrow and Dovie Westcott...who, as Rebecca Dew says, have been engaged for over a year but can't get any 'forrader.' Aunt Kate, who is a distant aunt of Dovie's...to be exact, I think she's the aunt of a second cousin of Dovie's on the mother's side...is deeply interested in the affair because she thinks Jarvis is such an excellent match for Dovie...and also, I suspect, because she hates Franklin Westcott and would like to see him routed, horse, foot and artillery. Not that Aunt Kate would admit she 'hated' anybody, but Mrs. Franklin Westcott was a very dear girlhood friend of hers and Aunt Kate solemnly avers that he murdered her.

"I am interested in it, partly because I'm very fond of Jarvis and moderately fond of Dovie and partly, I begin to suspect, because I am an inveterate meddler in other people's business...always with excellent intentions, of course.

"The situation is briefly this:—Franklin Westcott is a tall, somber, hard-bitten merchant, close and unsociable. He lives in a big, old-fashioned house called Elmcroft just outside the town on the upper harbor road. I have met him once or twice but really know very little about him, except that he has an uncanny habit of saying something and then going off into a long chuckle of soundless laughter. He has never gone to church since hymns came in and he insists on having all his windows open even in winter storms. I confess to a sneaking sympathy with him in this, but I am probably the only person in Summerside who would. He has got into the habit of being a leading citizen and nothing municipal dares to be done without his approval.

"His wife is dead. It is common report that she was a slave, unable to call her soul her own. Franklin told her, it is said, when he brought her home that he would be master.

"Dovie, whose real name is Sibyl, is his only child...a very pretty, plump, lovable girl of nineteen, with a red mouth always falling a little open over her small white teeth, glints of chestnut in her brown hair, alluring blue eyes and sooty lashes so long you wonder if they can be real. Jen Pringle says it is her eyes Jarvis is really in love with. Jen and I have actually talked the affair over. Jarvis is her favorite cousin.

"(In passing, you wouldn't believe how fond Jen is of me...and I of Jen. She's really the cutest thing.)

"Franklin Westcott has never allowed Dovie to have any beaus and when Jarvis Morrow began to 'pay her attention,' he forbade him the house and told Dovie there was to be no more 'running round with that fellow.' But the mischief had been done. Dovie and Jarvis were already fathoms deep in love.

"Everybody in town is in sympathy with the lovers. Franklin

Westcott is really unreasonable. Jarvis is a successful young lawyer, of good family, with good prospects, and a very nice, decent lad in himself.

"'Nothing could be more suitable,' declares Rebecca Dew. 'Jarvis Morrow could have any girl he wanted in Summerside. Franklin Westcott has just made up his mind that Dovie is to be an old maid. He wants to be sure of a housekeeper when Aunt Maggie dies.'

"'Isn't there any one who has any influence with him?' I asked.

"'Nobody can argue with Franklin Westcott. He's too sarcastical. And if you get the better of him he throws a tantrum. I've never seen him in one of his tantrums but I've heard Miss Prouty describe how he acted one time she was there sewing. He got mad over something...nobody knew what. He just grabbed everything in sight and flung it out of the window. Milton's poems went flying clean over the fence into George Clarke's lily pond. He's always kind of had a grudge at life. Miss Prouty says her mother told her that the yelps of him when he was born passed anything she ever heard. I suppose God has some reason for making men like that, but you'd wonder. No, I can't see any chance for Jarvis and Dovie unless they elope. It's a kind of low-down thing to do, though there's been a terrible lot of romantic nonsense talked about eloping. But this is a case where anybody would excuse it.'

"I don't know what to do but I must do something. I simply can't sit still and see people make a mess of their lives under my very nose, no matter how many tantrums Franklin Westcott takes. Jarvis Morrow is not going to wait forever...rumor has it that he is getting out of patience already and has been seen savagely cutting Dovie's name out of a tree on which he had cut it. There is an attractive Palmer girl who is reported to be throwing herself at his head, and his sister is said to have said that his mother has said that her son has no need to dangle for years at any girl's apron-string.

"Really, Gilbert, I'm quite unhappy about it.

"It's moonlight tonight, beloved...moonlight on the poplars of the yard...moonlit dimples all over the harbor where a phantom ship is drifting outwards...moonlight on the old graveyard...on my own private valley...on the Storm King. And it will be moonlight in Lover's Lane and on the Lake of Shining Waters and the old Haunted Wood and Violet Vale. There should be fairy dances on the hills tonight. But, Gilbert dear, moonlight with no one to share it is just...just moonshine.

"I wish I could take little Elizabeth for a walk. She loves a moonlight walk. We had some delightful ones when she was at Green Gables. But at home Elizabeth never sees moonlight except from the window.

"I am beginning to be a little worried about her, too. She is going on ten now and those two old ladies haven't the least idea what she needs, spiritually and emotionally. As long as she has good food and good clothes, they cannot imagine her needing anything more. And it will be worse with every succeeding year. What kind of girlhood will the poor child have?"

6

Jarvis Morrow walked home from the High School Commencement with Anne and told her his woes.

"You'll have to run away with her, Jarvis. Everybody says so. As a rule I don't approve of elopements" ("I said that like a teacher of forty years' experience," thought Anne with an unseen grin) "but there are exceptions to all rules."

"It takes two to make a bargain, Anne. I can't elope alone. Dovie is so frightened of her father, I can't get her to agree. And it wouldn't be an elopement...really. She'd just come to my sister Julia's...Mrs. Stevens, you know...some evening. I'd have the minister there and we could be married respectably enough to please anybody and go over to spend our honeymoon with Aunt Bertha in Kingsport. Simple as that. But I can't get Dovie to chance it. The poor darling has been giving in to her father's whims and crotchets so long, she hasn't any will-power left."

"You'll simply have to make her do it, Jarvis."

"Great Peter, you don't suppose I haven't tried, do you, Anne? I've begged till I was black in the face. When she's with me she'll almost promise it, but the minute she's home again she sends me word she can't. It seems odd, Anne, but the poor child is really fond of her father and she can't bear the thought of his never forgiving her."

"You must tell her she has to choose between her father and you."

"And suppose she chooses him?"

"I don't think there's any danger of that."

"You can never tell," said Jarvis gloomily. "But something has to be decided soon. I can't go on like this forever. I'm crazy about Dovie...everybody in Summerside knows that. She's like a little red rose just out of reach...I must reach her, Anne."

"Poetry is a very good thing in its place, but it won't get you anywhere in this instance, Jarvis," said Anne coolly. "That sounds like a remark Rebecca Dew would make, but it's quite true. What you need in this affair is plain, hard common sense. Tell Dovie you're tired of shilly-shallying and that she must take you or leave you. If she doesn't care enough for you to leave her father for you, it's just as well for you to realize it."

Jarvis groaned.

"You haven't been under the thumb of Franklin Westcott all your life, Anne. You haven't any realization of what he's like. Well, I'll make a last and final effort. As you say, if Dovie really cares for me she'll come to me...and if she doesn't, I might as well know the worst. I'm beginning to feel I've made myself rather ridiculous."

"If you're beginning to feel like that," thought Anne, "Dovie would better watch out."

Dovie herself slipped into Windy Poplars a few evenings later to consult Anne.

"What shall I do, Anne? What can I do? Jarvis wants me to elope...practically. Father is to be in Charlottetown one night next week attending a Masonic banquet...and it would be a good chance. Aunt Maggie would never suspect. Jarvis wants me to go to Mrs. Stevens' and be married there."

"And why don't you, Dovie?"

"Oh, Anne, do you really think I ought to?" Dovie lifted a sweet, coaxing face. "Please, please make up my mind for me. I'm just distracted." Dovie's voice broke on a tearful note. "Oh, Anne, you don't know Father. He just hates Jarvis...I can't imagine why...can you? How can anybody hate Jarvis? When he called on me the first time, Father forbade him the house and told him he'd set the dog on him if he ever came again...our big bull. You know they never let go once they take hold. And he'll never forgive me if I run away with Jarvis."

"You must choose between them, Dovie."

"That's just what Jarvis said," wept Dovie. "Oh, he was so stern...I never saw him like that before. And I can't...I can't live without him, Anne."

"Then live with him, my dear girl. And don't call it eloping. Just coming into Summerside and being married among his friends isn't eloping."

"Father will call it so," said Dovie, swallowing a sob. "But I'm going to take your advice, Anne. I'm sure you wouldn't advise me to take any step that was wrong. I'll tell Jarvis to go ahead and get the license and I'll come to his sister's the night Father is in Charlottetown."

Jarvis told Anne triumphantly that Dovie had yielded at last.

"I'm to meet her at the end of the lane next Tuesday night...she won't have me go down to the house for fear Aunt Maggie might see me...and we'll just step up to Julia's and be married in a brace of shakes. All my folks will be there, so it will make the poor darling quite comfortable. Franklin Westcott said I should never get his daughter. I'll show him he was mistaken."

7

Tuesday was a gloomy day in late November. Occasional cold, gusty showers drifted over the hills. The world seemed a dreary outlived place, seen through a gray drizzle.

"Poor Dovie hasn't a very nice day for her wedding," thought Anne. "Suppose...suppose..." she quaked and shivered..."suppose it doesn't turn out well, after all. It will be my fault. Dovie would never have agreed to it if I hadn't advised her to. And suppose Franklin Westcott never forgives her. Anne Shirley, stop this! The weather is all that's the matter with you."

By night the rain had ceased but the air was cold and raw and the sky lowering. Anne was in her tower room, correcting school papers, with Dusty Miller coiled up under her stove. There came a thunderous knock at the front door.

Anne ran down. Rebecca Dew poked an alarmed head out of her bedroom door. Anne motioned her back.

"It's some one at the front door!" said Rebecca hollowly.

"It's all right, Rebecca dear. At least, I'm afraid it's all wrong...but, anyway, it's only Jarvis Morrow. I saw him from the side tower window and I know he wants to see me."

"Jarvis Morrow!" Rebecca went back and shut her door.

"This is the last straw."

"Jarvis, whatever is the matter?"

"Dovie hasn't come," said Jarvis wildly. "We've waited hours... the minister's there...and my friends...and Julia has supper ready...and Dovie hasn't come. I waited for her at the end of the lane till I was half crazy. I didn't dare go down to the house because I didn't know what had happened. That old brute of a Franklin Westcott may have come back. Aunt Maggie may have locked her up. But I've got to know. Anne, you must go to Elmcroft and find out why she hasn't come."

"Me?" said Anne incredulously and ungrammatically.

"Yes, you. There's no one else I can trust...no one else who knows. Oh, Anne, don't fail me now. You've backed us up right along. Dovie says you are the only real friend she has. It isn't late...only nine. Do go."

"And be chewed up by the bulldog?" said Anne sarcastically.

"That old dog!" said Jarvis contemptuously. "He wouldn't say boo to a tramp. You don't suppose I was afraid of the dog, do you? Besides, he's always shut up at night. I simply don't want to make any trouble for Dovie at home if they've found out. Anne, please!"

"I suppose I'm in for it," said Anne with a shrug of despair.

Jarvis drove her to the long lane of Elmcroft, but she would not let him come further.

"As you say, it might complicate matters for Dovie in case her father has come home."

Anne hurried down the long, tree-bordered lane. The moon occasionally broke through the windy clouds, but for the most part it was gruesomely dark and she was not a little dubious about the dog.

There seemed to be only one light in Elmcroft...shining from the kitchen window. Aunt Maggie herself opened the side door to Anne. Aunt Maggie was a very old sister of Franklin Westcott's, a little bent, wrinkled woman who had never been considered very bright mentally, though she was an excellent housekeeper.

"Aunt Maggie, is Dovie home?"

"Dovie's in bed," said Aunt Maggie stolidly.

"In bed? Is she sick?"

"Not as I knows on. She seemed to be in a dither all day. After supper she says she was tired and ups and goes to bed."

"I must see her for a moment, Aunt Maggie. I...I just want a little important information."

"Better go up to her room then. It's the one on the right side as you go up."

Aunt Maggie gestured to the stairs and waddled out to the kitchen.

Dovie sat up as Anne walked in, rather unceremoniously, after a hurried rap. As could be seen by the light of a tiny candle, Dovie was in tears, but her tears only exasperated Anne.

"Dovie Westcott, did you forget that you promised to marry Jarvis Morrow tonight...tonight?"

"No...no..." whimpered Dovie. "Oh, Anne, I'm so unhappy...I've put in such a dreadful day. You can never, never know what I've gone through."

"I know what poor Jarvis has gone through, waiting for two hours at that lane in the cold and drizzle," said Anne mercilessly.

"Is he...is he very angry, Anne?"

"Just what you could notice"...bitingly.

"Oh, Anne, I just got frightened. I never slept one wink last night. I couldn't go through with it...I couldn't. I...there's really something disgraceful about eloping, Anne. And I wouldn't get any nice presents...well, not many, anyhow. I've always wanted to be m...m...arried in church...with lovely decorations...and a white veil and dress...and s...s...ilver slippers!"

"Dovie Westcott, get right out of that bed...at once...and get dressed...and come with me."

"Anne...it's too late now."

"It isn't too late. And it's now or never...you must know that, Dovie, if you've a grain of sense. You must know Jarvis Morrow will never speak to you again if you make a fool of him like this."

"Oh, Anne, he'll forgive me when he knows..."

"He won't. I know Jarvis Morrow. He isn't going to let you play indefinitely with his life. Dovie, do you want me to drag you bodily out of bed?"

Dovie shuddered and sighed.

"I haven't any suitable dress..."

"You've half-a-dozen pretty dresses. Put on your rose taffeta."

"And I haven't any trousseau. The Morrows will always cast that up to me..."

"You can get one afterwards. Dovie, didn't you weigh all these things in the balance before?"

"No...no...that's just the trouble. I only began to think of them last night. And Father...you don't know Father, Anne..."

"Dovie. I'll give you just ten minutes to get dressed!"

Dovie was dressed in the specified time.

"This dress is g...g...getting too tight for me," she sobbed as Anne hooked her up. "If I get much fatter I don't suppose Jarvis will l...l...love me. I wish I was tall and slim and pale, like you, Anne. Oh, Anne, what if Aunt Maggie hears us!"

"She won't. She's shut in the kitchen and you know she's a little deaf. Here's your hat and coat and I've tumbled a few things into this bag."

"Oh, my heart is fluttering so. Do I look terrible, Anne?"

"You look lovely," said Anne sincerely. Dovie's satin skin was rose and cream and all her tears hadn't spoiled her eyes. But Jarvis couldn't see her eyes in the dark and he was just a little annoyed with his adored fair one and rather cool during the drive to town.

"For Heaven's sake, Dovie, don't look so scared over having to marry me," he said impatiently as she came down the stairs of the Stevens house. "And don't cry...it will make your nose swell. It's nearly ten o'clock and we've got to catch the eleven o'clock train."

Dovie was quite all right as soon as she found herself irrevocably married to Jarvis. What Anne rather cattishly described in a letter to Gilbert as "the honeymoon look" was already on her face.

"Anne, darling, we owe it all to you. We'll never forget it, will we, Jarvis? And, oh, Anne darling, will you do just one more thing for me? Please break the news to Father. He'll be home early tomorrow evening...and somebody has got to tell him. You can smooth him over if anybody can. Please do your best to get him to forgive me."

Anne felt she rather needed some smoothing-over herself just then; but she also felt rather uneasily responsible for the outcome of the affair, so she gave the required promise.

"Of course he'll be terrible...simply terrible, Anne...but he can't kill you," said Dovie comfortingly. "Oh, Anne, you don't know...you can't realize...how safe I feel with Jarvis."

When Anne got home Rebecca Dew had reached the point where she had to satisfy her curiosity or go mad. She followed Anne to the tower room in her night-dress, with a square of flannel wrapped round her head, and heard the whole story.

"Well, I suppose this is what you might call 'life,'" she said sarcastically. "But I'm real glad Franklin Westcott has got his come-uppance at last, and so will Mrs. Captain MacComber be. But I don't envy you the job of breaking the news to him. He'll rage and utter vain things. If I was in your shoes, Miss Shirley, I wouldn't sleep one blessed wink tonight."

"I feel that it won't be a very pleasant experience," agreed Anne ruefully.

8

Anne betook herself to Elmcroft the next evening, walking through the dream-like landscape of a November fog with a rather sinking sensation pervading her being. It was not exactly a delightful errand. As Dovie had said, of course Franklin Westcott wouldn't kill her. Anne did not fear physical violence...though if all the tales told of him were true, he might throw something at her. Would he gibber with rage? Anne had never seen a man gibbering with rage and she imagined it must be a rather unpleasant sight. But he would probably exercise his noted gift for unpleasant sarcasm, and sarcasm, in man or woman, was the one weapon Anne dreaded. It always hurt her...raised blisters on her soul that smarted for months.

"Aunt Jamesina used to say, 'Never, if you can help it, be the bringer of ill news,'" reflected Anne. "She was as wise in that as in everything else. Well, here I am."

Elmcroft was an old-fashioned house with towers at every corner and a bulbous cupola on the roof. And at the top of the flight of front steps sat the dog.

"'If they take hold they never let go,'" remembered Anne. Should she try going round to the side door? Then the thought that Franklin Westcott might be watching her from the window braced her up. Never would she give him the satisfaction of seeing that she was afraid of his dog. Resolutely, her head held high, she marched up the steps, past the dog and rang the bell. The dog had not stirred. When Anne glanced at him over her shoulder he was apparently asleep.

Franklin Westcott, it transpired, was not at home but was expected every minute, as the Charlottetown train was due. Aunt Maggie convoyed Anne into what she called the "liberry" and left her there. The dog had got up and followed them in. He came and arranged himself at Anne's feet.

Anne found herself liking the "liberry." It was a cheerful, shabby room, with a fire glowing cozily in the grate, and bearskin rugs on the worn red carpet of the floor. Franklin Westcott evidently did himself well in regard to books and pipes.

Presently she heard him come in. He hung up his hat and coat in the hall: he stood in the library doorway with a very decided scowl on his brow. Anne recalled that her impression of him the first time she had seen him was that of a rather gentlemanly pirate, and she felt a repetition of it.

"Oh, it's you, is it?" he said rather gruffly. "Well, and what do you want?"

He had not even offered to shake hands with her. Of the two, Anne thought the dog had decidedly the better manners.

"Mr. Westcott, please hear me through patiently before..."

"I am patient...very patient. Proceed!"

Anne decided that there was no use beating about the bush with a man like Franklin Westcott.

"I have come to tell you," she said steadily, "that Dovie has married Jarvis Morrow."

Then she waited for the earthquake. None came. Not a muscle of Franklin Westcott's lean brown face changed. He came in and sat down in the bandy-legged leather chair opposite

Anne.

"When?" he said.

"Last night...at his sister's," said Anne.

Franklin Westcott looked at her for a moment out of yellowish brown eyes deeply set under penthouses of grizzled eyebrow. Anne had a moment of wondering what he had looked like when he was a baby. Then he threw back his head and went into one of his spasms of soundless laughter.

"You mustn't blame Dovie, Mr. Westcott," said Anne earnestly, recovering her powers of speech now that the awful revelation was over. "It wasn't her fault..."

"I'll bet it wasn't," said Franklin Westcott.

Was he trying to be sarcastic?

"No, it was all mine," said Anne, simply and bravely. "I advised her to elo...to be married...I made her do it. So please forgive her, Mr. Westcott."

Franklin Westcott coolly picked up a pipe and began to fill it.

"If you've managed to make Sibyl elope with Jarvis Morrow, Miss Shirley, you've accomplished more than I ever thought anybody could. I was beginning to be afraid she'd never have backbone enough to do it. And then I'd have had to back down...and Lord, how we Westcotts hate backing down! You've saved my face, Miss Shirley, and I'm profoundly grateful to you."

There was a very loud silence while Franklin Westcott tamped his tobacco down and looked with an amused twinkle at Anne's face. Anne was so much at sea she didn't know what to say.

"I suppose," he said, "that you came here in fear and trembling to break the terrible news to me?"

"Yes," said Anne, a trifle shortly.

Franklin Westcott chuckled soundlessly.

"You needn't have. You couldn't have brought me more welcome news. Why, I picked Jarvis Morrow out for Sibyl when they were kids. Soon as the other boys began taking notice of her, I shooed them off. That gave Jarvis his first notion of her. He'd show the old man! But he was so popular with the girls that I could hardly believe the incredible luck when he did really take a genuine fancy to her. Then I laid out my plan of campaign. I knew the Morrows root and branch. You don't. They're a good family, but the men don't want things they can get easily. And they're determined to get a thing when they're told they can't. They always go by contraries. Jarvis' father broke three girls' hearts because their families threw them at his head. In Jarvis' case I knew exactly what would happen. Sibyl would fall head over heels in love with him...and he'd be tired of her in no time. I knew he wouldn't keep on wanting her if she was too easy to get. So I forbade him to come near the place and forbade Sibyl to have a word to say to him and generally played the heavy parent to perfection. Talk about the charm of the uncaught! It's nothing to the charm of the uncatchable. It all worked out according to schedule, but I struck a snag in Sibyl's spinelessness. She's a nice child but she is spineless. I've been thinking she'd never have the pluck to marry him in my teeth. Now, if you've got your breath back, my dear young lady, unbosom yourself of the whole story."

Anne's sense of humor had again come to her rescue. She could never refuse an opportunity for a good laugh, even when it was on herself. And she suddenly felt very well acquainted with Franklin Westcott.

He listened to the tale, taking quiet, enjoyable whiffs of his pipe. When Anne had finished he nodded comfortably.

"I see I'm more in your debt even than I thought. She'd never have got up the courage to do it if it hadn't been for you. And Jarvis Morrow wouldn't have risked being made a fool of twice...not if I know the breed. Gosh, but I've had a narrow escape! I'm yours to command for life. You're a real brick to come here as you did, believing all the yarns gossip told you. You've been told a-plenty, haven't you now?"

Anne nodded. The bulldog had got his head on her lap and was snoring blissfully.

"Every one agreed that you were cranky, crabbed and

crusty," she said candidly.

"And I suppose they told you I was a tyrant and made my poor wife's life miserable and ruled my family with a rod of iron?"

"Yes; but I really did take all that with a grain of salt, Mr. Westcott. I felt that Dovie couldn't be as fond of you as she was if you were as dreadful as gossip painted you."

"Sensible gal! My wife was a happy woman, Miss Shirley. And when Mrs. Captain MacComber tells you I bullied her to death, tick her off for me. Excuse my common way. Mollie was pretty...prettier than Sibyl. Such a pink-and-white skin...such golden-brown hair...such dewy blue eyes! She was the prettiest woman in Summerside. Had to be. I couldn't have stood it if a man had walked into church with a handsomer wife than me. I ruled my household as a man should but not tyrannically. Oh, of course, I had a spell of temper now and then, but Mollie didn't mind them after she got used to them. A man has a right to have a row with his wife now and then, hasn't he? Women get tired of monotonous husbands. Besides, I always gave her a ring or a necklace or some such gaud after I calmed down. There wasn't a woman in Summerside had more nice jewelry. I must get it out and give it to Sibyl."

Anne went wicked.

"What about Milton's poems?"

"Milton's poems? Oh, that! It wasn't Milton's poems...it was Tennyson's. I reverence Milton but I can't abide Alfred. He's too sickly sweet. Those last two lines of Enoch Arden made me so mad one night, I did fire the book through the window. But I picked it up the next day for the sake of the Bugle Song. I'd forgive anybody anything for that. It didn't go into George Clarke's lily pond—that was old Prouty's embroidery. You're not going? Stay and have a bite of supper with a lonely old fellow robbed of his only whelp."

"I'm really sorry I can't, Mr. Westcott, but I have to attend a meeting of the staff tonight."

"Well, I'll be seeing you when Sibyl comes back. I'll have to fling a party for them, no doubt. Good gosh, what a relief this has been to my mind. You've no idea how I'd have hated to have to back down and say, 'Take her.' Now all I have to do is to pretend to be heart-broken and resigned and forgive her sadly for the sake of her poor mother. I'll do it beautifully...Jarvis must never suspect. Don't you give the show away."

"I won't," promised Anne.

Franklin Westcott saw her courteously to the door. The bulldog sat up on his haunches and cried after her.

Franklin Westcott took his pipe out of his mouth at the door and tapped her on the shoulder with it..

"Always remember," he said solemnly, "there's more than

one way to skin a cat. It can be done so that the animal'll never know he's lost his hide. Give my love to Rebecca Dew. A nice old puss, if you stroke her the right way. And thank you...thank you."

Anne betook herself home, through the soft, calm evening. The fog had cleared, the wind had shifted and there was a look of frost in the pale green sky.

"People told me I didn't know Franklin Westcott," reflected Anne. "They were right...I didn't. And neither did they."

"How did he take it?" Rebecca Dew was keen to know. She had been on tenterhooks during Anne's absence.

"Not so badly after all," said Anne confidentially. "I think he'll forgive Dovie in time."

"I never did see the beat of you, Miss Shirley, for talking people round," said Rebecca Dew admiringly. "You have certainly got a way with you."

"'Something attempted, something done has earned a night's repose,'" quoted Anne wearily as she climbed the three steps into her bed that night. "But just wait till the next person asks my advice about eloping!"

9

(Extract from letter to Gilbert.)

"I am invited to have supper tomorrow night with a lady of Summerside. I know you won't believe me, Gilbert, when I tell you her name is Tomgallon...Miss Minerva Tomgallon. You'll say I've been reading Dickens too long and too late.

"Dearest, aren't you glad your name is Blythe? I am sure I could never marry you if it were Tomgallon. Fancy...Anne Tomgallon! No, you can't fancy it.

"This is the ultimate honor Summerside has to bestow...an invitation to Tomgallon House. It has no other name. No nonsense about Elms or Chestnuts or Crofts for the Tomgallons.

"I understand they were the 'Royal Family' in old days. The Pringles are mushrooms compared to them. And now there is left of them all only Miss Minerva, the sole survivor of six generations of Tomgallons. She lives alone in a huge house on Queen Street...a house with great chimneys, green shutters and the only stained-glass window in a private house in town. It is big enough for four families and is occupied only by Miss Minerva, a cook and a maid. It is very well kept up, but somehow whenever I walk past it I feel that it is a place which life has forgotten.

"Miss Minerva goes out very little, excepting to the Anglican church, and I had never met her until a few weeks ago, when she came to a meeting of staff and trustees to make a formal gift of her father's valuable library to the school. She looks exactly as you would expect a Minerva Tomgallon to look...tall and thin, with a long, narrow white face, a long thin nose and a long thin mouth. That doesn't sound very attractive, yet Miss Minerva is quite handsome in a stately, aristocratic style and is always dressed with great, though somewhat old-fashioned, elegance. She was quite a beauty when she was young, Rebecca Dew tells me, and her large black eyes are still full of fire and dark luster. She suffers from no lack of words, and I don't think I ever heard any one enjoy making a presentation speech more.

"Miss Minerva was especially nice to me, and yesterday I received a formal little note inviting me to have supper with her. When I told Rebecca Dew, she opened her eyes as widely as if I had been invited to Buckingham Palace.

"'It's a great honor to be asked to Tomgallon House,' she said in a rather awed tone. I never heard of Miss Minerva asking any of the principals there before. To be sure, they were all men, so I suppose it would hardly have been proper. Well, I hope she won't talk you to death, Miss Shirley. The Tomgallons could all talk the hind leg off a cat. And they liked to be in the front of things. Some folks think the reason Miss Minerva lives so retired is because now that she's old she can't take the lead as she used to do and she won't play second fiddle to any one. What are you going to wear, Miss Shirley? I'd like to see you wear your cream silk gauze with your black velvet bows. It's so dressy.'

"'I'm afraid it would be rather too "dressy" for a quiet evening out,' I said.

"'Miss Minerva would like it, I think. The Tomgallons all liked their company to be nicely arrayed. They say Miss Minerva's grandfather once shut the door in the face of a woman who had been asked there to a ball, because she came in her second-best dress. He told her her best was none too good for the Tomgallons.'

"Nevertheless, I think I'll wear my green voile, and the ghosts of the Tomgallons must make the best of it.

"I'm going to confess something I did last week, Gilbert. I suppose you'll think I'm meddling again in other folks' business. But I had to do something. I'll not be in Summerside next year and I can't bear the thought of leaving little Elizabeth to the mercy of those two unloving old women who are growing bitterer and narrower every year. What kind of a girlhood will she have with them in that gloomy old place?

"'I wonder,' she said to me wistfully, not long ago, 'what it would be like to have a grandmother you weren't afraid of.'

"This is what I did: I wrote to her father. He lives in Paris and I didn't know his address, but Rebecca Dew had heard and remembered the name of the firm whose branch he runs there, so I took a chance and addressed him in care of it. I wrote as diplomatic a letter as I could, but I told him plainly that he ought to take Elizabeth. I told him how she longs for and dreams about him and that Mrs. Campbell was really too severe and strict with her. Perhaps nothing will come of it, but if I hadn't written I would be forever haunted by the conviction that I ought to have done it.

"What made me think of it was Elizabeth telling me very seriously one day that she had 'written a letter to God,' asking Him to bring her father back to her and make him love her. She said she had stopped on the way home from school, in the middle of a vacant lot, and read it, looking up at the sky. I knew she had done something odd, because Miss Prouty had seen the performance and told me about it when she came to sew for the widows next day. She thought Elizabeth was getting 'queer'...'talking to the sky like that.'

"I asked Elizabeth about it and she told me.

"'I thought God might pay more attention to a letter than a prayer,' she said. 'I've prayed so long. He must get so many prayers.'

"That night I wrote to her father.

"Before I close I must tell you about Dusty Miller. Some time ago Aunt Kate told me that she felt she must find another home for him because Rebecca Dew kept complaining about him so that she felt she really could not endure it any longer. One evening last week when I came home from school there was no Dusty Miller. Aunt Chatty said they had given him to Mrs. Edmonds, who lives on the other side of Summerside from Windy Poplars. I felt sorry, for Dusty Miller and I have been excellent friends. 'But, at least,' I thought, 'Rebecca Dew will be a happy woman.'

"Rebecca was away for the day, having gone to the country to help a relative hook rugs. When she returned at dusk nothing was said, but at bedtime when she was calling Dusty Miller from the back porch Aunt Kate said quietly:

"'You needn't call Dusty Miller, Rebecca. He is not here. We have found a home for him elsewhere. You will not be bothered with him any more.'

"If Rebecca Dew could have turned pale she would have done so.

"'Not here? Found a home for him? Good grief! Isn't this his home?'

"'We have given him to Mrs. Edmonds. She has been very lonely since her daughter married and thought a nice cat would be company.'

"Rebecca Dew came in and shut the door. She looked very wild.

"'This is the last straw,' she said. And indeed it seemed to be. I've never seen Rebecca Dew's eyes emit such sparkles of rage. 'I'll be leaving at the end of the month, Mrs. MacComber, and sooner if you can be suited.'

"'But, Rebecca,' said Aunt Kate in bewilderment, 'I don't understand. You've always disliked Dusty Miller. Only last week you said...'

"'That's right,' said Rebecca bitterly. 'Cast things up to me! Don't have any regard for my feelings! That poor dear Cat! I've waited on him and pampered him and got up nights to let him in. And now he's been spirited away behind my back without so much as a by-your-leave. And to Sarah Edmonds, who wouldn't buy a bit of liver for the poor creature if he was dying for it! The only company I had in the kitchen!'

"'But, Rebecca, you've always...'

"'Oh, keep on...keep on! Don't let me get a word in edgewise, Mrs. MacComber. I've raised that cat from a kitten...I've looked after his health and his morals...and what for? That Jane Edmonds should have a well-trained cat for company. Well, I hope she'll stand out in the frost at nights, as I've done, calling that cat for hours rather than leave him out to freeze, but I doubt it...I seriously doubt it. Well, Mrs. MacComber, all I hope is that your conscience won't trouble you the next time it's ten below zero. I won't sleep a wink when it happens, but of course that doesn't matter an old shoe to any one.'

"'Rebecca, if you would only...'

"'Mrs. MacComber, I am not a worm, neither am I a doormat. Well, this has been a lesson for me...a valuable lesson! Never again will I allow my affections to twine themselves around an animal of any kind or description. And if you'd done it open and aboveboard...but behind my back...taking advantage of me like that! I never heard of anything so dirt mean! But who am I that I should expect my feelings to be considered!'

"'Rebecca,' said Aunt Kate desperately, 'if you want Dusty Miller back we can get him back.'

"'Why didn't you say so before then?' demanded Rebecca Dew. 'And I doubt it. Jane Edmonds has got her claws in him. Is it likely she'll give him up?'

"'I think she will,' said Aunt Kate, who had apparently reverted to jelly. 'And if he comes back you won't leave us, will you, Rebecca?'

"'I may think it over,' said Rebecca, with the air of one making a tremendous concession.

"Next day, Aunt Chatty brought Dusty Miller home in a covered basket. I caught a glance exchanged between her and Aunt

Kate after Rebecca had carried Dusty Miller out to the kitchen and shut the door. I wonder! Was it all a deep-laid plot on the part of the widows, aided and abetted by Jane Edmonds?

"Rebecca has never uttered a word of complaint about Dusty Miller since and there is a veritable clang of victory in her voice when she shouts for him at bedtime. It sounds as if she wanted all Summerside to know that Dusty Miller is back where he belongs and that she has once more got the better of the widows!"

10

It was on a dark, windy March evening, when even the clouds scudding over the sky seemed in a hurry, that Anne skimmed up the triple flight of broad, shallow steps flanked by stone urns and stonier lions, that led to the massive front door of Tomgallon House. Usually, when she had passed it after dark it was somber and grim, with a dim twinkle of light in one or two windows. But now it blazed forth brilliantly, even the wings on either side being lighted up, as if Miss Minerva were entertaining the whole town. Such an illumination in her honor rather overcame Anne. She almost wished she had put on her cream gauze.

Nevertheless she looked very charming in her green voile and perhaps Miss Minerva, meeting her in the hall, thought so, for her face and voice were very cordial. Miss Minerva herself was regal in black velvet, a diamond comb in the heavy coils of her iron-gray hair and a massive cameo brooch surrounded by a braid of some departed Tomgallon's hair. The whole costume was a little outmoded, but Miss Minerva wore it with such a grand air that it seemed as timeless as royalty's.

"Welcome to Tomgallon House, my dear," she said, giving Anne a bony hand, likewise well sprinkled with diamonds. "I am very glad to have you here as my guest."

"I am..."

"Tomgallon House was always the resort of beauty and youth in the old days. We used to have a great many parties and entertained all the visiting celebrities," said Miss Minerva, leading Anne to the big staircase over a carpet of faded red velvet. "But all is changed now. I entertain very little. I am the last of the Tomgallons. Perhaps it is as well. Our family, my dear, are under a curse."

Miss Minerva infused such a gruesome tinge of mystery and horror into her tones that Anne almost shivered. The Curse of the Tomgallons! What a title for a story!

"This is the stair down which my Great-grandfather Tomgallon fell and broke his neck the night of his house-warming given to celebrate the completion of his new home. This house was consecrated by human blood. He fell there..." Miss Minerva pointed a long white finger so dramatically at a tiger-skin rug in the hall that Anne could almost see the departed Tomgallon dying on it. She really did not know what to say, so said inanely, "Oh!"

Miss Minerva ushered her along a hall, hung with portraits and photographs of faded loveliness, with the famous stained-glass window at its end, into a large, high-ceilinged, very stately guest-room. The high walnut bed, with its huge headboard, was covered with so gorgeous a silken quilt that Anne felt it was a desecration to lay her coat and hat on it.

"You have very beautiful hair, my dear," said Miss Minerva admiringly. "I always liked red hair. My Aunt Lydia had it...she was the only red-haired Tomgallon. One night when she was brushing it in the north room it caught fire from her candle and she ran shrieking down the hall wrapped in flames. All part of the Curse, my dear...all part of the Curse."

"Was she..."

"No, she wasn't burned to death, but she lost all her beauty. She was very handsome and vain. She never went out of the house from that night to the day of her death and she left directions that her coffin was to be shut so that no one might see her scarred face. Won't you sit down to remove your rubbers, my dear? This is a very comfortable chair. My sister died in it from a stroke. She was a widow and came back home to live after her husband's death. Her little girl was scalded in our kitchen with a pot of boiling water. Wasn't that a tragic way for a child to die?"

"Oh, how..."

"But at least we knew how it died. My half-aunt Eliza...at least, she would have been my half-aunt if she had lived...just disappeared when she was six years old. Nobody ever knew what became of her."

"But surely..."

"Every search was made but nothing was ever discovered. It was said that her mother...my step-grandmother...had been very cruel to an orphan niece of my grandfather's who was being brought up here. She locked it up in the closet at the head of the stairs, one hot summer day, for punishment and when she went to let it out she found it...dead. Some people thought it was a judgment on her when her own child vanished. But I think it was just Our Curse."

"Who put...?"

"What a high instep you have, my dear! My instep used to be admired too. It was said a stream of water could run under it...the test of an aristocrat."

Miss Minerva modestly poked a slipper from under her velvet skirt and revealed what was undoubtedly a very handsome foot.

"It certainly..."

"Would you like to see over the house, my dear, before we have supper? It used to be the Pride of Summerside. I suppose everything is very old-fashioned now, but perhaps there are a few things of interest. That sword hanging by the head of the stairs belonged to my great-great-grandfather who was an officer in the British Army and received a grant of land in Prince Edward Island for his services. He never lived in this house, but my great-great-grandmother did for a few weeks. She did not long survive her son's tragic death."

Miss Minerva marched Anne ruthlessly over the whole huge house, full of great square rooms...ballroom, conservatory, billiard-room, three drawing-rooms, breakfast-room, no end of bedrooms and an enormous attic. They were all splendid and dismal.

"Those were my Uncle Ronald and my Uncle Reuben," said Miss Minerva, indicating two worthies who seemed to be scowling at each other from the opposite sides of a fireplace. "They were twins and they hated each other bitterly from birth. The house rang with their quarrels. It darkened their mother's whole life. And during their final quarrel in this very room, while a thunderstorm was going on, Reuben was killed by a flash of lightning. Ronald never got over it. He was a haunted man from that day. His wife," Miss Minerva added reminiscently, "swallowed her wedding-ring."

"What an ex..."

"Ronald thought it was very careless and wouldn't have anything done. A prompt emetic might have...but it was never heard of again. It spoiled her life. She always felt so unmarried without a wedding-ring."

"What a beautiful..."

"Oh, yes, that was my Aunt Emilia...not my aunt really, of course. Just the wife of Uncle Alexander. She was noted for her spiritual look, but she poisoned her husband with a stew of mushrooms...toadstools really. We always pretended it was an accident, because a murder is such a messy thing to have in a family, but we all knew the truth. Of course she married him against her will. She was a gay young thing and he was far too old for her. December and May, my dear. Still, that did not really justify toadstools. She went into a decline soon afterwards. They are buried together in Charlottetown...all the Tomgallons bury in Charlottetown. This was my Aunt Louise. She drank laudanum. The doctor pumped it out and saved her, but we all felt we could never trust her again. It was really rather a relief when she died respectably of pneumonia. Of course, some of us didn't blame her much. You see, my dear, her husband had spanked her."

"Spanked..."

"Exactly. There are really some things no gentleman should do, my dear, and one of them is spank his wife. Knock her down...possibly...but spank her, never! I would like," said Miss Minerva, very majestically, "to see the man who would dare to spank me."

Anne felt she would like to see him also. She realized that there are limits to the imagination after all. By no stretch of hers could she imagine a husband spanking Miss Minerva Tomgallon.

"This is the ballroom. Of course it is never used now. But there have been any number of balls here. The Tomgallon balls were famous. People came from all over the Island to them. That chandelier cost my father five hundred dollars. My Great-aunt Patience dropped dead while dancing here one night...right there in that corner. She had fretted a great deal over a man who had disappointed her. I cannot imagine any girl breaking her heart over a man. Men," said Miss Minerva, staring at a photograph of her father...a person with bristling side-whiskers and a hawk-like nose..."have always seemed to me such trivial creatures."

11

The dining-room was in keeping with the rest of the house. There was another ornate chandelier, an equally ornate, gilt-framed mirror over the mantelpiece, and a table beautifully set with silver and crystal and old Crown Derby. The supper, served by a rather grim and ancient maid, was bountiful and exceedingly good, and Anne's healthy young appetite did full justice to it. Miss Minerva kept silence for a time and Anne dared say nothing for fear of starting another avalanche of tragedies. Once a large, sleek black cat came into the room and sat down by Miss Minerva with a hoarse meow. Miss Minerva poured a saucer of cream and set it down before him. She seemed so much more human after this that Anne lost a good deal of her awe of the last of the Tomgallons.

"Do have some more of the peaches, my dear. You've eaten nothing...positively nothing."

"Oh, Miss Tomgallon, I've enjoyed..."

"The Tomgallons always set a good table," said Miss Minerva complacently. "My Aunt Sophia made the best sponge-cake I ever tasted. I think the only person my father ever really hated to see come to our house was his sister Mary, because she had such a poor appetite. She just minced and tasted. He took it as a personal insult. Father was a very unrelenting man. He never forgave my brother Richard for marrying against his will. He ordered him out of the house and he was never allowed to enter it again. Father always repeated the Lord's Prayer at family worship every morning, but after Richard flouted him he always left out the sentence, 'Forgive us our trespasses as we forgive those who trespass against us.' I can see him," said Miss Minerva dreamily, "kneeling there leaving it out."

After supper they went to the smallest of the three drawing-rooms...which was still rather big and grim...and spent the evening before the huge fire...a pleasant, friendly enough fire. Anne crocheted at a set of intricate doilies and Miss Minerva knitted away at an afghan and kept up what was practically a monologue composed in great part of colorful and gruesome Tomgallon history.

"This is a house of tragical memories, my dear."

"Miss Tomgallon, didn't any pleasant thing ever happen in this house?" asked Anne, achieving a complete sentence by a mere fluke. Miss Minerva had had to stop talking long enough to blow her nose.

"Oh, I suppose so," said Miss Minerva, as if she hated to admit it. "Yes, of course, we used to have gay times here when I was a girl. They tell me you're writing a book about every one in Summerside, my dear."

"I'm not...there isn't a word of truth..."

"Oh!" Miss Minerva was plainly a little disappointed. "Well, if ever you do you are at liberty to use any of our stories you like, perhaps with the names disguised. And now what do you say to a game of parchesi?"

"I'm afraid it is time I was going..."

"Oh, my dear, you can't go home tonight. It's pouring cats and dogs...and listen to the wind. I don't keep a carriage now...I have so little use for one...and you can't walk half a mile in that deluge. You must be my guest for the night."

Anne was not sure she wanted to spend a night in Tomgallon House. But neither did she want to walk to Windy Poplars in a March tempest. So they had their game of parchesi...in which Miss Minerva was so interested that she forgot to talk about horrors...and then a "bedtime snack." They ate cinnamon toast and drank cocoa out of old Tomgallon cups of marvelous thinness and beauty.

Finally Miss Minerva took her up to a guest-room which Anne at first was glad to see was not the one where Miss Minerva's sister had died of a stroke.

"This is Aunt Annabella's room," said Miss Minerva, lighting the candles in the silver candlesticks on a rather pretty green dressing-table and turning out the gas. Matthew Tomgallon had blown out the gas one night...whereupon exit Matthew

Tomgallon. "She was the handsomest of all the Tomgallons. That's her picture above the mirror. Do you notice what a proud mouth she had? She made that crazy quilt on the bed. I hope you'll be comfortable, my dear. Mary has aired the bed and put two hot bricks in it. And she has aired this night-dress for you..." pointing to an ample flannel garment hanging over a chair and smelling strongly of moth balls. "I hope it will fit you. It hasn't been worn since poor Mother died in it. Oh, I nearly forgot to tell you..." Miss Minerva turned back at the door..."this is the room Oscar Tomgallon came back to life in—after being thought dead for two days. They didn't want him to, you know—that was the tragedy. I hope you'll sleep well, my dear."

Anne did not know if she could sleep at all or not. Suddenly there seemed something strange and alien in the room...something a little hostile. But is there not something strange about any room that has been occupied through generations? Death has lurked in it...love has been rosy red in it...births have been here...all the passions...all the hopes. It is full of wraths.

But this was really rather a terrible old house, full of the ghosts of dead hatreds and heart-breaks, crowded with dark deeds that had never been dragged into light and were still festering in its corners and hidy-holes. Too many women must have wept here. The wind wailed very eerily in the spruces by the window. For a moment Anne felt like running out, storm or no storm.

Then she took herself resolutely in hand and commanded common sense. If tragic and dreadful things had happened here, many shadowy years agone, amusing and lovely things must have happened, too. Gay and pretty girls had danced here and talked over their charming secrets; dimpled babies had been born here; there had been weddings and balls and music and laughter. The sponge-cake lady must have been a comfortable creature and the unforgiven Richard a gallant lover.

"I'll think on these things and go to bed. What a quilt to sleep under! I wonder if I'll be as crazy as it by morning. And this is a spare room! I've never forgotten what a thrill it used to give me to sleep in any one's spare room."

Anne uncoiled and brushed her hair under the very nose of Annabella Tomgallon, who stared down at her with a face in which there were pride and vanity, and something of the insolence of great beauty. Anne felt a little creepy as she looked in the mirror. Who knew what faces might look out of it at her? All the tragic and haunted ladies who had ever looked into it, perhaps. She bravely opened the closet door, half expecting any number of skeletons to tumble out, and hung up her dress. She sat down calmly on a rigid chair, which looked as if it would be insulted if anybody sat on it, and took off her shoes.

Then she put on the flannel nightgown, blew out the candles and got into the bed, pleasantly warm from Mary's bricks. For a little while the rain streaming on the panes and the shriek of the wind around the old eaves prevented her from sleeping. Then she forgot all the Tomgallon tragedies in dreamless slumber until she found herself looking at dark fir boughs against a red sunrise.

"I've enjoyed having you so much, my dear," said Miss Minerva when Anne left after breakfast. "We've had a real cheerful visit, haven't we? Though I've lived so long alone I've almost forgotten how to talk. And I need not say what a delight it is to meet a really charming and unspoiled young girl in this frivolous age. I didn't tell you yesterday but it was my birthday, and it was very pleasant to have a bit of youth in the house. There is nobody to remember my birthday now..." Miss Minerva gave a faint sigh..."and once there were so many."

"Well, I suppose you heard a pretty grim chronicle," said Aunt Chatty that night.

"Did all those things Miss Minerva told me really happen, Aunt Chatty?"

"Well, the queer thing is, they did," said Aunt Chatty. "It's a curious thing, Miss Shirley, but a lot of awful things did happen to the Tomgallons."

"I don't know that there were many more than happen in any

large family in the course of six generations," said Aunt Kate.

"Oh, I think there were. They really did seem under a curse. So many of them died sudden or violent deaths. Of course there is a streak of insanity in them...every one knows that. That was curse enough...but I've heard an old story...I can't recall the details...of the carpenter who built the house cursing it. Something about the contract...old Paul Tomgallon held him to it and it ruined him, it cost so much more than he had figured."

"Miss Minerva seems rather proud of the curse," said Anne.

"Poor old thing, it's all she has," said Rebecca Dew.

Anne smiled to think of the stately Miss Minerva being referred to as a poor old thing. But she went to the tower room and wrote to Gilbert:

"I thought Tomgallon House was a sleepy old place where nothing ever happened. Well, perhaps things don't happen now but evidently they did. Little Elizabeth is always talking of Tomorrow. But the old Tomgallon house is Yesterday. I'm glad I don't live in Yesterday...that Tomorrow is still a friend.

"Of course I think Miss Minerva has all the Tomgallon liking for the spotlight and gets no end of satisfaction out of her tragedies. They are to her what husband and children are to other women. But, oh, Gilbert, no matter how old we get in years to come, don't let's ever see life as all tragedy and revel in it. I think I'd hate a house one hundred and twenty years old.

I hope when we get our house of dreams it will either be new, ghostless and traditionless, or, if that can't be, at least have been occupied by reasonably happy people. I shall never forget my night at Tomgallon House. And for once in my life I've met a person who could talk me down."

12

Little Elizabeth Grayson had been born expecting things to happen. That they seldom happened under the watchful eyes of Grandmother and the Woman never brighted her expectations in the least. Things were just bound to happen some time...if not today, then tomorrow.

When Miss Shirley came to live at Windy Poplars Elizabeth felt that Tomorrow must be very close at hand and her visit to Green Gables was like a foretaste of it. But now in the June of Miss Shirley's third and last year in Summerside High, little Elizabeth's heart had descended into the nice buttoned boots Grandmother always got for her to wear. Many children at the school where she went envied little Elizabeth those beautiful buttoned kid boots. But little Elizabeth cared nothing about buttoned boots when she could not tread the way to freedom in them. And now her adored Miss Shirley was going away from her forever. At the end of June she would be leaving Summerside and going back to that beautiful Green Gables. Little Elizabeth simply could not bear the thought of it. It was of no use for Miss Shirley to promise that she would have her down to Green Gables in the summer before she was married. Little Elizabeth knew somehow that Grandmother would not let her go again. Little Elizabeth knew Grandmother had never really approved of her intimacy with Miss Shirley.

"It will be the end of everything, Miss Shirley," she sobbed.

"Let's hope, darling, that it is only a new beginning," said Anne cheerfully. But she felt downcast herself. No word had ever come from little Elizabeth's father. Either her letter had never reached him or he did not care. And, if he did not care, what was to become of Elizabeth? It was bad enough now in her childhood, but what would it be later on?

"Those two old dames will boss her to death," Rebecca Dew had said. Anne felt that there was more truth than elegance in her remark.

Elizabeth knew that she was "bossed." And she especially resented being bossed by the Woman. She did not like it in Grandmother, of course, but one conceded reluctantly that perhaps a grandmother had a certain right to boss you. But what right had the Woman? Elizabeth always wanted to ask her that right out. She would do it some time...when Tomorrow came.

And oh, how she would enjoy the look on the Woman's face!

Grandmother would never let little Elizabeth go out walking by herself...for fear, she said, that she might be kidnaped by gypsies. A child had been once, forty years before. It was very seldom gypsies came to the Island now, and little Elizabeth felt that it was only an excuse. But why should Grandmother care whether she were kidnaped or not? Elizabeth knew that Grandmother and the Woman didn't love her at all. Why, they never even spoke of her by her name if they could help it. It was always "the child." How Elizabeth hated to be called "the child" just as they might have spoken of "the dog" or "the cat" if there had been one. But when Elizabeth had ventured a protest, Grandmother's face had grown dark and angry and little Elizabeth had been punished for impertinence, while the Woman looked on, well content. Little Elizabeth often wondered just why the Woman hated her. Why should any one hate you when you were so small? Could you be worth hating? Little Elizabeth did not know that the mother whose life she had cost had been that bitter old woman's darling and, if she had known, could not have understood what perverted shapes thwarted love can take.

Little Elizabeth hated the gloomy, splendid Evergreens, where everything seemed unacquainted with her although she had lived in it all her life. But after Miss Shirley had come to Windy Poplars everything had changed magically. Little Elizabeth lived in a world of romance after Miss Shirley's coming. There was beauty wherever you looked. Fortunately Grandmother and the Woman couldn't prevent you from looking, though Elizabeth had no doubt they would if they could. The short walks along the red magic of the harbor road, which she was all too rarely permitted to share with Miss Shirley, were the high lights in her shadowy life. She loved everything she saw...the far-away lighthouse painted in odd red and white rings...the far, dim blue shores...the little silvery blue waves...the range lights that gleamed through the violet dusks...all gave her so much delight that it hurt. And the harbor with its smoky islands and glowing sunsets! Elizabeth always went up to a window in the mansard roof to watch them through the treetops...and the ships that sailed at the rising of the moon. Ships that came back...ships that never came back. Elizabeth longed to go in one of them...on a voyage to the Island of Happiness. The ships that never came back stayed there, where it was always Tomorrow.

That mysterious red road ran on and on and her feet itched to follow it. Where did it lead to? Sometimes Elizabeth thought she would burst if she didn't find out. When Tomorrow really came she would fare forth on it and perhaps find an island all her own where she and Miss Shirley could live alone and

Grandmother and the Woman could never come. They both hated water and would not put foot in a boat for anything. Little Elizabeth liked to picture herself standing on her island and mocking them, as they stood vainly glowering on the mainland shore.

"This is Tomorrow," she would taunt them. "You can't catch me any more. You're only in Today."

What fun it would be! How she would enjoy the look on the Woman's face!

Then one evening in late June an amazing thing happened. Miss Shirley had told Mrs. Campbell that she had an errand next day at Flying Cloud, to see a certain Mrs. Thompson, who was convener of the refreshment committee of the Ladies' Aid, and might she take Elizabeth with her. Grandmother had agreed with her usual dourness...Elizabeth could never understand why she agreed at all, being completely ignorant of the Pringle horror of a certain bit of information Miss Shirley possessed...but she had agreed.

"We'll go right down to the harbor mouth," whispered Anne, "after I've done my errand at Flying Cloud."

Little Elizabeth went to bed in such excitement that she didn't expect to sleep a wink. At last she was going to answer the lure of the road that had called so long. In spite of her excitement, she conscientiously went through her little ritual of retiring. She folded her clothes and cleaned her teeth and brushed her golden hair. She thought she had rather pretty hair, though of course it wasn't like Miss Shirley's lovely red-gold with the ripples in it and the little love-locks that curled around her ears. Little Elizabeth would have given anything to have had hair like Miss Shirley's.

Before she got into bed little Elizabeth opened one of the drawers in the high, black, polished old bureau and took a carefully hidden picture from under a pile of hankies...a picture of Miss Shirley which she had cut out of a special edition of the Weekly Courier that had reproduced a photograph of the High School staff.

"Good night, dearest Miss Shirley." She kissed the picture and returned it to its hiding-place. Then she climbed into bed and cuddled down under the blankets...for the June night was cool and the breeze of the harbor searching. Indeed, it was more than a breeze tonight. It whistled and banged and shook and thumped, and Elizabeth knew the harbor would be a tossing expanse of waves under the moonlight. What fun it would be to steal down close to it under the moon! But it was only in Tomorrow one could do that.

Where was Flying Cloud? What a name! Out of Tomorrow again. It was maddening to be so near Tomorrow and not be able to get into it. But suppose the wind blew up rain for tomorrow! Elizabeth knew she would never be allowed to go anywhere in rain.

She sat up in bed and clasped her hands.

"Dear God," she said, "I don't like to meddle, but could You see that it is fine tomorrow? Please, dear God."

The next afternoon was glorious. Little Elizabeth felt as if she had slipped from some invisible shackles when she and Miss Shirley walked away from that house of gloom. She took a huge gulp of freedom, even if the Woman was scowling after them through the red glass of the big front door. How heavenly to be walking through the lovely world with Miss Shirley! It was always so wonderful to be alone with Miss Shirley. What would she do when Miss Shirley had gone? But little Elizabeth put the thought firmly away. She wouldn't spoil the day by thinking it. Perhaps...a great perhaps...she and Miss Shirley would get into Tomorrow this afternoon and then they would never be separated. Little Elizabeth just wanted to walk quietly on towards that blueness at the end of the world, drinking in the beauty around her. Every turn and kink of the road revealed new lovelinesses...and it turned and kinked interminably, following the windings of a tiny river that seemed to have appeared from nowhere.

On every side were fields of buttercups and clover where bees buzzed. Now and then they walked through a milky way of daisies. Far out the strait laughed at them in silver-tipped waves. The harbor was like watered silk. Little Elizabeth liked it better that way than when it was like pale blue satin. They drank the wind in. It was a very gentle wind. It purred about them and seemed to coax them on.

"Isn't it nice, walking with the wind like this?" said little Elizabeth.

"A nice, friendly, perfumed wind," said Anne, more to herself than Elizabeth. "Such a wind as I used to think a mistral was. Mistral sounds like that. What a disappointment when I found out it was a rough, disagreeable wind!"

Elizabeth didn't quite understand...she had never heard of the mistral...but the music of her beloved's voice was enough for her. The very sky was glad. A sailor with gold rings in his ears...the very kind of person one would meet in Tomorrow...smiled as he passed them. Elizabeth thought of a verse she had learned in Sunday-school..."The little hills rejoice on every side." Had the man who wrote that ever seen hills like those blue ones over the harbor?

"I think this road leads right to God," she said dreamily.

"Perhaps," said Anne. "Perhaps all roads do, little Elizabeth. We turn off here just now. We must go over to that island...that's Flying Cloud."

Flying Cloud was a long, slender islet, lying about a quarter of a mile from the shore. There were trees on it and a house. Little Elizabeth had always wished she might have an island of her own, with a little bay of silver sand in it.

"How do we get to it?"

"We'll row out in this flat," said Miss Shirley, picking up the oars in a small boat tied to a leaning tree.

Miss Shirley could row. Was there anything Miss Shirley couldn't do? When they reached the island, it proved to be a fascinating place where anything might happen. Of course it was in Tomorrow. Islands like this didn't happen except in Tomorrow. They had no part or lot in humdrum Today.

A little maid who met them at the door of the house told Anne she would find Mrs. Thompson on the far end of the island, picking wild strawberries. Fancy an island where wild strawberries grew!

Anne went to hunt Mrs. Thompson up, but first she asked if little Elizabeth might wait in the living-room. Anne was thinking that little Elizabeth looked rather tired after her unaccustomedly long walk and needed a rest. Little Elizabeth didn't think she did, but Miss Shirley's lightest wish was law.

It was a beautiful room, with flowers everywhere and wild sea-breezes blowing in. Elizabeth liked the mirror over the mantel which reflected the room so beautifully and, through the open window, a glimpse of harbor and hill and strait.

All at once a man came through the door. Elizabeth felt a moment of dismay and terror. Was he a gypsy? He didn't look like her idea of a gypsy but of course she had never seen one. He might be one...and then in a swift flash of intuition Elizabeth decided she didn't care if he did kidnap her. She liked his crinkly hazel eyes and his crinkly brown hair and his square chin and his smile. For he was smiling.

"Now, who are you?" he asked.

"I'm...I'm me," faltered Elizabeth, still a little flustered.

"Oh, to be sure...you. Popped out of the sea, I suppose...come up from the dunes...no name known among mortals."

Elizabeth felt that she was being made fun of a little. But she didn't mind. In fact she rather liked it. But she answered a bit primly.

"My name is Elizabeth Grayson."

There was a silence...a very queer silence. The man looked at her for a moment without saying anything. Then he politely asked her to sit down.

"I'm waiting for Miss Shirley," she explained. "She's gone to see Mrs. Thompson about the Ladies' Aid Supper. When she comes back we are going down to the end of the world."

Now, if you have any notion of kidnaping me, Mr. Man!

"Of course. But meanwhile you might as well be comfortable. And I must do the honors. What would you like in the way of light refreshment? Mrs. Thompson's cat has probably brought something in."

Elizabeth sat down. She felt oddly happy and at home.

"Can I have just what I like?"

"Certainly."

"Then," said Elizabeth triumphantly, "I'd like some ice-cream with strawberry jam on it."

The man rang a bell and gave an order. Yes, this must be Tomorrow...no doubt about it. Ice-cream and strawberry jam didn't appear in this magical manner in Today, cats or no cats.

"We'll set a share aside for your Miss Shirley," said the man.

They were good friends right away. The man didn't talk a great deal, but he looked at Elizabeth very often. There was a tenderness in his face...a tenderness she had never seen before in anybody's face, not even Miss Shirley's. She felt that he liked her. And she knew that she liked him.

Finally he glanced out of the window and stood up.

"I think I must go now," he said. "I see your Miss Shirley coming up the walk, so you'll not be alone."

"Won't you wait and see Miss Shirley?" asked Elizabeth, licking her spoon to get the last vestige of the jam. Grandmother and the Woman would have died of horror had they seen her.

"Not this time," said the man.

Elizabeth knew he hadn't the slightest notion of kidnaping her, and she felt the strangest, most unaccountable sensation of disappointment.

"Good-by and thank you," she said politely. "It is very nice here in Tomorrow."

"Tomorrow?"

"This is Tomorrow," explained Elizabeth. "I've always wanted to get into Tomorrow and now I have."

"Oh, I see. Well, I'm sorry to say I don't care much about Tomorrow. I would like to get back into Yesterday."

Little Elizabeth was sorry for him. But how could he be unhappy? How could any one living in Tomorrow be unhappy?

Elizabeth looked longingly back to Flying Cloud as they rowed away. Just as they pushed through the scrub spruces that fringed the shore to the road, she turned for another farewell look at it. A flying team of horses attached to a truck wagon whirled around the bend, evidently quite beyond their driver's control.

Elizabeth heard Miss Shirley shriek...

13

The room went around oddly. The furniture nodded and jiggled. The bed...how came she to be in bed? Somebody with a white cap on was just going out of the door. What door? How funny one's head felt! There were voices somewhere...low voices. She could not see who was talking, but somehow she knew it was Miss Shirley and the man.

What were they saying? Elizabeth heard sentences here and there, bobbing out of a confusion of murmuring.

"Are you really...?" Miss Shirley's voice sounded so excited..

"Yes...your letter...see for myself...before approaching Mrs. Campbell...Flying Cloud is the summer home of our General Manager..."

If that room would only stay put! Really, things behaved rather queerly in Tomorrow. If she could only turn her head and see the talkers...Elizabeth gave a long sigh.

Then they came over to her bed...Miss Shirley and the man. Miss Shirley all tall and white, like a lily, looking as if she had been through some terrible experience but with some inner radiance shining behind it all...a radiance that seemed part of the golden sunset light which suddenly flooded the room. The man was smiling down at her. Elizabeth felt that he loved her very much and that there was some secret, tender and dear, between them which she would learn as soon as she had learned the language spoken in Tomorrow.

"Are you feeling better, darling?" said Miss Shirley.

"Have I been sick?"

"You were knocked down by a team of runaway horses on the mainland road," said Miss Shirley. "I...I wasn't quick enough. I thought you were killed. I brought you right back here in the flat and your...this gentleman telephoned for a doctor and nurse."

"Will I die?" said little Elizabeth.

"No, indeed, darling. You were only stunned and you will be all right soon. And, Elizabeth darling, this is your father."

"Father is in France. Am I in France, too?" Elizabeth would not have been surprised at it. Wasn't this Tomorrow? Besides, things were still a bit wobbly.

"Father is very much here, my sweet." He had such a delightful voice...you loved him for his voice. He bent and kissed her. "I've come for you. We'll never be separated anymore."

The woman in the white cap was coming in again. Somehow, Elizabeth knew whatever she had to say must be said before she got quite in.

"Will we live together?"

"Always," said Father.

"And will Grandmother and the Woman live with us?"

"They will not," said Father.

The sunset gold was fading and the nurse was looking her

disapproval. But Elizabeth didn't care.

"I've found Tomorrow," she said, as the nurse looked Father and Miss Shirley out.

"I've found a treasure I didn't know I possessed," said Father, as the nurse shut the door on him. "And I can never thank you enough for that letter, Miss Shirley."

"And so," wrote Anne to Gilbert that night, "little Elizabeth's road of mystery has led on to happiness and the end of her old world."

14

"Windy Poplars,

"Spook's Lane,

"(For the last time),

"June 27th.

"DEAREST:

"I've come to another bend in the road. I've written you a good many letters in this old tower room these past three years. I suppose this is the last one I will write you for a long, long time. Because after this there won't be any need of letters. In just a few weeks now we'll belong to each other forever...we'll be together. Just think of it...being together...talking, walking, eating. dreaming, planning together...sharing each other's wonderful moments...making a home out of our house of dreams. Our house! Doesn't that sound 'mystic and wonderful,' Gilbert? I've been building dream houses all my life and now one of them is going to come true. As to whom I really want to share my house of dreams with...well, I'll tell you that at four o'clock next year.

"Three years sounded endless at the beginning, Gilbert. And now they are gone like a watch in the night. They have been very happy years...except for those first few months with the Pringles. After that, life has seemed to flow by like a pleasant golden river. And my old feud with the Pringles seems like a dream. They like me now for myself...they have forgotten they ever hated me. Cora Pringle, one of the Widow Pringle's brood, brought me a bouquet of roses yesterday and twisted round the stems was a bit of paper bearing the legend, 'To the sweetest teacher in the whole world.' Fancy that for a Pringle!

"Jen is broken-hearted because I am leaving. I shall watch Jen's career with interest. She is brilliant and rather unpredictable. One thing is certain...she will have no commonplace existence. She can't look so much like Becky Sharp for nothing.

"Lewis Allen is going to McGill. Sophy Sinclair is going to Queen's. Then she means to teach until she has saved up enough money to go to the School of Dramatic Expression in

Kingsport. Myra Pringle is going to 'enter society' in the fall. She is so pretty that it won't matter a bit that she wouldn't know a past perfect participle if she met it on the street.

"And there is no longer a small neighbor on the other side of the vine-hung gate. Little Elizabeth has gone forever from that sunshineless house...gone into her Tomorrow. If I were staying on in Summerside I should break my heart, missing her. But as it is, I'm glad. Pierce Grayson took her away with him. He is not going back to Paris but will be living in Boston. Elizabeth cried bitterly at our parting but she is so happy with her father that I feel sure her tears will soon be dried. Mrs. Campbell and the Woman were very dour over the whole affair and put all the blame on me...which I accept cheerfully and unrepentantly.

"'She has had a good home here,' said Mrs. Campbell majestically.

"'Where she never heard a single word of affection,' I thought but did not say.

"'I think I'll be Betty all the time now, darling Miss Shirley,' were Elizabeth's last words. 'Except,' she called back, 'when I'm lonesome for you, and then I'll be Lizzie.'

"'Don't you ever dare to be Lizzie, no matter what happens,' I said.

"We threw kisses to each other as long as we could see, and I came up to my tower room with tears in my eyes. She's been so sweet, the dear little golden thing. She always seemed to me like a little aeolian harp, so responsive to the tiniest breath of affection that blew her way. It's been an adventure to be her friend. I hope Pierce Grayson realizes what a daughter he has...and I think he does. He sounded very grateful and repentant.

"'I didn't realize she was no longer a baby,' he said, 'nor how unsympathetic her environment was. Thank you a thousand times for all you have done for her.'

"I had our map of fairyland framed and gave it to little Elizabeth for a farewell keepsake.

"I'm sorry to leave Windy Poplars. Of course, I'm really a bit tired of living in a trunk, but I've loved it here...loved my cool morning hours at my window...loved my bed into which I have veritably climbed every night...loved my blue doughnut cushion...loved all the winds that blew. I'm afraid I'll never be quite so chummy with the winds again as I've been here. And shall I ever have a room again from which I can see both the rising and the setting sun?

"I've finished with Windy Poplars and the years that have been linked with it. And I've kept the faith. I've never betrayed Aunt Chatty's hidy-hole to Aunt Kate or the buttermilk secret of each to either of the others.

"I think they are all sorry to see me go...and I'm glad of it. It would be terrible to think they were glad I am going...or that they would not miss me a little when I'm gone. Rebecca Dew has been making all my favorite dishes for a week now...she even devoted ten eggs to angel-cake twice... and using the 'company' china. And Aunt Chatty's soft brown eyes brim over whenever I mention my departure. Even Dusty Miller seems to gaze at me reproachfully as he sits about on his little haunches.

"I had a long letter from Katherine last week. She has a gift for writing letters. She has got a position as private secretary to a globe-trotting M. P. What a fascinating phrase 'globe-trotting' is! A person who would say, 'Let's go to Egypt,' as one might say, 'Let's go to Charlottetown'...and go! That life will just suit Katherine.

"She persists in ascribing all her changed outlook and prospects to me. 'I wish I could tell you what you've brought into my life,' she wrote. I suppose I did help. And it wasn't easy at first. She seldom said anything without a sting in it, and listened to any suggestion I made in regard to the school work with an air of disdainfully humoring a lunatic. But somehow, I've forgotten it all. It was just born of her secret bitterness against life.

"Everybody has been inviting me to supper...even Pauline Gibson. Old Mrs. Gibson died a few months ago, so Pauline dared do it. And I've been to Tomgallon House for another supper with Miss Minerva of that ilk and another one-sided conversation. But I had a very good time, eating the delicious meal Miss Minerva provided, and she had a good time airing a few more tragedies. She couldn't quite hide the fact that she was sorry for any one who was not a Tomgallon, but she paid me several nice compliments and gave me a lovely ring set with an aquamarine...a moonlight blend of blue and green...that her father had given her on her eighteenth birthday...'when I was young and handsome, dear...quite handsome. I may say that now, I suppose.' I was glad it belonged to Miss Minerva and not to the wife of Uncle Alexander. I'm sure I could never have worn it if it had. It is very beautiful. There is a mysterious charm about the jewels of the sea.

"Tomgallon House is certainly very splendid, especially now when its grounds are all a-leaf and a-flower. But I wouldn't give my as yet unfounded house of dreams for Tomgallon House and grounds with the ghosts thrown in.

"Not but what a ghost might be a nice, aristocratic sort of thing to have around. My only quarrel with Spook's Lane is that there are no spooks.

"I went to my old graveyard yesterday evening for a last prowl...walked all round it and wondered if Herbert Pringle occasionally chuckled to himself in his grave. And I'm saying good-by tonight to the old Storm King, with the sunset on its brow, and my little winding valley full of dusk.

"I'm a wee bit tired after a month of exams and farewells and 'last things.' For a week after I get back to Green Gables I'm going to be lazy...do absolutely nothing but run free in a green world of summer loveliness. I'll dream by the Dryad's Bubble in the twilight. I'll drift on the Lake of Shining Waters in a shallop shaped from a moonbeam...or in Mr. Barry's flat, if moonbeam shallops are not in season. I'll gather starflowers and June bells in the Haunted Wood. I'll find plots of wild strawberries in Mr. Harrison's hill pasture. I'll join the dance of fireflies in Lover's Lane and visit Hester Gray's old, forgotten garden...and sit out on the back door-step under the stars and listen to the sea calling in its sleep.

"And when the week is ended you will be home...and I won't want anything else."

When the time came the next day for Anne to say good-by to the folks at Windy Poplars, Rebecca Dew was not on hand. Instead, Aunt Kate gravely handed Anne a letter.

"Dear Miss Shirley," wrote Rebecca Dew, "I am writing this to bid my farewell because I cannot trust myself to say it. For three years you have sojourned under our roof. The fortunate possessor of a cheerful spirit and a natural taste for the gaieties of youth, you have never surrendered yourself to the vain pleasures of the giddy and fickle crowd. You have conducted yourself on all occasions and to every one, especially the one who pens these lines, with the most refined delicacy. You have always been most considerate of my feelings and I find a heavy gloom on my spirits at the thought of your departure. But we must not repine at what Providence has ordained. (First Samuel, 29th and 18th.)

"You will be lamented by all in Summerside who had the privilege of knowing you, and the homage of one faithful though humble heart will ever be yours, and my prayer will ever be for your happiness and welfare in this world and your eternal felicity in that which is to come.

"Something whispers to me that you will not be long 'Miss Shirley' but that you will erelong be linked together in a union of souls with the choice of your heart, who, I understand from what I have heard, is a very exceptional young man. The writer, possessed of but few personal charms and beginning to feel her age (not but what I'm good for a good few years yet), has never permitted herself to cherish any matrimonial aspirations. But she does not deny herself the pleasure of an interest in the nuptials of her friends and may I express a fervent wish that your married life will be one of continued and uninterrupted Bliss? (Only do not expect too much of a man.)

"My esteem and, may I say, my affection for you will never lessen, and once in a while when you have nothing better to do will you kindly remember that there is such a person as

"Your obedient servant,

"REBECCA DEW.

"P.S. God bless you."

Anne's eyes were misty as she folded the letter up. Though she strongly suspected Rebecca Dew had got most of her phrases out of her favorite "Book of Deportment and Etiquette," that did not make them any the less sincere, and the P. S. certainly came straight from Rebecca Dew's affectionate heart.

"Tell dear Rebecca Dew I'll never forget her and that I'm coming back to see you all every summer."

"We have memories of you that nothing can take away," sobbed Aunt Chatty.

"Nothing," said Aunt Kate, emphatically.

But as Anne drove away from Windy Poplars the last message from it was a large white bath-towel fluttering frantically from the tower window. Rebecca Dew was waving it.

ANNE OF WINDY POPLARS
1st Printing : 1 JUNE 2025

Author : Lucy Maud Montgomery
Publisher : Jang, Youngjae
Publishing Co. : Thestory
Publication Register : 313-2012-81 (16 March 2012)
Address : 2F, 12 Seongmisan-ro 32-gil, Mapo-gu, Seoul, 03983, Republic of Korea
Tel : 02-3141-4421
Fax : 0505-333-4428
E-mail : sanhonjinju@naver.com

Damaged or defective books will be replaced.